It's the central challenge for any entrepreneur or leader: how can we think better? Dan Pontefract expertly guides us to go beyond facile answers and provides a new framework to help us make better decisions and achieve more successful outcomes in our lives.

DORIE CLARK, author of *Entrepreneurial You* and *Stand Out*, and adjunct professor at Duke University Fuqua School of Business

Our sound-bite, politicized, shortcut way of coming to solutions is exacerbating many of society's most significant problems. In the face of our perennial time famine, *Open to Think* offers a refreshing perspective on how we can take control of our thinking and ultimately get to a better solution more quickly.

RITA GUNTER MCGRATH, professor at Columbia Business School and author of *The End of Competitive Advantage*

We think we know how to think. And you do, kinda. But, as you'll see, you're mostly a high performing amateur. Why not up your game and "go pro"? Combining solid research and practical tools, *Open to Think* will get you thinking better. And that means acting smarter.

MICHAEL BUNGAY STANIER, *Wall Street Journal* best-selling author of *The Coaching Habit*

DAN PONTEFRACT

open to think

SLOW DOWN, THINK CREATIVELY, AND MAKE BETTER DECISIONS

Figure.1
Vancouver / Berkeley

Cataloguing data is available from
Library and Archives Canada
ISBN 978-1-77327-027-2 (hbk.)
ISBN 978-1-77327-028-9 (ebook)
ISBN 978-1-77327-029-6 (pdf)
ISBN 978-1-77327-075-3 (audio)

Jacket design by Jessica Sullivan
Text design by Naomi MacDougall
Author photograph by Denise Lamarche

Editing by Richard Martin
Copy editing by Gillian Scobie
Proofreading by Renate Preuss
Indexing by Stephen Ullstrom
Front cover images: left: Timquo/Shutterstock.com,
right: iStock.com/eternalcreative
Back cover image: Virtu Studio/Shutterstock.com
Printed and bound in Canada by Friesens
Distributed internationally by Publishers Group West

Figure 1 Publishing Inc.
Vancouver BC Canada
www.figure1publishing.com

The Road Not Taken

Two roads diverged in a yellow wood,
And sorry I could not travel both
And be one traveler, long I stood
And looked down one as far as I could
To where it bent in the undergrowth;

Then took the other, as just as fair,
And having perhaps the better claim,
Because it was grassy and wanted wear;
Though as for that the passing there
Had worn them really about the same,

And both that morning equally lay
In leaves no step had trodden black.
Oh, I kept the first for another day!
Yet knowing how way leads on to way,
I doubted if I should ever come back.

I shall be telling this with a sigh
Somewhere ages and ages hence:
Two roads diverged in a wood, and I—
I took the one less traveled by,
And that has made all the difference.

ROBERT FROST

For Dad, for everything.

contents

ACKNOWLEDGMENTS

In the Trenches . . .

Richard Martin, you are the author whisperer. Although we are separated by an eight-hour time zone difference between Victoria, Canada, and Whitstable, UK, your gift as a substantive editor shows no gap. I look forward to several more books with you, Richard. Thank you for everything. Vive le Tour.

My thanks to Don Loney, Roger L. Martin, Stephen Lamb, Mike Desjardins, Kelsy Trigg, Elango Elangovan, Mark Colgate, Peter Johnston, Bryan Acker, and Denise Lamarche for listening to me ramble on about the book's theory, only to provide helpful counterpoints, suggestions, and "don't do that" comments along the way. I am forever grateful. I suspect the reader will be, too.

To my new team at Figure 1 Publishing. I cannot thank you enough for welcoming me into the spine of your book business. Many thanks to Jennifer Smith and Chris Labonté and everyone at "FI" for refilling my fountain pen. Jess Sullivan, you are a gifted artist. Gillian Scobie, ain't you the best copy editor ever! Renate Preuss and Lara Smith, thank you for getting me to the finish line.

In the Book . . .

The sincerest of thanks to everyone who put up with my questions, phone calls, emails, and face-to-face interviews. They are the people behind the stories that surfaced the Open Thinking framework. These folks helped make *Open to Think* come alive. Cheers to: Mark Mattson, James Stewart, James Perry, Tania Miller, Marc Kielburger, Alison Galloway, Eric Jordan, Greg Moore, Dominic Reid, Dave Gray, Lisa Helps, Tim Hockey, Kathryn Calder, Sameer Patel, Joel Plaskett, Eva Clayton, Brian Scudamore, Jonathan Becher, Yong Zhao, Peter Gilmore, John Dalla Costa, Adele Diamond, Rohan Light, Dion Hinch-cliffe, Elango Elangovan, Allen Devine, Kyna Leski, Daniel Levitin, Brianna Wettläufer, Karl Moore, Charlene Li, and Mike Desjardins. Gord Downie, may your 1,000-pound feather continue to be "a beautiful thing" up there. Blessed are we to have known Wicapi Omani.

Also a very special thank-you to Karyn Ruiz of Lilliput Hats. You are an extraordinary person. Thank you for crystalizing the essence of Open Thinking.

In Thought . . .

I am forever indebted to friends and colleagues who continue to aid my ongoing practice of Open Thinking. In addition to those named above, thank you in no particular order for the conversations—recent-ish or in the past—that helped shape the book: Kathryn Barnett, Mark and Orla Colgate, Céline Schillinger, Jill Schnarr, Keith and Michelle Driscoll, Luke and Annie Mills, Steven Hill, Keven and Jen Fletcher, Kenneth Mikkelsen, Henry Mintzberg, Rick Wartzman, Becky and Eliot Anderson, Saul Klein, Michael Bungay Stanier, Bev Patwell, Bob and Joan Snowden, Charles Handy, Dan Gunn, Jon Husband, Matthew Wood, Darren Entwistle, Josh Blair, Andrew Turner, Jeffrey Puritt, Marilyn Tyfting, Anna Carreon-Rivera, Paul Bleier, Erin Dermer, Frances Picherack, Roman Picherack, Bruce Duthie, Mary Hewitt, Laura Jamieson, Greg and Shannon Southgate, the grads of TELUS MBA 2018, Kim Morgan, Kevin McCardle, Megan "Megs" Mittler, Kevin Jones, Jen Murtagh, Michelle Moore, Kevin Oakes, Alison van Buuren, John Ambrose, Dan Klein, Marcia Conner, Richard Straub, Ross Porter, Grant and Darcy Evans, Val Litwin, Ehren Lee, Sandra

Daniel, Lynette Van Steinburg, James Tyer, Kiran Mohan, Rasool Rayani, Antonio Nieto-Rodriguez, Chuck Hamilton, Raymond Hofmann, Ludo Van der Heyden, Jocelyn Berard, Grainne and Martin McElroy, Vince Molinaro, Tim Kastelle, Eric Moeller, Stephen McDermott, Brian Reid, Nilofer Merchant, Shawn Hunter, Dan Sheehan, Deborah Wickins, Phil LeNir, the gang from Speak and Spill as well as Write and Rant, Alex Rothwell, Anne Glazier, Blair and Tracy Hagkull, and Shelly Berlin. To the Air Canada service directors who seem to always check in on me and my writing, thank you! (A lot of writing gets done at 35,000 feet.) Undoubtedly I have missed a few. For that, I am profusely apologetic. Hit me up for a scotch or latte next time we meet.

. . . and In Love

My love for family begins my thinking, for they have always encouraged me to dream. Love ya: Mia, Roy, Nicole, Alana, Natasha, Adam, Michelle, Zoe, Rich, Suzanne, Chris, Madeleine, Tyler, Debbie, Diane, Ron, Jane, and Lawrence. To the growing-ever-so-fast goats—Claire, Cole, and Cate—I love you to the moon and back. Keep writing! Stop growing! Remember, love yourself first. "To be that self which one truly is." And finally, to Denise, the true rock of our family, the ultimate quarry master. Thank you for always balancing the tightrope of chaos as if there were no worries below. I don't know how you do it. Yer amazing. Love ya. "Onward. Daily. Forward. Away."

Introduction

Nothing in all the world is more dangerous than
sincere ignorance and conscientious stupidity.
MARTIN LUTHER KING, JR

ROBERT FROST'S MOST famous poem is probably "The Road Less Traveled." For many, the final three lines are its most important. With those closing words, Frost elegantly depicts a traveler who first thinks about and then decides to traverse the road that was less traveled; a road that ultimately delivers a difference.

Two roads diverged in a wood, and I—
I took the one less traveled by,
And that has made all the difference.

I am certain you have crossed paths with these well-known lines at some point in your life. Before we proceed, however, there is a problem to surface, which relates to the thesis of this book: thinking.

The poem is not called "The Road Less Traveled," as I suggested above. Its proper title is "The Road Not Taken." Perhaps many readers knew that already.

It is possible that some just went with it. Why contest a poem title this early in a book? In fact, Professors Lewandowsky, Ecker, Seifert, Schwarz, and Cook have proven that it requires more cognitive effort—our brains need to work harder—to reject misinformation, lies, and other falsities. They write, "Weighing the plausibility and the source of a message is cognitively more difficult than simply accepting that the message is true—it requires additional motivational and cognitive resources. If the topic isn't very important to you or you have other things on your mind, misinformation is more likely to take hold."

Therefore, a reader might have accepted the name of the poem as "The Road Less Traveled" because their brain was too tired to think. Or they were just being lazy. Perhaps they wanted to rush through the introduction, eager to dive into the "real" writing in Chapter 1. "What's an introduction for, anyway?" they might have pondered. They may even have trusted this author enough to take it at face value. "Of course it's called 'The Road Less Traveled,' Dan said it was."

In the modern world, our senses are bombarded daily by political propaganda and fake news. We fluctuate between high filtering and gullibility. The truth is becoming harder and harder to discern. This situation introduces another important factor. Speed has become a weapon against thoughtfulness. Time to market, time to innovate, and time to exploit have become bullets in the gun. And that gun seems perpetually cocked. In a world governed by growth, we are under stress to complete things as quickly as possible. Indeed, we now scamper from task to task or action to action in a continuous peripatetic state. We are unable to pause and reflect to make better decisions. Convenience has become king.

No wonder some readers may have glossed over my use of a fake title. In fact, we do know that the title of Frost's 1916 poem is frequently mistaken. Google provides over 3 million search results for it. Wikipedia even has an entry for "The Road Less Traveled," urging visitors to click "The Road Not Taken" instead. It is a common mistake. But the question I want to explore in this book is why.

The biggest reason could be because people have simply not bothered to read the poem in its entirety. Instead, they rely on fridge magnets and Hallmark motivational cards containing those last three lines as the basis of the poem's underlying meaning, a road less traveled. As David Orr points out in his 2016 book, *The Road Not Taken:*

Finding America in the Poem Everyone Loves and Almost Everyone Gets Wrong, "It's almost possible to forget the poem is actually a poem."

"The Road Not Taken" offers a metaphor for life. Indeed, it is an introductory metaphor to this book about thinking. Our actions have always been impacted by our levels of reflection, our decision-making abilities, and our actions. The poem provides insight into our penchant for shortcut thinking, obstructed thinking.

In a world that thrives on rushing to complete things before thorough analysis—in a world of work where we do not spend enough time "marinating in the moment" dreaming up ideas and deciding what to do with them—those last three lines of the poem represent the shortsightedness of today's thinking culture. We mistake the name of the poem, and then we misconstrue its meaning because we do not bother to think deeper.

In fact, the poem spans 20 lines rather than the 3 that are regularly cited. Better thinking is hard, not easy. Better thinking takes time, not haste. There is no shortcut. There is no mobile phone app to truly make you think. Siri or Alexa are not going to help you with this one. "The Road Not Taken" is not about a concluding triumph or delivering on a conviction like the fridge magnets urge. Even Frost himself advised his friend Edward Thomas, "You have to be careful of that one; it's a tricky poem—very tricky."

It turns out—as many scholars have articulated—the poem's roads are equal: "Though as for that the passing there / Had worn them really about the same." One is not better than, less visited than, the other. The traveler in the poem is not making a brilliant decision, electing to wander down one of the roads. The traveler is subject to and acts upon choices similar to those of many other travelers who have preceded them.

If we do not take the time to understand the fundamental meaning of Frost's poem, we run the risk of becoming a closed thinker. This is the opposite of what we aim for in this book. Because we do not scrutinize the likelihood that there might be more to the poem and its meaning—neglecting the other 17 lines—we ignore it and move on. This obliviousness is becoming problematic in our society. Convenience is not only king, it has also become a crutch.

"I'll bet not half a dozen people can tell who was hit and where he was hit by my 'Road Not Taken,'" Frost commented to Louis Untermeyer. The poem is not about choosing a road less traveled. But millions of people continue to think this is Frost's message. Too often people rush to judgment, ignoring misinformation, gliding over nuance, imposing their own worldview, jumping to conclusions. Decisions made without pause for reflection—balancing criticality with creativity—often lead to further work down the line. Worse, they can lead to otherwise avoidable errors.

This book focuses on thinking. Throughout the following chapters, I argue that both individuals *and* organizations need a more reflective and responsive thinking mindset. Our thinking ought to be shaped by constantly changing inputs and information. We should recognize that our thinking is only as good as our ability to continually challenge and question. Better thinking is dependent on how open we are to new ideas, how evidence-based our decision-making can be, how capable we remain to get things done.

Dream, decide, do. The interplay of these three concepts sits at the heart of something I have termed "Open Thinking." In *Open to Think*, we will explore three phases of thinking that ought to be continuously in motion: Creative Thinking, Critical Thinking, and Applied Thinking. Our investigation will examine the following elements of Open Thinking:

CHOICES
- Thinking should include periods of ideation and reflection. Can we build a new road? How? Thinking ought to be creative.

JUDGMENT
- We must decide why one road is chosen before the other. Is there a need to return to the junction? Why? Thinking must be critical.

ACTION
- To achieve our goals, we should travel the roads. One cannot scheme and analyze ad infinitum. With experience come more ideas and more decisions. Thinking needs to be applied.

INFINITE

- Reflection and analysis are never-ending. There are more roads to build, to travel on. Thinking occurs in a continuum.

The questions below provide a quick litmus test.

- Am I a dreamer?
- Am I a decision-maker?
- Am I a doer?
- Am I an Open Thinker?
- Am I all of the above?

To be open is to be inclusive. In his poem, Frost depicts a situation in which the narrator stands at the crossroads between observing, decision-making, and executing. The poem shows the potential between Creative Thinking, Critical Thinking, and Applied Thinking. The poet/narrator contemplates his surroundings and carefully reviews what decisions he can make. Roads are definitely traveled. But the narrator is not thinking in isolation. He has not quarantined ideation, judgment, and application. Instead, they act in unison. I argue that the narrator is behaving like an Open Thinker.

Open Thinking is the type of thinking that we will define and unpack over the coming pages. My goal? Through the various interviews I have conducted, my professional observations, academic research, historical evidence, and the *Open to Think* model that I will introduce in the first chapter, I want to help you become an Open Thinker, one who aspires to consistently dream, decide, and do.

My ultimate aim is to help you become an improved thinker, and a better person. Open Thinking is the type of thinking we need for a more humanistic society. On the topic of atomic education in 1946, Albert Einstein said, "A new type of thinking is essential if mankind is to survive and move toward higher levels." Indeed, it is.

Life is far too short for fridge magnet advice.

I

thinking

1

Cogito Ergo Sum

The solution to adult problems tomorrow depends on large measure upon how our children grow up today.

MARGARET MEAD

THINK.

We all do it. We all think. But *think* is a rather strange word subject to countless interpretations and misinterpretations. There are hundreds of books and thousands of papers dedicated to the topic of thinking. Even so, *think* is a word and a concept that begs both greater attention *and* better understanding. It needs to be rescued, redefined. Adrian West, research director at the Edward de Bono Foundation, captures my sentiments: "Developing our abilities to think more clearly, richly, fully—individually and collectively—is absolutely crucial to solving world problems."

Many of us have forgotten how to think. Worse, some have surrendered the *responsibility* to think. In the process, minds have closed to the potential an improved form of thinking brings. For some, thinking has been outsourced in favor of artificial intelligence like Siri or Alexa. Consequently, some people have outsourced both Creative and Critical Thinking. Professor Tom Nichols of the U.S. Naval War College insists "we are witnessing the 'death of expertise': a Google-fueled, Wikipedia-based, blog-sodden collapse of any division between

9

professionals and laymen, students and teachers, knowers and won-
derers—in other words, between those of any achievement in an area
and those with none at all."

The impact of not thinking is troubling and far-reaching. Fake
news has become credible. Post-truth politics is now the norm. Social
media has replaced long reads and books. Employee engagement continues to wane. The wage and net worth gap between the C-Suite
and employees remains extraordinary, while for-profit companies
continue to believe there is logic in operating only for the short term.
Worse, levels of stress and anxiety are on the rise in the western world
and lifespans are shrinking. The World Health Organization predicts
that by 2020 depression will be the second leading cause of disease
worldwide. Indeed, the situation is alarming, given that depression
became the leading cause of illness and disability in 2017.

It is time to rethink how we think.

Early Steps

This book pays homage to previously defined thinking strategies such
as Integrative Thinking by Roger L. Martin and Design Thinking, put
forth separately and collaboratively by Roger and IDEO founder Tim
Brown. It recognizes the ground-breaking work of psychologist and
behavioral economist Daniel Kahneman, who wrote in his book *Thinking, Fast and Slow*, "Minds: we can be blind to the obvious, and we are
also blind to our blindness." As any management book ought to do,
Open to Think revisits great ideas that have previously been published
and attributes accordingly, including but not limited to Roger, Tim,
and Daniel.

The theory and accompanying model that I will take you through
is based on extensive research. It also comes from my own hands-on
experience working in for-profit companies and academic institu-
tions in addition to my role as Chief Envisioner at TELUS, where I
get to help other organizations with their quests for culture change.
For more than 20 years, I have observed people working, studying,

and operating in their roles. I have thought long and hard about what is missing from how people think and what is needed to improve it.

Furthermore, I interviewed people in a wide range of different professions—oncologists, musicians, mayors, CEOs, not-for-profit leaders, educators, engineers, symphony conductors, First Nations leaders, chefs, and even milliners—to crystallize the *Open to Think* thesis. They hail from countries in North America, Europe, and Asia. Together, between the old and the new, I have determined that for people to improve their level of thinking, a new, yet easy-to-remember framework just may do the trick. As I mentioned in the introduction, I call it Open Thinking.

My first book, *Flat Army*, explored ways to inculcate a more collaborative organizational culture. It contained five overlapping models to help leaders *and* team members work better together, in "a flow of corporate commonality." My second book, *The Purpose Effect*, investigated the importance of purpose, arguing that a sweet spot is achieved for both individuals and collectives when personal, organizational, and role purpose becomes aligned. I concluded the book with the idea, "Each of us deserves a life where we get paid to fulfill our purpose, in an organization that consciously chooses to do good."

If culture and purpose are two legs of a stool—one that aims to recreate and sustain a healthier society—the third leg is dedicated to improving our thinking. An autonomous and thriving society by its very nature is all about the freedom to think, the ability to assess, and the nurturing of creativity. It requires patience, judgment, collaboration, and action. Individuals and leaders ought to be striving for an environment where imagination is encouraged and critiquing leads to better decision-making, while thoughtful execution delivers positive and sustainable results. In fact, these are the hallmarks of a healthier society, of a better you: culture, purpose, and now the third leg, Open Thinking.

The way we focus on the short term, race to complete tasks, or sit on wonderful ideas because we are fearful of what may happen, is regrettable. At times, it is downright frightening. But this current state of thinking has created an opportunity to reconsider how we approach our work, our lives. There is hope. I have witnessed it, whether through my firsthand experiences as a leader, or through interviews, observations, and research. There are people, teams, and organizations out there that have already been using an Open Thinking mindset, I assure you. That's the good news. But we cannot believe for a second that how most of society thinks and operates today is working effectively. In the words of Facebook COO Sheryl Sandberg, "Option A is not available. So let's kick the shit out of option B."

Indeed, it is time to rethink our thinking.

When One Thinks

When we *think*, we are using our mind to actively form or connect an idea. But there is more to the word think. Thinking is also an approach, a possibility, a deliberation, an opinion, or an attitude. It can even be a belief or a conclusion.

Let's first contemplate the act of thinking.

Thinking can happen in parallel. That is, you can think about one thing while doing something completely different. When you take a shower, for example, you go through a routine that you have likely performed thousands of times. Your brain thinks through the routine and action ensues. Soak. Soap. Lather. Rinse. Repeat. It's been like that for years, so why change?

But maybe while lathering or rinsing you have a chance to simultaneously unleash thinking that may be more creative or critical than simply lathering soap over your body. I shave my head and face every morning in the shower. It has been a routine of mine for more than 20 years. But during the shave I often float into a state of endless possibility and wonderment. The medical community calls it automaticity, when a cell spontaneously generates action without an external stimulus. My morning ritual has become a daily five-minute instance of ideation and decision-making while I continue completing the task of shaving without cutting myself. I am getting things done in more ways than one.

Richard Martin, co-author of *The Neo-Generalist*, confirmed my point during a discussion we once had. "There are times when my mind is freed up to concentrate on other things. For example, when I ride a bike, my body is doing one thing that is very mechanical, while my mind is freed up to sift through bits and pieces of information, sorting them into ideas for action, writing, and so on. I've experienced blog posts and articles coming to me fully formed in this way."

Both of us are paying homage to what Daniel Kahneman calls "System 1 and System 2" thinking. Kahneman writes: "People who experience flow describe it as 'a state of effortless concentration so deep that they lose their sense of time, of themselves, of their problems,' and their descriptions of the joy of that state are so compelling that [colleague] Csikszentmihalyi has called it an 'optional experience.'" Some of my showers have lasted extra long because I ended up in a daydreaming trance as my brain tried to put disparate pieces of data or knowledge together. Even then I failed to cut myself, to the relief of my wife, Denise.

Thinking—like eating—is something we all do. In fact, we are all constantly thinking. But as with eating, there are both healthy and unhealthy habits we must become more aware of.

Thinking is both conscious and unconscious. It is voluntary and involuntary. It is equal parts contemplative, interrogative, and active. It is automatic and manual. We can control thought, but there are times when our thinking becomes instinctive. It is the quality and healthiness of thinking, however, that we must reconsider. While a chocolate donut or greasy fries are fine in moderation, when unhealthy food choices become the norm, our physique suffers. We become obese, subjecting our bodies to more complicated maladies such as diabetes or heart disease. Similarly, if you constantly employ poor thinking habits, don't be surprised if your life becomes detrimentally affected over time.

Let's consider a scenario at work in which your boss presents a series of customer service issues to solve. Ideally, you enter a state of reflection that should transition into a decision and, finally, action. You should consider the possibilities, deduce what will work, make the decision, and then act to fix the customer problem in a mutually acceptable timeframe. If you spend too much time white-boarding the possibilities and/or overanalyzing your options—or you immediately dive into action without devoting thinking time to being creative or critical—that is akin to eating a 12-pack of donuts for lunch every day of the week. Inevitably, the result is unhealthy. At some point your habit becomes set. In this case, the customer remains dissatisfied. Poor thinking has won.

A different example. Your team wishes to improve how its members share information with one another. In a perfect world, everyone gets together to first think of some new ideas, critique them, decide what will be used, and then move to implementing the ideas. Hopefully, the process is iterative and weaves in any new feedback or thoughts. But for many teams, either the leader mandates changes in a top-down fashion, or the team itself doesn't spend enough time on the various options. Inescapably, any so-called improvements that were applied miss the mark because a version of closed thinking is applied. It is not open. It is not engaging. Time is not invested. Consequently, the result is unsatisfactory. Everyone loses.

In my home, when I share my opinion about my young son Cole's latest "Jack and John" short story, I am thinking critically, providing thoughtful, patient feedback so he can become a better writer. If I am too flippant or quick, Cole loses out on additional learning and opportunities for improvement. If I interrupt the moment by attending to my mobile phone simply because it vibrated or lit up, how will he feel about my commitment to his learning? What type of example am I setting for him?

Conversely, in my place of work, if I am not regularly asking team members for feedback on an idea, what does that say about my own personal level of thinking? Closed or open? In fact, thinking is tied to your attitude or behavior. If you are closed-minded and fixated on dominating at all costs, what does that say about your ability to think openly, let alone being viewed as a respected leader?

But thinking is also intuitive and instinctual. When an erratic driver is about to collide head-on with my car, I am forced to think and then react quickly to take evasive action. The process is seamless and fast and quite different than the examples mentioned above. Similarly, when an emergency-room doctor is presented with a life-or-death case, she must make critical decisions right away based on her experience, then act to save the patient.

Thinking is multifaceted. The type of thinking we want to focus on in this book does not pertain to avoiding car crashes or saving a patient's life. *Open to Think* is not a book about the psychology or neuroscience of thinking, nor is it intended to rehash Design or Integrative Thinking. Furthermore, it is also not aimed at those who actually enjoy repetition in their role at work. The kind of thinking we are going to analyze is more conscious than unconscious, more interrogative and contemplative than innate or automatic. It is the type of thinking that you have control of in your daily lives—including your role at work—and the kind you, hopefully, want to improve.

To do so, I urge you to consider doing something throughout the book. As you delve into *Open to Think*, I encourage you to continuously assess how you think. In doing so, you are not simply reading the book, you are potentially developing better thinking habits along the way. Try asking yourself these three simple questions as you journey through the pages:

- Do I spend enough time reflecting and dreaming?
- Do I make thorough decisions based on facts and evidence?
- Do I rush to complete an action?

Are You Open to Think?

This book explores three distinct components of daily thinking. Open Thinking comprises three key categories:

- **Creative Thinking**: the generation of new ideas, unleashed from constraints.
  - » Do you reflect?

- **Critical Thinking**: the thorough analysis of ideas and facts to make an ethical and timely decision.
  - » How do you decide?

- **Applied Thinking**: commitment to execute a decision.
  - » Will you take thoughtful action?

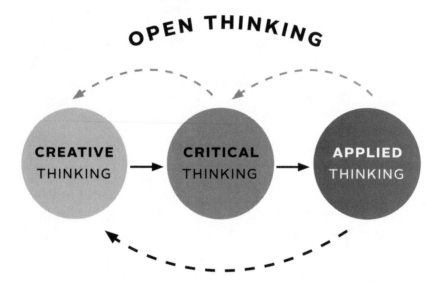

Open to Think recommends a fairly simple thinking model for you to carry out in your day-to-day life. The book is ultimately aimed at individuals who aspire to become better thinkers. To become an Open Thinker, one ought to understand the relationship between reflection and action—between the options we come up with, the choices we make, and the actions we then take—and how any of the *Open to Think* components can negatively or positively affect an outcome.

Through my research, interviews, and workplace experience, I have concluded that people who employ the Open Thinking mindset are engaged, purpose-driven, and innovative. They are resilient and often view mistakes or setbacks as the chance to go back and dream or decide some more. They are constantly learning, which aids their Open Thinking. In a nutshell, Open Thinkers are enlightened. They are patient and thoughtful but they also seem to get things done. They genuinely have fun doing it, too. In hindsight, those who employ Open Thinking are the types of people who are successful, defined not by their celebrity or riches but by life satisfaction. They understand Open Thinking is a philosophy—a behavior to be consistently practiced—not a step-by-step process performed in a meeting room.

We tend to be creatures of habit. Unfortunately, that can blind us to the potential for change, causing irreparable damage. The aim of this book is to not only introduce the *Open to Think* model for better thinking, it is to establish healthier thinking habits. Behaviors are learned, but they can also be unlearned. As futurist Alfred Toffler once wrote, "The illiterate of the 21st century will not be those who cannot read and write, but those who cannot learn, unlearn, and relearn."

Charles Duhigg, a Pulitzer Prize–winning reporter for *The New York Times*, gets to the heart of this point in his book *The Power of Habit*: "Habits are powerful, but delicate. They can emerge outside our consciousness, or can be deliberately designed. They often occur without our permission, but can be reshaped by fiddling with their parts. They shape our lives far more than we realize—they are so strong, in fact, that they cause our brains to cling to them at the exclusion of all else, including common sense."

Open to Think is laid out in five sections. After you complete this first section, there are three more that tackle the three unique components of Open Thinking. Section II focuses on Creative Thinking, Section III on Critical Thinking, and Section IV on Applied Thinking. The latter refers to getting things done within an Open Thinking method. There are two chapters in each section, one that outlines the inhibitors of each Open Thinking component, the other chapter delving into the behaviors that you can use to practice Open Thinking. Each chapter consists of stories, research, interviews, and examples that help put the Open Thinking model into context. The book concludes with Section V, a single chapter that brings together the *Open to Think* concept in its entirety. There is also a personal story of mine in the Afterword.

Bad Habits in Brief

Before we go any further we must first understand the antithesis of Open Thinking. As I introduce and discuss Creative, Critical, and Applied Thinking in the book, I will be simultaneously juxtaposing what prevents Open Thinking from happening. This goes beyond the simplistic notion of calling it closed thinking.

Many of people's day-to-day habits inhibit both the clarity *and* quality of their thinking. Productivity, engagement, purpose, personal growth, and innovation suffer as a result. I find this to be a major problem, and I suspect the issue is likely to grow if we do not address current thinking practices and bad habits.

The major block to Open Thinking is influenced by two factors: reflection and action. These factors must be balanced to become an Open Thinker. If the levers between reflection and action are misaligned, we end up in one of three bad habits I call Indifferent, Indecisive, and Inflexible Thinking. The three types are defined below using a graphic to illustrate their relationship to Open Thinking.

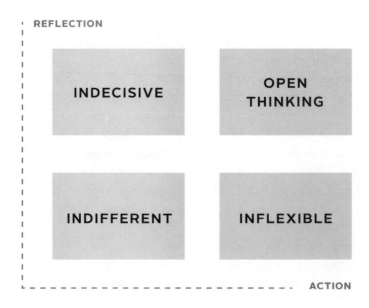

INDIFFERENT THINKING

Some of us become so accustomed to a previously learned habit we simply refuse the opportunity to try something different. Whether it is a routine, process, or system, once we have mastered something and become comfortable, the habit becomes hard to break. We like it. Why change when things are perfectly fine as they are? David DiSalvo, author of *What Makes Your Brain Happy and Why You Should Do the Opposite*, states, "We experience habits as patterns of thought and behavior imbued with automaticity. Automaticity—a sort of internal momentum that no longer needs overt, conscious fuel to keep going—is the result of learning. And in effect that's exactly what a habit is: the logical outcome of learning something, whether or not that something is beneficial or dangerous."

But this desire to hang on to the learned habit may be preventing new growth or ideas. Progress stalls when we remain stationary. I tend to side with Muhammad Ali, who once said, "If a man looks at the world when he is 50 the same way he looked at it when he was 20 and it hasn't changed, then he has wasted 30 years of his life." It results in generally being against change, uninterested in acting, closed to reflection, and averse to changing a previously learned habit. When individuals or groups behave with Indifferent Thinking as their default mode, they are, in effect, overlooking Open Thinking altogether. When they demonstrate Indifferent Thinking, they have become apathetic. They neither want to dream up new possibilities nor do they want to take charge of improving the outcome. They might even be a disengaged employee.

Indifferent Thinking can be thought of as a perfunctory stroll through the gardens of reflection and action. We would rather forgo the dreaming and decision-making because it is too hard or it would take too long. "Do we really have to brainstorm?" some may say. Others chime in, "Just make a decision, I really don't care." Conversely, our nonchalant attitude toward action means we will rush our tasks just to get them off our plate. Or we dismiss them altogether, pretending the work or objectives never existed in the first place. Indifferent Thinking is a calamitous situation in today's organizations. It not only prevents Open Thinking from coming to fruition, it downright encourages and props up anyone predisposed to remain in the status quo. Let's examine a few examples.

Imagine a staff meeting at your place of work. It occurs every Tuesday at 10:00 a.m. in Conference Room B. You sit in the same chair every week. Your boss sends out a replica agenda every Monday. It has been like this for three years. Nothing changes. As the meeting winds down, the usual any-other-business question is posed: "Does anyone have anything else to share?" No one says a word, heading back to the monotony of their daily routine. Disengaged and coasting, both leader and team exemplify Indifferent Thinking, caught in an endlessly repeating cycle.

How about a different example, this one personal? You decide to hop on a scale to weigh yourself for the first time in a few years. You knew you had picked up some girth along the way but now you stand there shocked. The scale indicates you are 15 pounds heavier since you last remember. You say to yourself, "Time to do something about this." A few weeks pass. Ultimately you don't do anything. Convinced that the pounds will shed naturally, you spend no time coming up with strategies for losing the extra weight. Subsequently, you make no decisions to enact a plan, and thus you never take any real action. A year passes by and you are now 20 pounds overweight. This is Indifferent Thinking at its finest, perhaps its heaviest.

INDECISIVE THINKING

Those of us unable to ever come to a decision—stuck in the habit of vacillating—demonstrate Indecisive Thinking. When the default habit is to take an extraordinarily long time critiquing or coming up with options, one can run the risk of employing what author H. Igor Ansoff called "paralysis by analysis." Ansoff had an epiphany shortly after the 1965 publication of his seminal book, *Corporate Strategy: An Analytic Approach to Business Policy for Growth and Expansion*. He recognized that his own approach to strategic planning was, ironically, causing managers and leaders to become indecisive. A strategy book about growth was having the opposite effect. After some consideration, he became his own most ardent critic. Ansoff eventually introduced an entirely new strategic planning model.

Indecisive Thinking not only accentuates a world of endless dreaming, it is a blatant disregard for making progress. If you demonstrate a proclivity to sit on the fence and ideate ad infinitum—refusing to either make a decision or move forward—you wind up affecting not only yourself but those you work with or lead. As we will discover throughout the book, taking the time to reflect, dream, and ideate is incredibly important to becoming an Open Thinker. But we cannot spend all of our time pondering the possibilities. Decisions must be made and action has to occur.

When exhibiting Indecisive Thinking, you might also be tempted to hesitate making a decision due to the sheer number of ideas at your disposal or through your creativity. Psychologist Barry Schwartz's 2004 book, *The Paradox of Choice: Why More Is Less*, stated that an abundance of options increases our levels of wasted time, depression, and anxiety. If we come up with too many ideas—or are exposed to them—and then become too overwrought to make a decision, the consequences can be alarming. Schwartz writes, "As the number of options increases, the effort required to make a good decision escalates as well, which is one of the reasons that choice can be transformed from a blessing into a burden."

Thus, Indecisive Thinking is a two-fold problem. We might develop issues with the quality and quantity of our dreaming *and* we may become mired in poor (or a lack of) decision-making due to an overabundance of options. Again, let's examine a few examples at work.

Consider the following situation set in mid-October. Your team has put forward its budget requirements for the next fiscal year starting in January. You notice a request for two new team members. The rationale is solid. One person would be dedicated to supporting the overflow of operational tasks that have slowed the team down. The other would be devoted to a business development role, aiding the team's pent-up demand for customer site visits. The added cost is $200,000 per year but the benefits laid out by the team predict revenue gains of approximately $500,000. You decide to mull it over. Three weeks pass. You ask for more information from the team, which provides it. Another three weeks go by. It is now the beginning of December. By mid-December, you decide to take the proposal to your boss for approval for next year's budget. You discover that late in October senior leaders earmarked new investments for the next fiscal year elsewhere in the unit. If only you had acted sooner. If only your thinking had been less indecisive.

Or how about a personal circumstance: you and your family have decided to build a new home. It is a big investment, both in time and money. The architectural plans have been created and approved. The process was relatively painless. You are now ahead of schedule. As construction begins and the foundation is being poured, your general contractor asks you to begin picking the home's accoutrements. You need to make decisions about appliances, bathroom fixtures, back-splash tiles, cabinetry types, flooring, and so on. It seems like there are a million decisions to make. Worse, there seem to be a billion ideas to look through. Because you believe in reviewing every possible option for your home's interior design, you delay decisions. What was supposed to be an 8-month build ends up taking 12 months, based solely on your tardiness to make a decision. Those extra two months cost you $6,000 in additional rent and another $25,000 in labor charges. Was it worth it?

INFLEXIBLE THINKING

When we demonstrate Inflexible Thinking—the third and final blockage to Open Thinking—we tend to immediately jump to action without properly reflecting. We demonstrate an inflexibility to reflect, focusing instead on getting something accomplished. People will choose activity over a weighted blend of ideation, pause, consideration, and response. They relinquish breathing space because it takes too long. There is more joy in firefighting than fire prevention. The act of doing becomes *the* most important thing. Brené Brown, author of *Daring Greatly: How the Courage to Be Vulnerable Transforms the Way We Live, Love, Parent, and Lead*, captures it perfectly: "One of the most universal numbing strategies is what I call crazy-busy. I often say that when they start having 12-step meetings for busy-aholics, they'll need to rent out football stadiums. We are a culture of people who've bought into the idea that if we stay busy enough, the truth of our lives won't catch up with us."

Being constantly busy and defaulting to "getting things done" is how an Inflexible Thinking–type of individual operates. If you are leading people, and have that attitude, it will likely cause excessive stress on your team and potentially others. Individual contributors might be fooled by the belief that being (or looking) busy is the only way to behave. An inflexible thinker tends to rush to judgment. Their default habit is to make breathless decisions and take action as quickly as possible. They are the type of thinker who operates on gut instinct or, worse, quick guesses. They may even believe demonstrating a frenetic and discombobulated demeanor is a badge of honor.

There are several risks to operating with an Inflexible Thinking mindset. Being an absolutist for action means there is no time for imagination. When we do not make the time to envision—when the extremeness of being busy overcomes our thinking—we can miss out on developing our intelligence. We become so preoccupied and hell-bent to act, there is simply no time to learn. And when we are not learning, we are doing a disservice to ourselves and anyone we interact with. People who possess Inflexible Thinking habits are often oblivious to their own bias for action. They create a culture of freneticism. They pressure themselves and others to get tasks done quickly and to sign up for more when they complete them. The toxic cycle of doing for the sake of doing becomes the norm. Let's investigate a couple of examples.

Imagine there is a highly innovative idea that you and a number of colleagues dreamed up several months ago that remains untouched. It is a project that could save the organization several thousand dollars. Why does it remain untouched? Your organization spends most of its time in firefighting mode and by necessity you are right there with your hose. Whether you are a leader or team member, you are constantly being called in to fix something that has gone wrong. You keep asking yourself, "Why can't I ever do what I signed up for when I joined this organization?" The pressure mounts. As you continue to address problems that may not have occurred within an Open Thinking culture, you insist that at some point soon things will be different. But nothing changes. You and your organization are in thrall to the urgent. Panic reigns. Every issue seems like a burning platform. It becomes tyrannical. Indeed, it is a tyranny of the urgent. That innovative idea you dreamed up is never going to be touched because you keep getting called in to fight the next fire. This is an Inflexible Thinking organizational culture.

Let's look at another example, this time in your home. Each night after work you come home, eat dinner, and lament about the issues with your backyard deck. It's made of wood and is about 10 years old, but several defects have become noticeable, including the stairs, the railing, and portions of the flooring. You keep saying to yourself, "I want to learn how to fix a deck." But each night, instead of learning about woodworking repair or taking a class at the local college, you fill your time by watching mindless television on Netflix. The act of watching dopamine-driven programming night after night serves the magnetic draw of Inflexible Thinking. You are busy watching television, too concerned about what is happening elsewhere, rather than learning, ideating, and planning to fix something in your own backyard. This is another form of Inflexible Thinking, caught up in the busyness of binge-watching.

Throughout this book I will refer to these habits, often using the terms "reflection" and "action" as the twin engines of Open Thinking. When we maximize our time spent on both reflection and action—when we are conscious of continuously dreaming, deciding, and doing—the result is Open Thinking. If, however, we spend our time in any combination that does not maximize reflection and action, we end up exhibiting Indifferent, Indecisive, and/or Inflexible–type Thinking. These are the bad thinking habits you ought to keep in mind as you move through the book.

The Strategy of Stratego

When I was a child, I used to enjoy playing Stratego, a two-person board game that has much in common with Dou Shou Qi and L'Attaque. Reflecting back on my Stratego-playing days, I realized that not only did it help me learn how to think, it taught me the significance of strategy. Researching this book has brought the relationship between thinking and strategy more clearly into focus for me. I'm going to spend a few lines highlighting this importance through the example of Stratego.

Stratego, like chess, is a game played on a grid—10-by-10 rather than chess's 8-by-8. In chess, the purpose of the game is to checkmate your opponent's king. In Stratego, the objective is to capture your enemy's flag.

Each player has 40 plastic pieces of different military ranks. The teams are either blue or red. One side of each piece depicts the rank—the number 1 signifies the general, the highest-ranking playing piece—while the other side is blank. When two pieces collide in the game, the one with the lower number wipes out the other. For example, if a number 5 and a number 7 collide, the number 5 would be left standing and the number 7 would be removed from the board. Before play begins, each player places the 40 pieces—not including six immovable bombs—on their side of the board, 4 rows deep and 10 squares across. Unlike chess, your opponent only sees blank pieces from their side of the table.

The first phase of the game is entirely strategic, determining the placement of your flag and planning the positioning of pieces for both defense and offense, culminating, hopefully, in the capture of your opponent's flag. You might mentally muse on a few things. Do you protect your flag with all six bombs in a defensive shell? Should you place one of your bombs in your first row to invoke immediate collateral damage to your opponent? How will you launch an offensive and with what ranks of military personnel? Where do you place your number 8 pieces—called miners—who can defuse your opponent's bombs? Do you sacrifice a few mid-ranking officers at the beginning of the contest to throw off your enemy? Do you protect your general by positioning the piece alongside your flag? There is much thinking to do, many options to consider, and several decisions to make. There is even a "spy" piece that can assassinate a general. The "sly spy," as I referred to it, was my favorite piece.

Before you ever make a move in Stratego, you are constantly working through possible scenarios and debating with yourself what your strategy ought to be. I recall once playing against my neighbor, who was in the grip of Indecisive Thinking. He spent over 25 minutes planning the distribution of his pieces, an eternity when you are only 10 years old. It was my first inkling that we do not all think in the same way, that not everyone is as creative or critical in their thinking as they could be. I also recall an instance playing with that same neighbor when I hastily arranged the pieces without much thought. "I'll outsmart him during gameplay," I thought to myself. My demonstration of Inflexible Thinking saw me losing the match in a matter of minutes.

We can pick up a key lesson from games like Stratego. Successful players are constantly planning, assessing, deciphering, and shifting back and forth between the Creative, Critical, and Applied Thinking phases. They experiment and innovate, testing out different scenarios, revising as early plans prove unsuccessful, making new decisions and acting upon them. Sun Tzu once wrote, "In the midst of chaos, there is also opportunity." How do we respond when our best-laid plans come up short? How do we reassess, shift our strategy, and adapt? How do we remain fluid in thought and deed? Stratego serves as a second useful metaphor for the *Open to Think* framework.

As play begins in Stratego, each player takes a turn moving pieces vertically or horizontally. Your army can't move in a diagonal direction and may only move one space at a time. In the midst of the game you must be constantly reflecting *and* taking action. If your memory fails, you may be providing your opponent with an edge. If you act too quickly and telegraph your intentions, catastrophe may be on the horizon. If you take too long to make a decision to move a piece, your opponent may sense a weakness with your current positioning. You also need to keep track of your opponent's pieces. Which ones are not moving? Could those be bombs, the flag, or are they decoys? Keeping track of what personnel you have left—and equally important, what pieces your opponent has left—will help you make decisions on how to attack.

Stratego is not made up of three discrete phases of thinking. It is characterized instead by a continuum of deliberation, judgment, and response. Perhaps this is why it's called Stratego. There is strategy and then you go. Strategy-go. Stratego. But in reality the game is made up of continual strategy changes and constant movement. Strategy *and* go. Constant strategy and go. Constant Stratego.

The same can be said for life in general. If we are unwilling to spend time thinking in creative and critical ways, completing an action can be fraught with issues. The defined strategy will consequently fail. Conversely, if we find ourselves completing an objective but running into obstacles we did not plan for, we are obliged to rethink our overall strategy and return to conjuring up new ideas and resulting decisions. Finally, if we fixate solely on action—obsessing over busyness—the likelihood of additional stress in our lives will increase. What is the counter-argument? Dream. Decide. Do. Repeat.

The word strategy comes from the Greek *strategia* and *strategos*. Each of these words can loosely be translated as "office or command of a general" or "commander of an army." You are the general of your own strategy, responsible for your own thinking. You are the one in charge of your own game of Stratego, your own life. Your strategy and the way in which you think and take action are intertwined. Which begs the question, are you open to continuously strategizing? Or perhaps you are content to fall victim to an opponent's flanking moves, suffering the ignominy of defeat because you were too stubborn to revisit your original ideas and decisions.

The Gavel of Thinking

"We need a slow thinking movement. We have a crisis of thought. Empathy needs to resurface."

Those were the unexpectedly blunt words of Lisa Helps, mayor of Victoria, the capital city of British Columbia. Victoria is also my adopted hometown. I moved to Victoria in the summer of 2011 after having spent the previous 17 years in Vancouver. Victoria is populated by roughly 400,000 people throughout various municipalities in what is known as the Capital Regional District (CRD). It is about 60 miles southwest of Vancouver and separated by the Georgia Strait, a large body of water full of seals, orca whales, and breathtaking beauty. There is no bridge, so to get from Vancouver to Victoria there is a 90-minute car ferry, a 35-minute float plane or helicopter service, or a 12-minute airline flight. (I use all of them.)

Lisa won her first election as mayor in November 2014. I was intrigued by her platform, but even more so there was something about the way she conducted herself that piqued my interest. After her victory, I paid more attention to her behavior, actions, and decisions. I have interviewed, met, and socialized with many politicians over the years. Lisa was different from the others. "I think the key thing that I brought into this office," she said when interviewed in her modest work place, "is Critical Thinking." Lisa abandoned her PhD in history in favor of politics, and she believes it is her ability to think laterally—to assess how three or four completely disparate things can be woven together—that has helped her in the role of mayor.

"I am always looking for those connections, the ones that are obvious and those that are not. My desire is to make the world different, a better place." Lisa believes society has become stuck in its thinking. "It's a worry of mine," she confessed. "People make up their mind too quickly because they might have read three things on Facebook. On the other hand, I like to come into every situation with the option of changing my mind. It's one of the strengths that I bring to this job. My thinking ability. And one of the biggest challenges in the job of mayor is that there is not a lot of thoughtfulness in politics. All of us, politicians and citizens, need to accept that we are building on ideas and thoughts. We need more thoughtfulness for each other, and for the idea to change."

Lisa's candor reminded me of another mayor in the province of British Columbia, Greg Moore. Greg has been the mayor of the city of Port Coquitlam since 2008. Port Coquitlam is a city of just over 58,000 people 21 miles east of Vancouver in what is known as the

Lower Mainland. After 10 years in office, Greg announced in 2017 that he would not seek re-election in 2018. Since 2012, Greg has also served as the chair of Metro Vancouver, a federation of 21 municipalities and First Nations groups that collaboratively plans for and delivers regional-scale services, representing the more than 2.5 million inhabitants across the greater Vancouver area.

"My thinking style has always been about empowering people around me," said Greg. "It is so important to have as many conversations as you can with as many people as is possible. In those conversations, even if you have an opinion, you have to be open-minded. You have to literally be ready to change your opinion." Ultimately, Greg learned to create an environment within his community in which the thinking style is open by default.

Greg stressed that his own success, or that of any well-regarded politician, is based on the ability to create an environment characterized by Open Thinking. "Show that you can creatively think, and that you are open to change during decisions and actions," he stated, "and you will be far more successful."

Greg elaborated on his open-minded approach. "Politicians have a sense that they must always have an answer, if not *the* answer. I don't believe that. Someone may say to me at an open Q&A session, 'Have you thought of this?' I'll say, 'No I haven't. That's great. Let me consider your feedback, think about it, and get back to you.'" Greg's propensity to take an idea from someone, and then work it into the mix of the conversation or ideas going forward is one of his biggest strengths. But it is a difficult task to do. It takes an Open Thinker to say "I don't know."

As Steven D'Souza and Diana Renner outline in their 2014 book, *Not Knowing*, "In spite of the potential risks, admitting that we don't know can develop a sense of connection with those around us. The vulnerability and humility in that admission can bring us closer to the people we work with, and can engage them in the challenge of moving forward and trying to solve the problem at hand. The power differential and the hierarchical structure become inconsequential when we are facing our biggest challenges together."

Lisa believes that any mayor is supposed to be doing "public work in public." She insists that, as a result of this, her thinking and that of her municipal government ought to be open. But she runs into the same issues as Greg. "If I say something on the radio, publicly it quickly becomes 'Oh, the mayor is going to do this.' But if I modify the approach, then the mayor is flip-flopping. It has everything to do with an idea being in stone. Ideas are never in stone. It is directly opposite of human thought. We need to accept that we are building on ideas and thoughts. This is how progress is made. This is Open Thinking."

Both mayors were driving home a key point concerning Open Thinking. Be open. It sounds simple if not trite, but it is their ability to remain open to new ideas and thoughts—conversations and feedback from just about anyone—during all three categories of Open Thinking that has allowed them to accomplish great things in their cities. It is not enough to demonstrate Creative, Critical, and Applied Thinking once. We must stay vigilant and be open to the possibility that new concepts or ideas from others may improve the end result. Open Thinking must be thought of as constantly being in flow. It is iterative.

Academic and architect Kyna Leski argues that being open also leads to serendipitous discovery. "I feel that ideas strike at moments when you least expect it," she said. Over a 30-year career, Kyna has observed that when people are outside their normal day-to-day habits, a new idea can often appear. It might alter what was in progress. Kyna highlighted a passage by the poet Rainer Maria Rilke on the topic of the passing glance:

> I owe my intimacy with it, in part, to the passing glance with which we unconsciously examine and take in our customary environment, if it has even some slight relationship with us. It was this kind of glance that I suddenly stopped in its course and focussed, exactly and attentively.

Kyna continued, "Pausing as a suspension of the methodical search for something makes way for the passing glance. That doesn't mean that you can sit in a relaxed state awaiting its arrival. Hard work makes us receptive to recognizing the source of discovery. It is a discovery precisely because it is not a part of the defined schema; because it doesn't fit your thinking. It overturns some aspect of what you know or thought you knew. This shift is the seed of creativity. As a teacher, and designer, artist myself, I always return to discovery, the passing glance, as the guiding compass point throughout the process."

Greg shared a valuable lesson concerning a time when he learned about the differences between Inflexible and Open Thinking. It was his own version of the passing glance. "I almost had the biggest disaster of my life," he acknowledged. When he first became mayor in 2008, the Port Coquitlam community had a large homeless population. Before being sworn in, Greg looked out the window of City Hall one day and noticed that someone had decided to make a bus shelter their home. Greg sent his chief administrations officer to remove the glass from the shelter's roof. He did not want a homeless person living in plain view of City Hall; he took action, but ultimately failed to balance the need to reflect.

Greg now recognizes this as a myopic act of Inflexible Thinking. "My decision went through the entire homeless community," he said. "And they were mad. They made plans to set up a large camp on the lawn of City Hall in an act of defiance." As the new mayor of his hometown, he knew if "tent city" was about to become a fixture at City Hall it would not be well-received by the community. "I recognized my error, and decided to chat with the homeless. I invited them into City Hall, and let them know that I was setting up a homelessness task force." Greg not only wanted to right the wrong, he knew that by listening to and involving the homeless the end result would be better.

Greg's ultimate aim was to end homelessness, not to pick a fight. He apologized for his error in judgment, listened to their initial thoughts, and then reminded himself of his Open Thinking style. "Right then and there, I asked them to be on the committee." Greg realized that for change to happen, a different and more inclusive way of thinking was needed. He not only asked various members of the homeless community to join the task force, he also asked local business leaders to join. "The business community ended up saying to me that it was the most important piece of work, the most important committee that we've ever had. Empowering two different types of audiences helped greatly. But it would not have occurred if I had remained closed-minded."

Lisa shares another example about the value of Open Thinking over Inflexible or Indifferent Thinking. As a result of its 2015 strategic planning process, the City of Victoria voted to install a massive bicycle network across major thoroughfares. The City hired a team of international experts from biking friendly cities, such as Copenhagen and Amsterdam, to help with the plan. The City's first mistake was to rush into naming it something. "We called it 'Biketoria,' and it was a colossal mistake." Instead of asking others, reaching out to the community for opinion and ideas, the City rushed to name the network because everyone at Victoria City Hall felt it appropriate to quickly give the project a catchy name.

"I was getting a lot of feedback about the name, and our approach," admitted Lisa. "It wasn't great. One day I received a request from a local CEO to go out for a coffee. We sat down, and just talked about the entire plan. He captured what much of the feedback was indicating. It's not about bikes. It should be about health and wellness. Through iterative feedback and listening to others, we realized we were too focused on a name and the approach, and not enough on involving people to help us make it as good as can be." Lisa shifted from Inflexible Thinking—quick and myopic action with low reflection—back to Open Thinking, with the result that the City Council banned the name Biketoria.

Even during the installation of the bike lanes themselves, Lisa acknowledged the need to be more open and inclusive. "The first phase of the bike lanes on Pandora Street went relatively well," she said. "People were mostly happy. But as we shifted to another phase of the project—we began to have different conversations. There were different opinions and business needs on Fort Street versus Pandora Street. We paused and began asking these people how to make the project better for everyone." The project team ended up conducting a meter-by-meter analysis with every business and interested residents at the Fort Street location to better understand their issues, and to identify potential solutions. The same approach will be used for other phases of the project. It is important to recognize that Open Thinking can get lost if we become too anxious to complete. If we forget about the opinion of others, we just may be missing out on something better.

Lisa added, "I do think the greatest barrier in our society is a lack of genuine dialogue and critical practice. There is a massive lack of empathy out there. Empathy is a critical practice of Open Thinking; it makes us do things differently. A lack of willingness to engage in dialogue is what we need to overcome." Both Lisa and Greg provide important lessons about the need to be empathetic as we conduct Open Thinking. Losing sight of or ignoring the feelings of others can easily lead to a path of closed-mindedness.

In their 2017 Workplace Empathy survey, technology firm Businessolver discovered that fewer than half of all employees would call their organization empathetic, while 85 percent believe empathy is highly undervalued. As we will discover in Chapter 7, cognitive, emotional, and sympathetic empathy are critical success factors for Open Thinking. Henry Ford was quoted in Dale Carnegie's 1937 book, How to Win Friends and Influence People: "If there is any one secret of success, it lies in the ability to get the other person's point of view and see things from that person's angle as well as from your own." Over 80 years ago, Ford put himself in the shoes of regular citizens and felt their pain. It was not a faster horse that was needed but an economical motor vehicle, something that could help others in society.

Leaders like Lisa and Greg help us understand the importance of empathy in our communities and with Open Thinking. As academic George Couros wrote in his 2015 book, The Innovator's Mindset, "To create new and better ways of doing things, we need to first understand who we are creating them for."

WE: The Open Thinking Renegades

"My team hears me say this all the time, at least five times a day: 'Begin with the end in mind.' What are we trying to accomplish? Then, let's dream and work backwards to achieve it."

These are the words of Marc Kielburger, the co-founder of WE, a social enterprise that brings people together who seek to change the world. Legendary leaders to millions of young people across the globe, Marc and his brother Craig's story of Open Thinking began at a very young age. Through their teens and into their early 20s, the Kielburgers demonstrated a curiosity to understand why and how children were suffering in third world regions. Whether volunteering in the slums of Jamaica, the sweat shops in South Asia, or the streets of Thailand, the Kielburgers' penchant to assist those in need was remarkable. It's a clue. To be an Open Thinker one must possess an open mind. Marc, Craig, and WE provide us with some additional hope in this first chapter.

The numerous trips—which included the brothers inviting others to join them—planted an important seed that saw them found a charity, one that would help build schools in places such as Kenya, Nicaragua, and India. "Because we were able to think in a prolific way," said Marc, "we didn't realize that what we were trying to achieve was not possible." The brothers and their new foundation started out by building one school, then 10, then 100. They have now built over 700 schools where today more than 200,000 children around the world receive an education. This was only the beginning of their Creative, Critical, and Applied Thinking ways. "Adults told us to go to school, not to build a school," Marc said as he laughed. "But we knew that our work was about a deep purpose, and it was what we wanted to accomplish. We definitely were thinking differently at an early age."

That idea of the Kielburgers giving back through the establishment of schools eventually led them to their present-day enterprise, WE, "a movement that brings people together and gives them the tools to change the world." WE is made up of a number of entities, including WE Charity, ME to WE, and the extraordinarily popular WE Day—an annual daylong celebration of youth making a difference in their local and global communities, held in arenas around the world. Tens of thousands of young people attend WE Day every year. The likes of Selena Gomez, Magic Johnson, Justin Trudeau, Michelle Obama, Shawn Mendes, Al Gore, Shaquille O'Neal,

Jane Goodall, and the Dalai Lama have spoken at the event. The entire WE enterprise now employs over 400 people, with its efforts affecting millions of people.

"Our thinking process is simple: begin with the end in mind," Marc reaffirmed. "It's not about us, it's about them. We think about our stakeholders first, and all the time. It's about who are we talking to and what we are doing to reach our goals. We are challenging the charity world with our thinking." During our discussions, it became clear to me that Marc, his brother Craig, and the entire WE team's thought process was one that was always in motion, constantly threatening to squash the status quo, never resting on its laurels, while fervently believing an ego-driven thinking culture runs counter to the benefits of an Open Thinking ethos.

"We have changed the parameters of our thinking such that we identify the objectives of our partners and shape the ideas backwards from that," Marc said. "A lot of people get caught up with a lack of self-awareness. They think about themselves too much. They think about how great they are. Self-based thinking mechanisms end up causing them harm in the end. But for us at WE, we think about who we're trying to engage with first, find the areas of intersection as a team, and then work through the cycle of dreaming, decision-making, and doing to get it done."

It was apparent to me that Marc's and by extension the WE organization's model of thinking was akin to Open Thinking. WE is a thriving family of organizations, and its thinking culture is one where the employees—regardless of rank or job title—are open and in turn are trusted to do what is right. By starting with the end in mind (their main goal), the organization unleashes its Creative and Critical Thinking habits to sort out how it can get accomplished. From there, during the Applied Thinking phase, Marc was adamant that they are unafraid to shift back into Creative or Critical Thinking if things are not going smoothly—another example of how important it is to be iterative as an Open Thinker.

Marc's insights also put a spotlight on the closed-minded thinking habits of many organizations. "We have a hard time bringing older adults into WE because they historically have worked in big companies where they have been used to a very specific, focused, and narrow task mindset. It seems hard for them to dream and decision-make—let alone do—like our WE culture. I find that today's companies tend to limit your thinking to a two-inch box. 'Here is your area of responsibility, so don't deviate.' This is not our thinking culture at WE. At the end of the day, we're all on deck to help with the dreaming, decision-making, and the doing. For example, if I get an email blast for approval, I will say, 'It's not about us, it's about them—you make the call.' Thinking like this has to start from the top. Otherwise, patterns in many cases become normalized and that's not what our culture will ever be like."

Throughout the book we will hear from people like Marc, Lisa, and Greg as they express their thoughts and share their insights on Open Thinking. For Marc specifically, the success of WE can be attributed to the fact he and his brother refused to be closed-minded in their thinking from an early age. Today, tens of thousands of citizens from all walks of life and countries are positively impacted by their refusal to be beholden to Indifferent, Indecisive, or Inflexible Thinking.

Hat Tip to the Millinery

Through a brief statement posted to their website on May 24, 2016, fans of The Tragically Hip were left shocked and disheartened when the band released news that its lead singer, Gord Downie, had been diagnosed with glioblastoma multiforme, a rare form of brain cancer. The word "terminal" closely followed. The next day the band made another announcement. The five men who made up The Hip divulged they would tour Canada one last time, starting in Victoria on July 22 and concluding in Kingston, Ontario, the band's hometown, on August 20.

I was fortunate to attend half of the concerts that summer, starting in Victoria and ending in Kingston. I have been a fan of this rock-blues-alternative band since 1989. When Gord appeared onstage for the first time in Victoria during that tour, it was a moment I will never forget. He emerged wearing a shiny, hot pink, metallic suit crafted by Toronto designer Izzy Camilleri. "What a way to go out," I thought to myself. The cheering from the crowd seemed to last an eternity. A fedora that brimmed with utter uniqueness further complemented his bedazzling stage outfit. It was big and bold and it sported what looked like peacock feathers sprouting out of its left side. As a self-proclaimed "hat guy," I was instantly impressed. Even a little jealous.

Gord had six distinctive hats made for that tour. Each of them was designed by Karyn Ruiz of Lilliput Hats, a traditional millinery in Toronto's Little Italy neighborhood. I contacted Karyn asking if I could come by her shop. In part, I wanted to see where Gord Downie's famous hats were made. But my curiosity quickly veered toward the millinery itself. At Lilliput Hats, the design, construction, and selling of hats occurs simultaneously. Each hat is handmade, crafted by a half-dozen employees. While I interviewed over 50 people for this book—and pored over reams of data, history, and academic research—Lilliput Hats and Karyn Ruiz's leadership stuck with me as a wonderful symbol *and* example of Open Thinking.

As you pull open the solid oak door framed by the pink and black trim that adorns the Lilliput building, your eyes are met by a carnival of colors, an aroma of indelible smells, a symphony of discussions, and the creaking of an old wooden floor. While the exterior building beams with the pride of Little Italy, inside the shop lies a truly incandescent jewel.

There are hats for sale on the walls as you first walk in, with a few placed on knee-level display racks. Take a few more paces—past the chaise longue—and you are smack in the middle of the working area of the milliners. There is no backroom. There is no divider. A table has fabric strewn about, several sewing machines are humming, steamers are steaming, and there is what looks to be a wall full of wooden hat molds spanning the head shape of every human on the planet. As you spin around you can't help but notice you are parading through the middle of a working rainbow. The colors are electric, vibrant, and seemingly endless. The chatter among milliners and between customers is ongoing. It is a magical mystery tour that I immediately fell in love with.

Whether in the moment or planning for the long term, what I discovered is that Lilliput Hats has a team constantly dreaming, deciding, and doing. Using only the finest materials and the time-honored traditions of millineries from days past, Lilliput Hats has remained in business since the late 1980s because of its Open Thinking culture. Karyn and her associates are accustomed to simultaneously thinking creatively and critically, all the while under the pressure of client deadlines. Hats must get made. Incomplete action is not an option. But creativity and critical decision-making is where the art meets the science. As I observed the milliners working in their eclectic shop, I felt so moved by their Open Thinking habits that I came up with the idea of closing each chapter in this book with an observation or two from Karyn and her team.

For now, hold on to your hat and let's begin discussing Creative Thinking in earnest.

II

creative thinking

2

At the Lonely End of the Think

Others have seen what is and asked why.
I have seen what could be and asked why not.

PABLO PICASSO

I F YOU FOUND yourself swimming in some body of water during the early 2000s and there was a white volleyball nearby for whatever reason, chances are you probably heard someone screaming "Wilson" with comedic panic in their voice.

Tom Hanks starred in the 2000 fiction film *Cast Away* as Chuck Noland, a FedEx systems analyst whose job requires him to travel the world to ensure FedEx shipping depots are operating as efficiently as possible. During an unexpected trip on Christmas Eve, Noland finds himself on an aircraft headed for Malaysia. But Noland never makes it to his destination, surviving a crash that kills the plane's crew. He finds himself washed up on a remote Pacific island without any form of communication or supplies except what can be salvaged from a handful of FedEx boxes. These provide Noland with a few rudimentary tools and a friend: Wilson, the volleyball.

Cast Away provides us with a pop culture example of the Open Thinking framework; a useful place to begin our exploration of the Creative Thinking component. Noland's compulsiveness, obsessiveness, and addiction to work is typical of so many people today. First, he neglects his girlfriend, Kelly, and her wishes for a proper relationship. Second, he is roughly 50 pounds overweight, a telltale sign that work is either consuming him or causing stress. The job comes first while health and personal relationships are secondary. The viewer is left with the impression of an Everyman workaholic.

A character flaw of Noland's that many people wrestle with today is his overzealousness to get things done—to be constantly busy—without thinking creatively beforehand. To be continually busy is how he views his professional existence. His only thought is to finish a task, doing so as quickly as possible. To pause and think creatively is an alien concept to Noland. Such is the life of a FedEx systems analyst, whose success is measured in terms of the speed of package delivery to clients.

Following the crash, Noland exhibits not only fear but the same rush-to-judgment behaviors that characterize his professional life. On one of his first nights on the island, Noland notices a light from a freight ship miles away from shore, and believes a rescue to be imminent. When dawn breaks, he grabs a broken oar and begins to paddle out to the ship on a dinghy with only half of the hull inflated. He is thwarted by the force of the ocean, injuring himself in the process as he capsizes and cuts his leg on some coral. Instead of creatively thinking through his options, Noland jumps to Applied Thinking—to get things done fast—and ends up failing miserably. This tendency is evident again when his attempt to start a fire to cook crabs results in further injury.

Four years into his island existence, the viewer is presented with a lean, fit, and savvy Noland, who has learned to adapt to his new environment. He clearly is a man with time on his hands, one who has been forced to think creatively to survive. Life has become a thinking continuum for the only inhabitant of the island. His circumstances have exposed an impressively advanced version of himself. Noland is now an Open Thinker.

For example, Noland devises a calendar on a cave wall using the sun and a crack in the rocks to determine time. He calculates the day and the month without recourse to expensive stationery or digital devices. He constructs an elaborate freshwater gathering system, reliant on empty coconuts and rainfall. There are other examples that demonstrate how Noland cognitively and physically transforms himself into a better thinker. He is in a new continuum of thinking *and* doing, of reflecting *and* taking action. He is constantly dreaming, deciding, and doing.

Perhaps the best story to illustrate Noland's new Open Thinking mindset is when a portable toilet door appears on shore. Noland sits on the beach—with trusty Wilson by his side—and stares contemplatively at the door wondering what he might do with it. There is an excruciatingly long spell of silence. It seems like he is thinking for days, kicking around ideas about what to do with this door. Suddenly, Noland screams to Wilson, "This could work! This could work…"

The door becomes a sail for Noland's escape from the island. For years, he has been considering how to overcome those overpowering waves and attempt a return home. Not only does he envisage how the door might be used, he goes through the pros and cons of how it might work. Once that decision is made, it becomes time to build the raft. He also has to ensure it is stocked with rations and supplies for the journey. Over a three-month period, Noland is in a continuous cycle of Creative, Critical, and Applied Thinking to get the raft built with the new sail. His thinking and action habits are now synchronized for the task at hand. Noland is brainstorming, deducing, testing, and acting in succession. Arguably he is exhibiting the Open Thinking continuum in full.

If the portable toilet door had washed up on shore a few days after the airplane crash, it is quite possible Tom Hanks's character would have immediately used it not as a sail, but as a roof. This is the plight of many employees and leaders in today's organizations. Rushed thinking has become an issue for many. We jump to action—because we have inculcated a mindset to "do more with less" and to get things done quickly—rather than to pause and creatively think what we might do. We do not take a break to consider the possibilities, and this makes our decision-making weak.

Our organizations are rife with versions of the Chuck Noland who landed on the island rather than the one who vacated it. Both employees and leaders are reacting far too quickly to the portable toilet door that washes up on shore, to the immediate allure of a light in the distance, and the incessant desire to make a fire without creatively thinking through the ways it might properly be accomplished. Why don't we hesitate and creatively think before taking action? Why do we jump to quick conclusions? Why must we insist on action before dreaming up the possibilities? Why do we seem so distracted? Why do we make such rash decisions?

This chapter explores those questions. Specifically, we'll analyze the various obstacles and limitations to Creative Thinking.

The Tower is Missing Its Pieces

In the late 1990s and early 2000s, I led the delivery of higher education programs at the British Columbia Institute of Technology (BCIT) for adult career changers. In one program, I would regularly run an exercise with a new cohort of students once they had completed the first week of their studies. This program was a year-long diploma aimed to help adults—who already had a degree—learn about business, leadership, and high tech.

On that first Friday afternoon, I would separate the class of 30 into five teams of six and add their names to the whiteboard. I then instructed them to shift from the main classroom to an assigned meeting room. It might be down the hall or on the floor above. The only verbal instructions I gave were as follows: "Go to the room you have been assigned to, read the instructions found in the envelope on the table, and complete your task." I provided no further rules other than to tell them I would be observing and that they were not permitted to speak to me. We would meet back in the large classroom to discuss the activity as a group once it wrapped up. Giddy with excitement, the students went rushing through the main classroom door to complete their quest.

For additional context, the average age of each cohort was approximately 35 years old and the students usually possessed a cumulative working age of over 300 years. They had professional experience in abundance. There were plenty of diverse and tenured academic backgrounds in each class, too. Generally, the students had 40 higher education degrees and diplomas, totaling approximately 140 years of higher education learning.

Inside each envelope was a piece of paper outlining some rudimentary instructions. There were a variety of materials as well. Pens, construction paper of various colors, glue, staplers, scissors, rulers, tape, and so on, were also included. The instructions went something like this:

> Using only the materials found in this envelope, you and the team have 45 minutes to build the following structure. Once you've completed it, head back to the classroom.

Underneath that meager line of information was a diagram outlining very specifically (with precise dimensions, scale, and colors) what the object had to look like. The students were asked to build a tower made of several layers of paper and straws. I provided some initial hope by including materials to get them all started. This way the students could get off on the right foot. But for this experiment to be successful a twist had to be introduced. Unbeknownst to the teams, I withheld certain materials from each envelope. Lacking the correct items to successfully build the tower, each team's project was destined to fail.

For example, the students may have needed scissors to accurately cut the paper, but they were missing. A specific color of paper was required for an additional layer to the tower, but it too was nowhere to be found in the envelope. One of the groups would be without anything to keep the tower together, such as glue, tape, or staples. Some would be missing a ruler, thereby forcing the team to guess the measurements.

I conducted this thinking experiment 15 times over a five-year period. In each case I wandered from room to room, observing what was transpiring with these highly educated and experienced people. Invariably, the groups would initially react in one of three ways:

- **Dictatorial.** An alpha male or alpha female would immediately take charge and read out the instructions to the team. From there, they would also play the part of general contractor, instructing people to build the tower according to their own unique thoughts or ideas. They immediately dove in. The leader was aggressive. Everyone else fell in line. Things got done fast. It was an example of Inflexible Thinking.

- **Panic.** Whether one person read the instructions or the group contorted their bodies so that everyone was reading at the same time, after quickly sorting through all available materials, the group quickly reached a consensus that the task was impossible. It was obvious they might not have a ruler or scissors, and so a sense of panic gripped the room on what to do next. They were about to fail, so they sat on the fence. "What should we do?" was often screamed. The group's tentativeness got in the way of thinking more creatively. Indecisive Thinking took hold.

- **Hopelessness.** Instead of panicking, the groups devoid of hope rested on past thinking habits. After reading the instructions, these groups typically assigned roles to everyone. They were far more methodical. But even after assigning roles, the team would come to the conclusion that the task was impossible. They may have been able to finish a few floors, but when they could not complete the task, the status quo of Indifferent Thinking became the norm. They neither took action nor did they reflect.

On five occasions when I ran the activity, something magical happened. It was the point at which some of the students figured out, much like Chuck Noland from *Cast Away*, that their current way of thinking had to change. If they were going to accomplish the goal, they had to begin thinking differently, injecting some new dreaming and deciding into the team to complete the activity successfully.

What was that magic? Nowhere did the instructions indicate that the students had to remain in the room where they were assigned. Sure, they were only permitted to use the materials in the envelope.

However, that did not preclude the group from working with *other* groups. At no time were the groups locked in their meeting room, nor were they told to stay put. Every single time I ran the exercise, the teams assumed from the outset that they were to work alone in their assigned room.

On those five occasions, the idea to work with another team would always materialize after several failed attempts to build the tower. Not once did a team first stop to think through the various ways the tower might be built. Instead, they invoked one of the three Open Thinking inhibitors and most teams ultimately failed. The idea to work with other teams usually happened around the 25-minute mark for those that were successful. Once the idea surfaced, the team members would quickly rush out of their assigned room, stampeding down the hall or riding the elevator to find the other teams. No one ever took notice of where the other four groups were stationed *before* they left the larger classroom at the beginning of the activity, so now there was further work to do.

On one occasion, two teams came out of their rooms at the same time, virtually bumping into one another. I know because they almost ran me over. The teams quickly rallied other teams and completed the goal. On another occasion, three teams emerged at roughly the same time. But the three other times when the "aha" moment had arrived, it was a lone team running around trying to convince other teams that they had to work together to complete the tower. For the teams that had come to the conclusion that everyone had to work together, it became an intense exercise in collaboration. In the end, they managed to beat the 45-minute clock.

But on 10 other occasions, the teams remained in their rooms. They tried in earnest to build that paper tower, but because it was impossible to do so without working with other teams, no group ever properly completed it. They all failed. But there were always a few unique ideas. Some would use a pen and scribble "Imagine this blue is actually red," if a layer required red paper but their envelope did not contain any. Some tried to recreate the required dimensions by instituting their own measurement system, to their own defined scale of course.

Regardless of whether the teams were successful or not, after the 45 minutes had passed, we always met as a 30-person cohort back in the large classroom to debrief what had happened.

Unfailingly, students would remark that they were so excited at venturing off to the meeting room that they completely forgot there were other people they could have been liaising with from the beginning of the activity. Many wondered why they sped off to the meeting room right away. Some would discuss why they felt the need to close the door of their meeting room. "It was a competition, and we wanted to win," was a normal response. But I never made it a competition, and there was no prize to win.

Once they got to the meeting room, the students often questioned, in hindsight, why, after they read the provided instructions, they immediately launched into the execution phase of building the tower. "If only we had first paused and thought about all the different ways in which to build the tower, I'm sure we might have been successful," was another common reaction.

With roughly 400 adults having gone through this exercise over the years, none of them began it by asking the question, "Why don't we work with other teams first?" Not one. With two-thirds of all teams never having completed the tower, it has often served as a reminder to me that many people either have forgotten or never learned the meaning of Open Thinking. It requires being open to think differently. We cannot use our cognitive biases and penchant for past thinking habits as the basis for better thinking in the future. As Daniel Kahneman remarked, "Confirmation bias comes from when you have an interpretation, and you adopt it, and then, top down, you force everything to fit that interpretation. That's a process that we know occurs in perception that resolves ambiguity, and it's highly plausible that a similar process occurs in thinking."

The paper tower exercise demonstrated to me that each of us has a degree of Chuck Noland in our existing thinking habits. The Noland that landed on the island. The objective of Open Thinking is to continuously dream, decide, and do, not to be overly indifferent, indecisive, or inflexible.

Open Thinking Inhibitors

Joseph Campbell is one of my favorite writers. The well-known American mythologist and lecturer is credited with affecting the lives of many screenwriters, directors, and novelists through his "hero's journey" archetype. Campbell depicts the journey as follows: "A hero ventures forth from the world of common day into a region of supernatural wonder: fabulous forces are there encountered and a decisive victory is won: the hero comes back from this mysterious adventure with the power to bestow boons on his fellow man." My favorite use of the model may be how director George Lucas incorporated it into the journey of Luke Skywalker and the original *Star Wars* saga.

But what sometimes gets overlooked in Campbell's theory—and in the way he lived his life—is the invaluable component of time. It's something I'm going to harp on throughout the book. Campbell insisted on living his life by incorporating periods of deep reflection. He gave himself permission to think creatively, and did so by allowing himself the time in which to do so. He paused before taking action. He reflected before moving ahead. This is where (and perhaps when) the magic happened.

For example, Campbell dropped out of a doctoral program at Columbia University in his 20s when his professors told him mythology was an unsuitable choice for a dissertation. He spent the next few years traveling, listening, and soaking up what life had to offer. On his own, Campbell was brewing the theory behind the hero's journey. Time was spent in Paris and other parts of Europe. He eventually made his way to Woodstock, New York, where he spent the better part of two years reading and reflecting some more. Out of this entire experience came what is arguably his most famous work, *The Hero With a Thousand Faces*, the book that cemented the hero's journey framework.

In it, Campbell writes: "The aim is not to see, but to realize that one is, that essence; then one is free to wander as that essence in the world. Furthermore: the world too is of that essence. The essence of oneself and the essence of the world: these two are one. Hence separateness, withdrawal, is no longer necessary. Wherever the hero may wander, whatever he may do, he is ever in the presence of his own essence, for he has perfected the eye to see. There is no separateness. Thus, just as the way of social participation may lead in the end to a realization of the all in the individual, so that of exile brings the hero to the self in all." The key word here is "wander." When you permit yourself to pause, to reflect, to wander, it becomes part of your self. If you can incorporate wandering into your overall behavior, you are more likely to practice Creative Thinking. Once you give yourself the permission to reflect, the Open Thinking mindset becomes easier to attain. If you are a leader or part of the C-Suite, reflection is one of the key ways you can bring about new ideas, innovations, and breakthroughs.

As mentioned in Chapter 1, when you do not spend enough time reflecting—coupled with a disdain for action—you become an Indifferent Thinker. Your thinking is lazy, informed by an acceptance of the status quo. Change will be arduous, whether for you specifically or the team and organization you work with. However, as with Chuck Noland in *Cast Away*, if you spend no time allowing your mind to wander or dream and you jump to conclusions or actions, you block any chance of becoming an Open Thinker. You are someone who might never be able to inject new ideas or innovations into a particular situation. Of course, if you spend too much time reflecting—without taking any action—you are largely indecisive and unable to progress your goals.

Eric Jordan is the CEO of Codename Entertainment and offers valuable insight. Wearing a kilt, knee-high leather boots, and a plaid shirt, he chatted with me over several coffees about his gaming company. Codename has produced several popular games in the clicker/idle game space. Also known as incremental games, these video games consist of players performing simple and repeatable actions on a screen to gain a form of currency. The currency acts as a reward to unlock new features.

One of Codename's most popular games is *Crusaders of the Lost Idols*, the award-winning clicker/idle game where players unlock new Crusaders, level them up, collect gear, and earn achievements to progress through a fantasy universe. It is one of the most-played games on

Kongregate.com out of more than 109,000 available and it is consistently found within the top 1 percent of games played on Steam, the computer-based entertainment platform. *Crusaders of the Lost Idols* is the only idle/clicker game to include a formation feature where players learn to master the strategy of organizing their party of characters into the most powerful, monster-destroying formation possible. But *Crusaders of the Lost Idols* almost never came to be. Even though Codename Entertainment was a gaming company—one that has to be thinking creatively in its line of work—Inflexible Thinking mindsets had crept into the company's operating ethos.

Before publishing *Crusaders of the Lost Idols*, the company had released another game called *Shards of Titan*. In the words of Eric, "It was an exercise in being too focused on action and mind, forgetting about heart and reflection." Although not a disaster, *Shards of Titan* was nowhere near the success that *Crusaders of the Lost Idols* is today. Why? "We stopped development and put *Crusaders* on the shelf to breathe," explained Eric. "And that made all the difference." In the case of *Shards of Titan*, the team at Codename Entertainment was in a constant state of action, using their minds only to pump the product into the hands of game players as quickly as possible. It was an exercise in production versus the balance of action and reflection. As a result, although enjoyed by a subset of gamers, *Shards of Titan* was not the runaway success that *Crusaders* has become.

Nowadays, Eric has steered the company over a four-year period to use the terminology he calls "bets." About 50 percent of the company's time is spent ensuring that existing games and operations meet their revenue targets. That leaves 50 percent of the company's time to focus on the bets, where the people in the company can dream, reflect, and let their minds wander on new initiatives. I ascertained that the bets Eric referred to this time involved many Creative Thinking moments. They allowed multiple games (or parts of games) to be simultaneously developed or dreamed up, improving their chances for market success. Employees may let one game sit on the shelf for several months, turning their reflecting and wandering minds to work on another game.

This was the strategy employed from the outset of developing *Crusaders of the Lost Idols*. The game was built over a much longer period of time so that proper and thorough reflection would make it a truly engaging experience for its customers. It proved to be a very successful culture change, too. "If our strategy had remained the same, *Crusaders* would not be the success it is today," said Eric. "And now, we have taken greater time to more fully develop our new bets. With dedicated Creative Thinking time in our process, there are far more options for us in the pipeline."

When we allow our minds to daydream or sit idle, creativity tends to flourish. Research published in 2015 by Professor Jonathan Schooler of the University of California, Santa Barbara and Professor Jonathan Smallwood of the University of York suggests people are more creative when they allow their minds to wander. Furthermore, the researchers discovered that when people are working on a difficult objective, it is better for them to work on something that promotes mind-wandering first. When they go back to the more difficult objective, creativity is unleashed. The researchers found that the optimal way to be more creative is to switch between difficult and easy tasks, with easy ones allowing for innovative ideas to be hatched.

Codename Entertainment has become a company that ensures Creative Thinking is a strategic part of its operations and its culture. It will not develop any new game without the game spending time in the incubation period. As was the case with Joseph Campbell, for Creative Thinking to be truly successful, individuals and organizations should recognize that building in time for reflection can be a critical enabler to Open Thinking. Imagine what you or your organization might dream up if you employed this sort of strategy.

Life Saver Thinking

Swiss psychiatrist Carl Jung, the founder of analytical psychology, was heavily influenced by Sigmund Freud's research on the unconscious mind. In fact, they were once close confidantes. Jung eventually deviated from Freud's work—and the friendship suffered—by exploring the concept of archetypes: universal, mythic characters that reside in each of our collective unconscious. Joseph Campbell's hero's journey was in turn especially influenced by Jung's ideas.

Jung wrote: "The conscious mind is a bad judge of its own situation and often persists in the illusion that its attitude is just the right one." He argued that our brains possess an unconscious process that tends to take over when our attitude and position on a given situation become unfavorable or inadequate. We might panic or freeze, rush to judgment, and even suspend action altogether if circumstances start to wobble. Jung's theory reminded me of the scenario that played out over and over again with those students of mine and the tower activity.

I turned to Daniel Levitin for additional context. I wanted his opinion on what he thought were some of the inhibitors of Creative Thinking. Daniel is the James McGill Professor Emeritus of Psychology and Behavioral Neuroscience at McGill University. He is the author of best-selling books like *This Is Your Brain on Music*, *The World in Six Songs*, *The Organized Mind*, and *Weaponized Lies: How to Think Critically in the Post-Truth Era*, as well as a practicing cognitive psychologist and neuroscientist. Daniel is also a musician and record producer, having worked with the likes of The Grateful Dead, Stevie Wonder, Steely Dan, and Chris Isaak.

"There are a number of reasons," he replied. "Being overly self-critical is one factor. Or fear of what others will think is another." The most prominent aspect that stood out for Daniel, however, centered on tools and what he referred to as a person's skills-at-the-ready. "If you're a painter and you don't have paint—or your paint is so disorganized you can't find anything—you're not going to get very far, and you're likely to sap a lot of your creative energy with frustration. Have your paints and brushes and paper or canvases orderly so that when you walk into your studio, you're ready to go." Daniel meant this literally as well as metaphorically. If you want to think creatively and make better decisions, you had better get organized before you start rushing to action.

Daniel also believes that bad thinking is avoidable. People who make difficult decisions later in the day—when their neural resources are at their lowest—can often run into difficulties. Daniel encourages people to make demanding or strenuous decisions early in the day, not in the afternoon or at night. "Recognize that you are not an expert on everything," he added, "and seek expertise from others to help guide your decision-making." Would Chuck Noland have fared better if more of his colleagues had been stranded on the island? Would my students have solved the challenge if they had thought to work with others much earlier on in the tower-building activity? Would your Creative Thinking juices flow more easily if you were to first reach out to others in the morning?

Samsung Electronics provides a glimpse into the repercussions on our thinking when we are stressed or overtired. The example is brief, but it packs a punch about the relationship between health and wellness and our thinking at work.

In 2015, the senior leadership team at Samsung was hungry for a win against its major competitor, Apple. With industry knowledge that Apple would likely launch its new iPhone 7 in the fall of 2016, Samsung issued a corporate edict to team members. It wanted its new phone, dubbed the Galaxy 7, to be available for consumer purchase before the iPhone 7. Ultimately, Samsung wanted a first-to-market advantage. This forced time pressure—where employees worked 80-hour weeks, often sleeping the night at the company's headquarters in Seoul, South Korea—not only bogged down their Creative Thinking, it caused several inadequate decisions to be made. Consequently, as employees became increasingly fatigued and tense, they failed to detect a flaw in the battery design. That missed flaw caused the phone to explode and catch fire. A global recall of all Samsung 7 devices resulted in a write-down of more than US$5.3 billion.

Daniel insists that if we were to break large problems into smaller ones, our thinking would improve. Take, for example, the origin of Life Savers. In 1912, when Clarence Crane—Cleveland chocolate maker and owner of the Queen Victoria Chocolate Company—recognized his customers were not buying chocolate in the hot summer months, he decided to do something about it. The problem? Crane's chocolate easily melted in hot temperatures. Customers wouldn't buy Queen Victoria's chocolate in the summer months. This was a revenue issue as much as an operating one.

Instead of trying to solve the issue of preventing his chocolate from melting, Crane chose a different path. He broke the problem down into smaller parts, and eventually decided to create something sweet that did not melt. Noticing that his local pharmacist used a special pill-making device to make flat and round drugs, he borrowed it and began to produce "Crane's Peppermint Life Savers." The name emerged once Crane decided to punch holes in the middle of the disc-like peppermint candies he was now making. The shape reminded him of flotation devices that lifeguards would use at the pool or beach. Today, Life Savers endure as an iconic candy to children and adults alike.

But, as we will discover next, there are more inhibitors to Creative Thinking to highlight.

The Burning Platform of Bad Thinking

Chuck Noland eventually figured out that the secret to Open Thinking was to be continuously reflective, judgmental, and action-oriented. When he arrived on the island, Noland's thinking jumped to conclusions. It was indifferent and inflexible. He gave no time to dream, often jumping right to performance and action. His thinking style was closed and myopic. The consequences were severe. Like Noland, the students in my paper tower experiment too often rushed to respond, failing to pause and consider all available options. Ergo, most of the groups floundered and did not achieve the goal of the exercise. Eric Jordan and his Codename Entertainment team reviewed their tendency to exhibit Inflexible Thinking, and decided to add more reflection and dreaming time into the process of making an online game.

Why do some people bypass this important element of thinking? Why is Creative Thinking cast away, so to speak? In addition to the points Daniel Levitin raises, there are other researchers who provide some clues. Roy F. Baumeister and Ellen Bratslavsky of Case Western Reserve University, for example, discovered in 2001 through meta-analyses that "bad is stronger than good, as a general principle across a broad range of psychological phenomena." The researchers found that whether through personal or professional relationships, stereotypes, self-image, health, learning patterns, or language, people tend to be more affected by bad things than good. In fact, the academics uncovered evidence suggesting it takes five positive interactions to undo every bad one: "Bad interactions have stronger, more pervasive, and longer-lasting effects."

Put this in context with where you work today. If the culture at your workplace demonstrates incivility, fear, and disengagement— where command-and-control leadership practices are prevalent—it will be onerous for team members to work with one another in creative ways, let alone independently. They will easily fall into the Indifferent Thinking mindset because input into decision-making is missing. People will simply keep their heads down and do as they are told for fear of reprisal. When someone is exhibiting an Indifferent Thinking mindset, they neither pause nor take action. It is a form of thinking purgatory, one in which an individual deliberately chooses to be uninformed. Think of these types of people as not being engaged at work, lacking purpose. Apathy becomes the norm because there are too many dreadful interactions, comments, and moments in the work environment. Those in the organization considered to be high performers may then say to themselves, "Forget this, I'm out of here," and begin their search for a new job elsewhere.

Similarly, if the organization is focused entirely on profit or in some cases maximizing shareholder return, there may be a large swath of employees unwilling to be creative because they do not believe in the organization's "bad" or misguided purpose.

In the parlance of economics, Daniel Kahneman and Amos Tversky posited that when making a financial decision, people look at the potential for losses before the potential for gains. This is known as prospect theory. According to Kahneman and Tversky, "Losses have more emotional impact than an equivalent amount of gains." Again, bad is much stronger than good. Our natural human tendency is to be more affected by things that are negative (or are potentially negative) than those that are positive. Is it any wonder then that an authoritative, top-down, power-hungry organizational culture negatively affects Creative Thinking? Further, should we be surprised that Creative Thinking is forgotten when an organization fails to conduct itself with a higher purpose, choosing instead to serve only profit-mongers or shareholders as opposed to all stakeholders?

Of course, this was the central argument in my second book, *The Purpose Effect*. During its composition, I visited for several hours with Dr. A.R. (Elango) Elangovan of the University of Victoria, someone who has spent a lifetime researching purpose, meaning, and callings. In fact, Elango has lived by the following declaration of purpose for years: "To help others live a fulfilled life." Elango suggested that when your role provides clarity and you are able to work in an arena of positivity—working for good—it is far more likely to result in sparking your Creative Thinking. He also indicated that this enhances your resilience, which allows you to handle eventual setbacks. Together, your personal purpose and the organization's purpose can affect your Creative Thinking and militate against the tendency to be swayed by the "bad."

Nokia's story illustrates this point. In early 2011, then-CEO Stephen Elop gave a talk to employees shortly after arriving from Microsoft, where he had been responsible for the popular Office suite of applications. Known as a motivator and a workaholic, Elop's speech was transcribed, posted on an internal Nokia blog, and then leaked to *The Wall Street Journal*. It has since become known as the "burning platform" memo.

Between 1999 and 2007, Nokia—the Finnish Telecommunications Company and maker of popular mobile phones—increased annual revenues from roughly €20 billion to just over €50 billion. The company was flourishing in many ways. It accounted for more than 40 percent of all global mobile phone sales. Not only was Nokia financially successful, its culture was collaborative and creative products were being shipped quarterly. Its customers were loyal, too.

But by the end of 2010, revenues had fallen by about 20 percent. Not insurmountable, but dropping steadily. Following a similar pattern, net profit at Nokia had risen from €2.6 billion in 1999 to a whopping €10.5 billion in 2007. But by 2010 it had plummeted to €2.5 billion. Elop was hired in late 2010 to combat the likes of Apple, Google, and Research in Motion (BlackBerry). His initial game plan left many questioning his ability to lead. Cost-cutting measures swept the company while high-performing employees began to leave voluntarily. In a demonstration of Inflexible Thinking, Elop partnered with his old employer, Microsoft, to replace Nokia's Symbian mobile phone operating system with Microsoft's Windows Phone. This decision proved rough sailing for the company. Nokia engineers hated it. Customers were questioning the company's sanity. The press was having a field day.

But it was Elop's speech and subsequent memo that shriveled up any hope for a return to Nokia's once formidable Creative Thinking days. The negative words Elop chose—summarizing the company's condition in 2011 as a "burning platform"—went over poorly with employees. Elop began the speech by introducing a story about a man working on an oil platform in the North Sea. After waking up from a loud explosion on the rig, surrounded by fire, the man had to make a decision: let the fire consume him or jump into the frigid waters of the North Sea and hope for the best. Like many management consultants and business executives who use the metaphor inappropriately, Elop was framing his message with a distasteful allusion to real events: 167 people had lost their lives on July 6, 1988, following an explosion on the Piper Alpha oil platform.

Elop's attempts to reinvigorate his Nokia colleagues backfired, creating a seismic rift between executives and the workforce. Many could neither forgive nor forget, and the culture shifted to one of angst and fear, with the effect of inhibiting Creative Thinking throughout the organization. Between 2011 and 2013 losses totaled more than €6.5 billion, and without the backing of the board, Elop left his post and returned to Microsoft. He did so already having negotiated both the Windows Phone partnership and the sale of Nokia's Devices and Services division to Microsoft in April of 2014.

After interviewing hundreds of current and former Nokia employees, authors Pekka Nykänen and Merina Salminen concluded: "By many measures Elop is one of the world's worst—if not the worst—chief executives." Under his leadership, Nokia became a culture where the purpose was unclear, engagement low, and rifts between teams evident. The negative atmosphere overrode any chance for a positive one. Is it any wonder the company found itself in such a predicament? What if the organization could have rallied around a more positive tone through a culture that was creative and open in its thinking?

About Those Bad Bosses

While Elop used negative reinforcement in his attempt to right the Nokia ship, there is another behavior leaders use that also stifles Creative Thinking in the organization. This behavior is known as psychological safety.

Research conducted in 2009 by academics Jin Nam Choi, Troy Anderson, and Anick Veillette and published in *Group & Organization Management* found that leaders who demonstrate unfavorable behavior toward an employee end up repressing that individual's ability to think creatively. The researchers found that leaders who use threats or intimidation tactics at work erase any chance for psychological safety. In return, without any sense of workplace safety, creativity is drastically diminished. The authors went on to say that of all the various workplace characteristics they researched, it was the organization's leaders who played the most significant role in enabling *or* preventing Creative Thinking.

In 2010, IBM released the results of a survey of more than 1,500 global chief executive officers leading organizations in 60 different countries and 33 industries. Titled the "Global CEO Study," the report specified that "more than rigor, management discipline, integrity, or even vision—successfully navigating an increasing complex world will require creativity." CEOs from across the world believed that Creative Thinking was *the* trait that was going to fuel growth and future success. Six years later, in 2016, more evidence came from a report published by the World Economic Forum (WEF), titled "The Future of Jobs." Researchers asked hundreds of C-Suite leaders—representing more than 13 million employees across the globe—what skills were going to be needed by 2020 to stimulate growth. Firmly placed at the top of the pack was none other than Creative Thinking.

Where's the irony? The organization's most senior leaders continue to talk a good game about Creative Thinking. Yet, rather unfortunately, these same organizations continue to be mired by poor employee engagement and a negative operating culture. According to Gallup, for example, disengaged employees continue to outnumber engaged employees by a ratio of nearly two-to-one. Aon Hewitt reports that only 25 percent of all employees are highly engaged. If you review the data as far back as 2000, there has not been a material change in employee engagement.

As a result, more employees than ever are contemplating leaving their jobs for new opportunities. Indeed, studies—such as that produced by iCIMS in 2016—confirm that 63 percent of all full-time employees are actively looking for a new job elsewhere. The non-profit organization Mental Health America partnered with the FAAS Foundation and found similar results in their 2017 report, "Mind the Workplace." More than 70 percent of employees were either "actively looking for new job opportunities" or had the topic on their minds "always, often or sometimes" at work.

What causes an employee to become unmotivated, disaffected, and disengaged? What pushes a team member to contemplate leaving their role? Over the course of my career, I have discovered that it almost always comes down to appalling leadership, misguided purpose, and poor organizational culture practices. Lodged in each of these is poor thinking. The irony, as I have noted, is that senior leaders crave Creative Thinking while they continue to display (or condone) disengaging leadership habits that ultimately snuff out any opportunity for creativity to take place. Even with data staring them in the face, leaders continue to gloss over the fact that an engaging and open organizational culture is necessary for Creative Thinking to materialize.

There is another inhibitor that can prevent Creative Thinking from happening. According to i4cp's 2014 study, "Six Talent Practices that Boost Engagement and Market Performance," leaders seem to believe Creative Thinking happens on its own. Based on research with more than 300 talent management leaders in organizations with more than 1,000 employees, i4cp discovered that setting time aside for Creative Thinking "is an approach used by only 26 percent of higher-performance organizations." Further, only 4 percent of low-performing organizations earmark time for Creative Thinking. We will explore this notion of time and constant action next.

Office of Net Assessment

The Office of Net Assessment (ONA) has been referred to as "America's safeguard against the perils of short-term thinking." Despite the deleterious legacy of Watergate, even President Richard Nixon had his moments of positive impact. By authorizing the creation of the ONA, Nixon can lay claim to approving an outfit that exclusively focused on long-term national safety interests. The organization was founded by Andrew Marshall in 1973 and its origins provide insights into the importance of *reflection* in the Open Thinking model.

After World War II, U.S. military, surveillance, security, and investigative spending grew steadily, so much so that bureaucracies began to spring up across multiple departments. Information and intelligence was hoarded by one group and hidden from another. The number of military and civilian employees expanded, as did the fiefdoms and the competition between different units. With increased bureaucracy, departmentalization, and growth came the development of several different strategies on how to handle the enemy. At the time, the United States was embroiled in the Cold War and dealing with the Vietnam War.

The ONA was established to think about the big picture, with an emphasis on the long-term safety interests of the United States. It was a group separate from the other agencies, owing to its singular goal to strategize protection policies for America's future. It did so by studying issues that may have been overlooked by other agencies. Its reports—dubbed net assessments, hence the name of the outfit—compared the policies, military strategy, and weapons of other countries to those of the United States. These top-secret analyses were not made public. The reports were deeply researched, prognosticating what societal and security calamities might happen in the future.

ONA employees thought constantly about future ramifications. The ONA's mandate was to be speculative but it did so by reflecting on the current conditions while simultaneously using Creative Thinking talents to forecast the future. The ONA's operating mechanism was a lot like Eric Jordan's example at his gaming company, Codename Entertainment. Spend a fair amount of your time contemplating the future—dreaming up the various what-if questions and answers—while continuously ensuring you are producing results for today.

The ONA not only reminded me of Codename Entertainment; I recalled reading a book, *The Clock of the Long Now: Time and Responsibility*, written by Stewart Brand. The book was a companion piece to Brand's previously established Long Now Foundation. The Foundation "hopes to provide a counterpoint to today's accelerating culture and help make long-term thinking more common." Both Brand's book and the Foundation are founded upon an aspiration to get people thinking about the next 10,000 years, not simply the span of their lifetime.

Most compelling are the guidelines Brand and his Long Now colleagues produced for organizations and individuals to create what they refer to as a "long-lived, long-valuable institution." The values are:

- Serve the long view
- Foster responsibility
- Reward patience
- Mind mythic depth
- Ally with competition
- Take no sides
- Leverage longevity

Taken as a whole, the values are exquisite reminders that to become better thinkers, we should consider pausing, observing, and making more time for dreaming. In a way, the ONA supports the adoption of the Long Now Foundation values. Codename Entertainment might unwittingly subscribe to them as well. While one need not follow any of the Long Now Foundation's values to the letter, what I have come to realize is that both individuals *and* organizations that consciously build in the time to reflect—to ponder the long term—end up being able to think more creatively in the moment. When we "serve the long view" or "reward patience" or "leverage longevity" we ultimately become better at Creative Thinking. However, if we are consumed solely by the short term, the likelihood of Open Thinking goes out the window.

Which begs the question, as we wrap up Chapter 2, how much time are you devoting to long-term, future-based, wistful Creative Thinking?

Hat Tip to the Millinery

Karyn Ruiz said something quite profound to me during one of my visits to her Lilliput Hats store. "Most people don't have creativity in their jobs, and some don't want it either. Either way, when customers come into our shop they are surrounded by creativity. We open up Pandora's Box, providing them with the ability to dream."

It was a compelling and insightful observation. Many of our organizations are awash with monotonous and transactional tasks. We focus on the short term and on being busy. When you enter Lilliput Hats, you are surrounded by creativity. "People who come into our shop for the first time," remarked Karyn, "are used to shopping on Amazon.com. They are confused by the process. First-time shoppers are usually blown away by the buzz that's in here. It's a hive of invention and dreaming. I wish more people had this type of creativity in their lives."

I also discovered that you cannot make a hat in an hour. It takes time to ideate and dream, to work with the customer on the pros and cons of certain styles, threads, felts, feathers, and so on. It may only be a hat, one might say, but its craftsmanship is shaped by reflection.

Creative Thinking cannot be forced. It is built over time. As with Chuck Noland, my BCIT students, Codename Entertainment, and Nokia, Creative Thinking can neither be forgotten nor rushed. It is vitally important to give it the breathing space it requires.

CREATIVE THINKING QUESTIONS FOR THE INDIVIDUAL

- When asked to complete a task, do you immediately jump into action or do you take the time to pause, to reflect?

- When a problem presents itself, do you build in time to allow your mind to wander? (i.e., do you brainstorm and ideate before taking action?)

- Do you have "skills-at-the-ready" when embarking on a Creative Thinking opportunity, or are you so disorganized it becomes a burden?

CREATIVE THINKING QUESTIONS FOR THE ORGANIZATION

- Is your organizational culture one that promotes reflection and dreaming as a core behavior?

- Are the leaders across your organization demonstrating command-and-control management practices, suffocating the chance for Creative Thinking to take place?

- Are team members permitted the time to think creatively, or do you espouse an organizational culture of constant busyness?

Come to Think of It

You can't use up creativity. The more you use, the more you have.

MAYA ANGELOU

S WEDEN'S ASTRID LINDGREN was a literary giant who changed the game of authoring, if not thinking. An introvert, but happily married to her extrovert husband, Sture, Lindgren worked as a secretary at the Royal Automobile Club in Stockholm in the 1920s and 1930s. In fact, this is where she met Sture, who happened to be the Club's office manager. The couple had two children—Lasse and Karin—and spent summers in Furusund, a part of the Stockholm Archipelago. By the early 1940s, shaped by the landscape of Sweden and the raising of her children, she began to write. Through the creation of an anti-authoritarian adventurer—nine-year-old Pippi Longstocking—Lindgren has educated thousands of young children across the world to think differently.

When Lindgren brought Pippi to life in 1945 with equal parts cleverness, noisiness, independence, and creativity, she encouraged young readers to think contrarily. Pippi was a heroine of exploration. She sought out adventure and freedom. More than 70 years ago, this was radical. In fact, Lindgren was vilified by many in the literary world.

One of the key points that Pippi had going for her was *time*. Unlike many of today's organizational leaders and employees, she was not being exploited for her time. Being consumed by repetitive tasks lacking purpose was a foreign concept to her. Remaining in the status quo was not Pippi's thing either. In fact, there was no status quo. There was no way she would fall into the trap of Indifferent Thinking, failing to reflect and taking no action. Indifferent Thinking was anathema to the way she operated. Pippi was continuously unshackling herself from the routine. In her eponymously titled book, she stoically remarks, "I have never tried that before, so I think I should definitely be able to do that."

Pippi was also never browbeaten by the endless need to look or be busy. She was constantly able to conjure up new plots, ideas, and ways to be mischievous. She was a girl exploring but she would set out on a path of discovery while remaining in charge of her time, using it to her advantage. Again, her behavior reminds me of Eric Jordan and what he learned at Codename Entertainment. When his team made a concerted effort to pause and reflect—taking their time in the production of the *Crusaders of the Lost Idols* game—the results proved far more successful than any of the previous games the company had released.

When we become too busy—unable to pause, reflect, and invoke Creative Thinking—a civil war erupts in our brains. Often, exploitation wins out over exploration. In a 1993 seminal paper titled "The Myopia of Learning," researchers Daniel Levinthal and James March discovered that "exploitation generates clearer, earlier, and closer feedback than exploration," and that exploitation will often yield more positive results in the near term. But for success to occur in the long term, exploration must be considered in lieu of exploitation.

When we exploit our time we are seeking an immediate result. When we exploit time, we jump to busyness or action. We deny ourselves the potential for longer-term benefits derived through appropriate pauses and reflection. When we explore our time, we discover a balance between reflection and action. We stop feeling pressure, reducing our stress levels, increasing both creativity and productivity, making better decisions.

It is Pippi's attitude toward Creative Thinking that makes such a difference in her life. She accepts that the prerequisite for Open Thinking is to generate the time for Creative Thinking to materialize.

At work, too many of us have denied ourselves the prospect of creativity by exploiting our time, not exploring it. The ramifications can be far-reaching for both personal development and organizational success. The consequences to Creative Thinking are also widespread.

One of the questions we ought to ask ourselves is whether or not a lack of Creative Thinking is due in part to our penchant to fall into a busyness trap, exploiting our time to remain moored to Indifferent, Indecisive, or Inflexible Thinking. Do we become blind to exploring the unknown? To fuel creativity, perhaps we can learn a lesson or two from Pippi Longstocking's example. Explore, don't exploit.

Paying Attention to Creativity

In an organizational setting, it may be as simple as paying attention to creative ideas that come from elsewhere. Take, for example, the story of John Lasseter. He is chief creative officer of Walt Disney and Pixar Animation Studios, and principal creative advisor of Walt Disney Imagineering.

Lasseter is one of the brilliant minds behind Pixar, the company that has given the world such wonderful films as *Wall-E*, *Finding Nemo*, *Cars*, and *Toy Story*. Before Pixar found success, Lasseter worked at the home of Mickey Mouse in the early 1980s as an animator. He was constantly thinking about the future of film animation. Lasseter was frequently unleashing his inner Pippi Longstocking, exploring where filmmaking might be heading. He was both reflecting and acting.

Lasseter began thinking about the future of Disney as a company. He felt that the decades-old approach of hand-drawn animation for its films was about to be replaced or at least augmented by computers. He pitched his bosses—and his bosses' bosses—the newfangled invention of computer-animated films. While Lasseter's prescient hunch was correct, Disney executives ultimately failed to think differently. They ignored Lasseter's prophetic vision—not giving the idea the time to incubate or materialize—and ended up firing him from the company. Disney leaders remained locked in an Inflexible Thinking mindset, unable to truly reconsider what their future might look like. They failed to properly reflect on Lasseter's Creative Thinking while simultaneously dismissing it and the opportunity to take action. Disney found comfort in the status quo.

It strikes me that Disney executives were either too busy to think differently or they were too distracted to rethink the studio's existing film-producing strategy. Either way, a question to consider is whether Disney executives were exploring or exploiting their time. Years later, as a key figure at Pixar alongside Ed Catmull and Steve Jobs, Lasseter ended up back at Disney. How? Among other factors, Disney recognized its error and in 2006 agreed to pay US$7.4 billion to acquire the entire Pixar team and film library. Disney executives then made Lasseter chief creative officer. The total global box office revenues of Pixar films up until that point were just shy of $1.8 billion. Since the acquisition closed, new Pixar films have grossed over $7 billion.

Listening for the Undercurrents

Warren Buffett, the famous American investor and philanthropist, offers an interesting perspective regarding the importance of reflection: "I insist on a lot of time being spent, almost every day, to just sit and think. That is very uncommon in American business. I read and think. So I do more reading and thinking, and make less impulse decisions than most people in business." Like Pippi Longstocking, Buffett does not suffer fools gladly. When it comes to leaders who do not spend enough time on reflection, Buffett has no time for them.

Sameer Patel is the CEO of Kahuna. As with Buffett, Sameer spends time every day sitting still and reflecting. Kahuna is a software start-up that offers artificial-intelligence-based marketing technology. Customers include the likes of the Dollar Shave Club, TickPick, and Yelp. Before Kahuna, Sameer was the general manager and senior vice president at SAP, where he led the team that was responsible for making SAP Jam, a collaboration platform for employees, partners, and customers. When he left SAP, Jam had over 35 million subscribers worldwide. Before SAP, Sameer led a boutique management consultancy.

I met Sameer while he was a principal at SpanStrategies, the consulting firm he founded. It was back in the days when collaboration software was referred to as "Enterprise 2.0," a term coined by MIT professor and author Andrew McAfee, during the mid-2000s. I have always wondered what has made Sameer tick as a consultant, as a general manager, and as a CEO. He has been successful in many different roles. His peers and those in the high-tech space hold him in high regard. "If there is one single trait—possibly every milestone that I've accomplished through a team and individually—it's what comes *before* the thinking," said Sameer.

"It's about being the best observer. I want to understand what is happening first. I don't rush to report it or talk about it with others. I want to understand the undercurrents, listening for signals, thinking about positive or negative repercussions. It really has to be about observing first. Observing is part of operating a collaborative culture. It cannot be solely about strategy, it's how you listen to everything that is going on around you before taking action or making a decision."

Sameer's success can be squarely attributed to this sage counsel: continually observe. Sameer believes that the only way you can scale an organization and be successfully creative is if you are observing the undercurrents around various ideas, thoughts, data, and information.

For example, let's pretend for a moment that a keen employee comes to you with an idea. It's a unique concept for a professional services software platform. It looks like it could make a lot of money, and quickly. If you say yes right away, have you let the possibility marinate long enough to catch all potential undercurrents related to it? What if the idea from this sharp team member is simply a ploy to build his resume, for he is more interested in becoming a chief corporate officer than this software idea? "You always have to observe before jumping in," said Sameer. "Every conversation with anyone is not just about the 'what,' but it's also about the 'how.' People need to get amazing at both the 'what' and the 'how' if they are going to become a successful thinker, one who observes before taking action."

In the case of Disney and the situation with John Lasseter, did the company wait too long to take action, allowing too much time to make a decision? It might be an example of Indecisive Thinking.

Or did the company disregard entirely the signals that Lasseter was providing, thus demonstrating Indifferent Thinking? Or, due to the overly busy schedule of a Disney executive, perhaps they were so preoccupied that there was not enough time to ponder the change in strategy, thus the third example of our thinking maladies, Inflexible Thinking? The lesson between Sameer's insight and the example with Disney and Lasseter is that we ought to be continually listening for signals and observing the undercurrents, but not at the expense of inaction. There is a delicate balance between reflection and action that each of us must heed.

"A learning organization is an organization that is continually expanding its capacity to create its future," wrote Peter Senge, author, systems scientist, and senior lecturer at the MIT Sloan School of Management. To create that future, leaders and team members alike should remember the importance of observation *and* reflection. Listening, watching, and paying attention to the meandering flow of information—the undertows and the overflows—will serve you well, as it does Open Thinkers like Sameer. The words of Anaïs Nin can also serve as a helpful guide: "My ideas usually come not at my desk writing, but in the midst of living."

Giving Time to Think Creatively

Pippi Longstocking had oodles of time to be creative. The culture that Lasseter helped to create at Pixar is also one steeped in Open Thinking. In fact, Pixar is an Open Thinking playground. The problem that we must face head-on with respect to Creative Thinking is the lack of time dedicated to it. "Creative Thinking is important in any organization, but it's often overlooked in one of the most important places: at the top," said Ryan Holmes, CEO of high-tech firm HootSuite. "For CEOs and founders, it's easy to get consumed with the demands of the day and the relentless cycles of business planning. This can leave little time for truly Creative Thinking and also sap energy from your work. Often, you don't even realize this is happening unless you happen to be pulled away from the daily grind and given a fresh chance to flex your creative and entrepreneurial muscles."

For the Open Thinking model to be fruitful, not only should time be devoted to Creative Thinking, the organizational culture should be one that supports it. If CEOs cannot act as Creative Thinking role models—succumbing to operational minutiae and constantly coming across as stressed out and too busy to dream—how is the rest of the organization going to behave? As with most aspects of an organization, the habits at the top are often mimicked by those below.

If our minds are constantly distracted and exploited by time and task pressures, none of us will be willing to employ Creative Thinking. We are far too consumed by competitors and organizational inanities. We become preoccupied by other things, not with what creativity may bring. It matters not if you are the CEO, team leader, or an individual contributor. In fact, our minds will be so engrossed and full we will not even pay attention to the possibility of fresh new ideas. Pippi Longstocking, Lasseter, and Pixar are examples of how to prevent such a scenario from happening. They make the time to explore creativity. They are not exploited by time. The culture of Pixar is one that supports and endorses Creative Thinking. It is "art of the possible" thinking versus "science of the impossible."

Bill Gates, former chairman and CEO of Microsoft, recognized the need to spend time away from the pressures of operational tasks and running a business during the height of his leadership at the Seattle-based high-tech firm. He introduced something known as "Think Week." Twice a year, he would sequester himself for a week of reading, thinking, listening, and letting the art of the possible permeate his brain. It was his planned time to think creatively. Mike Desjardins, CEO of VirTus, a leader I first interviewed in *The Purpose Effect*, employs a similar tactic. Instead of "Think Week," Mike sets out twice a year for what he calls "Reading Week," during which he devours books and articles to replenish and further his knowledge base. You will not be able to reach Mike on his phone because he immerses himself and blocks out any distractions from his Creative Thinking time.

Discussing the importance of pausing to dream, Bill McDermott, CEO of high-tech company SAP, said in an interview, "Most people today are so driven by the short term and the pressures of the day-to-day that they never take the time to put their feet up on the desk and look out the window and dream. They are constantly in meetings, many of them internal, burdened by PowerPoint. My recommendation is, free up some time on your calendar."

On a personal note, ever since 2002 I have refused to hold or take a meeting on Friday afternoons. Rarely do I answer the phone, texts, or email either. It is *my* time. In my calendar, I block it off so others cannot access me. I title it, rather appropriately, "DP Think Time." What I should be calling it is "My Divergent Thinking Time" but that comes across rather clumsily. It is my weekly dream time where I'm connecting dots and conjuring up new possibilities. I may read, write, whiteboard, sketch, or stare out the window. After 20 years of employing such a practice, I can assure you I will never relinquish it. You would have to fire me first.

Further, I head outside on my bicycle or strap into my indoor spinner at least four times a week, normally during lunch if I am working from home. If I am traveling, I visit the hotel gym daily after work. Not only is this good for my heart and health, the 100+ miles that I cycle each week provides another opportunity to dream, reflect, and ponder. Indeed, it is more Creative Thinking time.

Every day, each of us is equipped with 1,440 minutes. We all possess 168 hours a week and 8,736 hours a year to use to our advantage. If we do not earmark a significant portion of time to be creative we have little chance of erasing the Indifferent, Indecisive, or Inflexible Thinking mindsets. To help unleash your inner Pippi Longstocking and to be more like Sameer Patel, Mike Desjardins, Bill McDermott, or Bill Gates, Creative Thinking begs you to be more of an explorer—not an exploiter—of time. Setting aside time to be creative can potentially pay dividends in the long term.

Creative Culture: Part I

Creative Thinking is not solely an individual act, though. It can happen in teams. It may even be something implemented institution-wide. For Creative Thinking to emerge in an organization, however, the internal culture must be one that actually supports it. In my first book, Flat Army, I define an engaged organization as one that operates with "borderless collegiality." In my second book, The Purpose Effect, I point out that organizations that harness purpose "provide service to benefit all intended stakeholders." What I have also learned in my journey as an educator, professional, researcher, speaker, and as an author is that when an organization operates as an engaged and purpose-driven entity, it often promotes and exhibits the traits of Creative Thinking.

Brian Scudamore is the founder and CEO of O2E Brands, the parent company to such brands as 1-800-Got-Junk?, WOW 1 DAY PAINTING, You Move Me, and Shack Shine. He employs more than 300 people at O2E Brands headquarters and thousands more around the world by virtue of the franchising model he established. Over three decades, it has become a multi-million-dollar operation. I interviewed Brian for The Purpose Effect and decided to return to him for this book to gather his thoughts on Open Thinking. Not surprisingly, O2E Brands had many examples of its engaged operating culture and purpose-driven ethos nestling comfortably alongside its Creative Thinking practices.

Paying homage to the work of author Simon Sinek, Brian said, "We are big believers that 'leaders eat last' because you don't want to be the first person speaking in a meeting." Just before 11 a.m. every day, everyone at headquarters engages in a seven-minute huddle. It is an opportunity for Brian and senior leaders to listen to employees, their ideas or problems, as much as it is a chance to provide quick thoughts on what is going on within the leadership ranks. "It's a great way to bring all the brilliant minds into one room, ask 'what is going on' while making sure everyone is not only aligned, but able to surface feedback and input." The huddle is a daily rapid-fire Creative Thinking and sharing session.

Brian believes that the O2E Brands' culture and purpose are the reasons its Creative Thinking mindset is so evident. "We truly want to hear the employees' ideas first," said Brian. "Our responsibility as leaders is to provide guidance, but ultimately let our people decide the right direction to go." One way this Creative Thinking tradition is exemplified at O2E Brands is with the "Can You Imagine?" wall. "It's the way we breed creativity," he said. The wall is a place where employees can posit their ideas. "We encourage people to be creative—it is part of our culture—and the 'Can You Imagine?' wall is just another tool that gets our employees thinking outside of the box." Ideas such as being featured on Dr. Phil and *Harvard Business Review* might never have come to fruition had they not been dreamed up on the "Can You Imagine?" wall first.

Brian does confess, however, that over time both O2E Brands and he personally have learned how to better infuse Creative Thinking into the culture and purpose of the company. One of those lessons came from its hiring practices. "We had to learn how to hire creative people, but we also had to figure out how to find people who were *not* similar to us," he said. Brian recognized that O2E Brands needed diversity of thought to further its Creative Thinking. "If we don't have all sorts of different ideas, from different types of people, we're not going to be creative." Brian's comments about O2E Brands' Creative Thinking mindset, its culture, purpose, and even its hiring practices, reminded me again of Pixar.

Ed Catmull, the co-founder and president of Pixar Animation Studios, as well as president of Walt Disney Animation Studios, observed in 2008 that, "Creativity must be present at every level of every artistic and technical part of the organization." The Pixar leadership team was adamant that as the company continued to grow, it would maintain an environment that nurtured respect and trust. In doing so, it wanted to unleash the Creative Thinking mindset in everyone who worked there.

"If we get that right, the result is a vibrant community where talented people are loyal to one another and their collective work, everyone feels that they are part of something extraordinary, and their passion and accomplishments make the community a magnet for talented people coming out of schools or working at other places." Because it relates specifically to hiring, Catmull referenced the Pixar philosophy: "You get great creative people, you bet big on them, you give them enormous leeway and support, and you provide them with an environment in which they can get honest feedback from everyone. Getting people in different disciplines to treat one another as peers is just as important as getting people within disciplines to do so."

Creative Thinking cannot be overlooked, nor can it be left to the devices of a few. Not only does an organization's culture and purpose have to support it—new team members should be taught to embrace change and communicate freely their ideas and opinions. As Catmull states, "It must be safe for everyone to offer ideas."

Creative Culture: Part II

Brianna Wettläufer is the CEO of Stocksy United, a company she co-founded in 2012 that has reinvented the way stock photography and video footage is both curated and sold. Stocksy is an artist-run cooperative. Its motto is: "We believe in creative integrity, fair profit sharing, and co-ownership, with every voice being heard." As an artist, Brianna believes it is highly unethical to approach business from any angle other than transparency and accountability while continuously rallying to support and inspire the creators—the workers. "When you use this approach," she said, "you're investing in the long-term success, integrity, and people working for the product, so you shouldn't have to make choices that are intentionally designed for short-term gain at a huge cost."

Stocksy not only possesses a purpose-first company ethos, it maintains a culture that is highly collaborative. In doing so, Stocksy's Open Thinking mindset helps it to grow and thrive. "Stocksy is always focused on collaboration," said Brianna, "both internally with our staff, and as well with our membership." Brianna believes that being able to integrate and hear the feedback of others, no matter who they are or what their position, remains the singular focus in creating tangible equality and respect as a team. "This means we're very aware that we have to check our egos at the door and always be willing to be challenged on our assumptions, with the understanding that creating the best product versus just being right is more important."

The Stocksy approach is very much in line with research conducted by Teresa Amabile, the Edsel Bryant Ford Professor of Business Administration at Harvard Business School. In her 1996 book, *Creativity in Context*, Teresa purports that all tasks are either algorithmic or heuristic. But Creative Thinking and associated tasks are more heuristic than algorithmic—where exploratory problem-solving techniques are favored—hence the need for a collaborative culture is imperative.

Teresa argues that there is no proven way to solve a problem—no absolute or algorithmic way in which ideas come to life—so it behooves teams and organizations to collaborate. Creative Thinking and associated behaviors are based on a problem-discovery-discussion continuum. While there may be Eureka-like moments, creativity is more likely to happen when the culture of the organization is collaborative, when people are working together. It does not mean that every interaction in an organization ought to be collaborative. It simply means the operating behavior should be one in which employees think to share an idea, feedback, or a thought with others before either making a decision or moving to completion. In *Flat Army*, I refer to this as being a connected leader. That is, before taking action, connect with others first and consider all options second. Then make a decision, communicate it, and begin to take action. The same approach can be applied to Open Thinking. What you are doing then is shifting your mindset to become collaborative versus being closed-minded.

Brianna echoes this sentiment. "We have a team of incredibly challenging and intelligent people at Stocksy," she said. "My goal and hope is the team will challenge every angle of an idea before we agree it's the best option. If there's any language in an idea that is ambiguous or not completely articulated, we do our best to work through why that's happening. The opportunity to learn by identifying a weak point or where you're possibly wrong is an amazing opportunity to continue growing as a team and individuals."

But even in the most collaborative Open Thinking environments, Brianna provides a reminder about the risks of falling into the trap of Indecisive Thinking. When we spend too much time collaborating, subjecting ourselves to too many ideas and too much reflection, we ironically end up in a worse state. Collaboration requires balance between dreaming and doing, much as we have learned with Open Thinking itself. Brianna said, "Part of working through proposed projects or solutions is knowing when you need to commit to see the idea through before considering another angle or option. Otherwise you'll become distracted with constantly changing agendas that are never truly tested, which becomes disrespectful to people's time." In other words, remaining mired in indecision is as potentially troubling as being too quick to act.

These days, Stocksy earns more than $8 million in revenues and pays out $4.3 million in royalties to artists. It even pays out more than $200,000 to member artists as a dividend. Where will the company be in five or ten years? First, it will continue to support photographers and the community of platform cooperatives. Second, it is committed to carrying out creative integrity as a collaborative and Open Thinking organization. Brianna is "naively stubborn enough," as she puts it, to advocate that the Stocksy model of operating could help turn traditional business on its head. "Business can be fun," she said, "and it can be driven by creativity and purpose."

Creative Culture: Part III

Another purpose-first organization that sheds further light on the power and tactics of Creative Thinking is WE. We met Marc Kielburger, the co-founder and co-CEO, in Chapter 1. Marc believes incremental results are an important factor in an Open Thinking organization. These results come in the form of putting Creative Thinking on the list of attributes the organization embeds into its culture. But there is a catch.

"Instead of instituting big hairy audacious goals [BHAG] at your place of work—which are ridiculous—you really only need six-to-twelve-month plans," said Marc. BHAG is a concept made famous by authors Jim Collins and Jerry Porras in their 1994 book, *Built To Last: Successful Habits of Visionary Companies.*

"In really broad terms, we are trying to change the world by disrupting the entire industry of philanthropy, so Creative Thinking has to be done in small spurts. We need our WE employees, partners, and the public to feel empowered and focused. We need them to be creative, and that is never going to happen with a five-year plan." The success that WE has enjoyed, according to Marc, is that its Creative Thinking is realistic. "What world are you living in with a five-year plan?" he added, laughing while making the point. Marc's theory is that the shorter the planning cycle, the more likely employees are to think creatively, given the shorter runway space. Further, he is adamant that a shorter time frame allows you to celebrate the results and accomplishments more frequently, a key enabler of a more collaborative and purpose-driven organization.

Karl Moore is a professor of business at McGill University. Over coffee at his favorite café in Montreal, I asked him about the effectiveness of long-term planning with Creative Thinking. He reminded me of what is referred to as emergent strategy, a theory first defined by a colleague of his, management guru Henry Mintzberg. "I have seen the Open Thinking cycle many times on new masters programs that I have been involved in at McGill," remarked Karl. "The key is, you don't know how your strategy will evolve over time as events occur. Competitors react and the market changes. This is the real world that most industries now must inhabit. There is a back and forth between the three modes of thinking—Creative, Critical, and Applied—fairly regularly. Long-term strategy can become outdated rather quickly. It's quite a change from 10 or 15 years ago."

What is emergent strategy? Mintzberg suggests strategy itself can be over-managed. When it is emergent—when ideas are formulated out of observations and not through formulated exercises—it can become more important and successful. Mintzberg insists organizations cannot always rely on planning where their strategy may emerge, let alone plan the strategy itself. Mintzberg writes, "The most basic of all [concepts] is the intimate connection between thought and action. Smart strategists appreciate that they cannot always be smart enough to think through everything in advance."

In his 2007 book, *The Opposable Mind*, author Roger L. Martin introduced a thinking approach he calls Integrative Thinking, mentioned briefly in Chapter 1. Integrative Thinking suggests that instead of making a binary decision between two options that stand before you, create a new model that contains elements of each but is superior to both. He argues in the book that existing models ought not to represent reality and that opposing models need to be leveraged, not feared. While existing models are not perfect, Roger suggests that there is always a better model and you can find it or create it if you are patient enough. You must be comfortable getting into and out of the necessary complexity that is certain to manifest.

Roger observes, "Integrative Thinking produces possibilities, solutions, and new ideas. It creates a sense of limitless possibilities." Integrative Thinkers are not either/or people, rather they possess a both/and thinking style. Roger has not only embedded the Integrative Thinking model in Rotman School of Management core programs at the University of Toronto, he has consulted and provided executive coaching for some of the world's top CEOs of companies, including Procter & Gamble, LEGO, IDEO, and Verizon.

Roger released a follow-up to *The Opposable Mind* in 2017 titled *Creating Great Choices*, co-written with long-time colleague Jennifer Riel. They write, "We must redefine creativity as something each of us has the capacity to do." O2E, Stocksy, and WE are examples of organizations that not only create safe, transparent, inclusive, and collaborative environments to allow Creative Thinking to prosper, each of them is continually allowing its strategy to emerge by redefining creativity as something that all employees have the capacity to do. None of the companies' strategies has been set in stone—certainly not for a five-year period—nor have the companies become organizations that fail to enact Creative Thinking cultures.

The lesson for any organization is that—if it wishes to adopt Open Thinking—both culture and strategy must become integrated *and* emergent components. The more closed a culture is, the more likely it is to end up in either an Indifferent, Indecisive, or Inflexible–type Thinking culture. The more it chooses to forgo involving employees and other stakeholders in the Creative Thinking process—the more it prevents employees from unleashing their creative juices—the more it will focus on the short term and suffer dire consequences.

Baby Steps

Back when we were babies, every day was an opportunity for exploration. The journeys seemed endless. First, we explored our crib. Then we graduated and began to circumnavigate the floor. Eventually, we discovered that kitchen drawers were full of items to examine with our hands and mouths. As we began to walk there was more to explore: the velvety sand at the beach, the soft grass in the park, or the glistening snow found in a field. It was endless exploration. We felt it. Like Pippi Longstocking, we were a whirlwind of cleverness, noisiness, independence, and creativity. We were alive.

We did so because we had the luxury of time. Aside from a schedule of naps and snacks, no one was telling us to complete a task by day's end. There were no superiors badgering us to "do more with less." Our every minute was not being accounted for by overtaxing schedules, inane meetings, or rushed deadlines. Social media was as foreign to us as those objects we popped into our mouths. Most important, we had not developed any of the three inhibitors to Open Thinking: Indifferent, Indecisive, or Inflexible Thinking. Adventures built upon adventures and we liked it. There was no such thing as "business as usual." We were free to think creatively and were unafraid to do so. We simply had no cognitive biases.

If we fast-forward to our lives as adults, we now know there is conflict between our desire to be explorers and the reality of being exploited. In fact, Moshe Bar, a neuroscientist at Bar-Ilan University and a professor at Harvard Medical School, found in 2016 that Creative Thinking is the default cognitive mode we employ when our minds are clear. But there is a problem. The research that Bar and his peers conducted found that any chance for exploration is diminished by an occupied mind. To add insult to injury, our minds seem to be overly occupied these days, which is the very reason we resort to exploiting our time, not exploring it.

When our minds are overburdened with tasks or we have to put up with a high mental load, we consistently and quite effectively deliver something that we already know. When we become too busy, we choose the predictable. Ultimately, we dull down and desensitize our own selves. If our mental load exhausts us, any chance for increased creativity diminishes. Furthermore, as Jennifer Mueller of the Wharton School at the University of Pennsylvania discovered in her 2017 book, *Creative Change*, people often espouse creativity as something they want to do more of, but when presented with the opportunity to think creatively they end up spurning it. This is the crux of spending more time exploring versus exploiting. The balance between reflection and taking action has never been of greater concern.

Some personal questions to ponder as we push forward in the book:

- When you have a free moment, how are you spending that time?

- How often are you filling up moments of free time by aimlessly scrolling through social media streams and content?

- Has your life become one where even when you do have free time, you are too stressed or tired to think creatively?

- How much time do you dedicate to simply letting your mind wander? Do you daydream?

- What type of reading are you doing? Have you noticed that the number of long reads or books that you read is dwindling?

When stress, busyness, or even apathy set in at work, quality can suffer. If you fail to invest the time to enrich your knowledge, how do you formulate new ideas? If we over-program every second of the workday, we will eventually exhibit strain and fatigue. When we become too tense to dream and too dispirited to choose a different path, Indifferent Thinking is the result. It leads to low reflection and stagnant action. Ultimately, this indifferent behavior affects Creative

Thinking, and the consequences can be far-reaching, both for your career as well as for the organization's goals. As Bar pointed out, "The mind's natural tendency is to explore and to favor novelty but when occupied it looks for the most familiar and inevitably least interesting solution."

Creative Thinking in the workplace will not hatch innovations overnight. Ideas do not fall from the sky by chance. Many still believe, for example, that Charles Darwin devised his theory of natural selection while spending time on the Galapagos Islands in 1835. In fact, the theory of evolution and what he presented in his book, *On the Origin of Species*, only began to take shape once he returned to England. The book itself was not published until 1859, almost 25 years after his trip. Contrary to popular myths and beliefs, Darwin needed the time to ponder and then finalize the theory.

Creative Thinking requires you to both invest in *and* explore your use of time. Interestingly, in the IBM survey mentioned in the previous chapter, of over 1,500 CEOs from 60 countries in 33 different industries, Creative Thinking was cited as the most important organization-wide trait required for navigating the business environment.

"Big ideas take time" was the general motto of Bell Labs and a sublime example of instituting Creative Thinking as an organization-wide trait. Bell Labs employees were renowned for exploring their time (and creativity) delivering such Nobel Prize–winning advances as the laser beam and the transistor. Bell Labs was full of scientists and engineers. You would expect them to be explorers versus exploiters. But that does not mean their organization failed to capitalize on Creative Thinking.

A couple of paragraphs ago I asked you to consider some personal questions regarding your time. Now I'd like you to contemplate some professional questions:

- Is your role at work so isolating that there is no opportunity to be creative?

- Has your calendar become so overly scheduled that you wander zombie-like from meeting to meeting wondering why you're there in the first place?

- When you consider your organization's culture, is it one that openly shares, using collaboration techniques to ideate and brainstorm before taking action?

- Are ideas left to a few to come up with? Conversely, are ideas from any part of the organization embraced as opportunities for change or growth?

- During the process of Creative Thinking, are mistakes tolerated or even encouraged at your organization?

John Maeda, former president of Rhode Island School of Design, once wrote that creativity "can be re-kindled in people—all children are creative. They just lose their capability to be creative by growing up." Truer words may not have been written. Perhaps we should look back to those days when we were a baby crawling around the floor. Maybe it's a sign that we have to let go of a few things to induce Creative Thinking.

Functional Fixedness

In Chapter 2, I introduced the story about my students at BCIT and the tower activity. Let me introduce a Creative Thinking experiment with you right now.

Imagine you have walked into a room. There is a table, a wooden chair, and four empty walls. The walls are made of typical drywall plaster. Nothing else can be found on the floor or the walls. The room is properly lit by an overhead light, so you can see what you are doing. On the table are the following materials:

- A pack of regular matches
- A box of 30 normal-sized thumbtacks
- Two narrow candles

Here are your instructions: Using only the materials found on the table (i.e., you cannot use the table or the chair) I want you to think about how you might mount the candles to the wall. Then think through how you will light the candles to illuminate the room. You cannot use any other materials.

Were you successful? Psychologist Karl Duncker invented the "candle test" in 1945 to determine if we experience "functional fixedness" when given a problem to solve. It turns out we do. Often, when we are presented with information on a given situation, we tend to jump right into action, not stopping to creatively think how that information might be used for a different purpose. In calling it "functional fixedness," Duncker outlined the default behavior of humans. We possess a fixed mindset even when materials staring us in the face could alter an outcome.

When you considered the candle test, did you imagine using thumbtacks to stick the candles directly to the wall? Or did you first light the candles and then use some of the wax to glue the candles to the wall? Both of those options may have been successful.

There is another possibility, though. Did you consider using the thumbtack box as a tray for the candles? If you did, you could have emptied the thumbtacks from their box and used several of them to affix the box to the wall. From there you could have lit the candles, dripped wax into two spots in the box, then placed the candles onto the pools of melted wax so they remained upright and attached to the wall.

Which brings us back to Creative Thinking within the Open Thinking framework. Even when an answer looks as though it is staring us in the face, perhaps we should pause just a little longer—or involve other people in the creativity—to see if there are any other options before moving forward. We can liken this to atherosclerosis, a medical condition denoting hardening of the arteries. If we harden our minds and forgo dreaming or reflecting, a Creative Thinking stroke is bound to occur.

The Maginot Line provides us with a historical example of "functional fixedness" and the effects it had across Europe. Running nearly 200 miles on the eastern border of France, the Maginot Line was built by the French after World War I as a way to protect themselves from a potential German attack. This underground system of tunnels was a modern-day city of sorts. The heavily fortified labyrinth possessed shops, chapels, schools, hospitals, and even cinemas. How were the French demonstrating "functional fixedness"?

World War I was fought on the ground in thousands of trenches. That is where the term "trench warfare" originated. As Adolph Hitler assumed power in Germany during the early 1930s, the French prepared for the inevitability of another war. It developed the Maginot Line, assuming the next war would also be fought in trenches. Like Germany, France possessed a packet of matches, a box of thumbtacks, and two candles. But instead of looking at the materials that stood in front of them to think through different options, France and its military leaders fell into a state of Inflexible Thinking.

The complacency exhibited by various French leaders was a part of their collapse in World War II. Germany, on the other hand, failed to be lulled into "functional fixedness" and invented an entirely new type of warfare it called blitzkrieg. This "lightning war" would be fought in the air as well as on the ground in quick, sudden maneuvers that surprised opponents. When Germany invaded France in 1940—a year into World War II—it did not attempt to penetrate the Maginot Line. Instead, Germany flanked the French, attacking from the rear to eventually put its blitzkrieg strategy to effective use. The French lay waiting in their gigantic and elaborate trench, assuming the enemy would approach from the east and attack them head-on. France never saw it coming.

Creative Thinking requires imagination. "Functional fixedness" can strike anyone at any point in time if they are not careful. Even in scenarios where the answer seems obvious, we ought to remember how blinded we may become in choosing what seems to be the clearest path forward.

"Right" It Down

So far, I have introduced several ways you can question your Creative Thinking habits. They include concepts such as brainstorming, avoiding functional fixedness, scheduling, being less busy, and spending more time dreaming. One final inhibitor to introduce centers on your personal organizational skills and habits. Quite frankly, if you refuse to be organized during the normal course of your days, you may be less likely to exhibit Creative Thinking. One of the simplest and most successful habits that I have observed to help Creative Thinking come to life is to simply write things down.

Richard Branson, CEO of the Virgin Group, implores people to carry around a notebook. "I think the number one thing that I take with me when I'm traveling is the notebook," he once remarked. "You can use it for ideas, for contacts, for suggestions, for problems, and [to] get out and address the issues. Your life will be that much better organized for carrying it." When he reflected on the Virgin Group and how being organized helped him grow it into the £20 billion giant it is today, Branson said, "I could never have built the Virgin Group into the size it is without those few bits of paper. I think if you're going to run a really personal airline, it's those little details that matter and therefore the notebook is an essential part of my traveling day."

When I once asked Gord Downie—poet, lead singer, and lyricist of The Tragically Hip whom I introduced in Chapter 1—how he kept track of his ideas for lyrics or poems, he mentioned using an elaborate moleskin notebook system. Labeled A to Z, these notebooks were his way of filing all of life's observations, quips, and concepts that came to him purposefully or serendipitously. Gord passed away in October

2017 and was a multiple Juno award–winning artist. He was often seen carrying a moleskin notebook around with him wherever he went. Ever present was a four-colored Bic pen, so he could immediately shape his ideas in different ways. When he went to write a song or poem, the moleskin notebooks surfaced and the composition of sentences began.

As with Branson and Downie, musician Joel Plaskett believes his Creative Thinking is aided by continuously capturing what comes into his view. Joel is a Canadian singer and songwriter whose music, according to Billboard, "fuses the energetic melodies and hooks of power pop with the muscular strength of hard rock." Based in Halifax, and winner of the Queen Elizabeth II Diamond Jubilee Medal, Joel has been writing, recording, and playing music since the early 1990s. "I don't edit myself until I have to edit myself," Joel said to me. "I use my iPhone to constantly jot down ideas, memos, and notes to myself, but a lot of it is just gobbledygook." Joel teaches us that if we fail to capture the nonsense that pops into our heads, we are missing out on the possibility of new ideas.

"Often, I don't know what the words mean at the time I write it," he continued. "What I've previously written down may be corny, but then I twist it and I end up liking it. Those original words actually push me out of my comfort zone. In total, the process has allowed me to be relatively prolific as a writer and with my music."

I am not a professional musician like Gord or Joel, but as an author I am constantly using the Evernote application. On whatever device that is handy, ever since this cloud-based app came into existence in 2008 I have used it to not only write three books and hundreds of columns, it has become my repository of ideas. My poems are stored there, too. Without it, I am not certain how I would harvest the zany ideas that pop into my head on a daily basis. The simple lesson is to write your thoughts down in whatever manner suits you. Or, as philosopher and academic Marshall McLuhan once wrote, "A typewriter is a means of transcribing thought, not expressing it."

Hat Tip to the Millinery

When you walk into Lilliput Hats, the first thing you notice is the team's creativity. That's because as you pass through the arched doorway your eyes are gripped by a constellation of colors, feathers, and felts. As I mentioned in the first chapter, prominently positioned on walls to your left and right—as well as at waist-level displays—are various hats created by the Lilliput milliners. Although the shop is primarily a custom-hat millinery, the hats on display can be purchased on-site as is. But the real purpose of these sprightly displays is to showcase the collective imagination of the millinery. It is their Creative Thinking showcase. It is the art of the possible.

"A hat is a crown and glory," said Karyn of Lilliput Hats. "It's your lid, your head covering, and it can be a bad-hair-day hat. We want people coming into the shop seeing what is possible right away." The hats on display reminded me of Brian Scudamore, founder and CEO of O2E Brands, and the "Can You Imagine?" wall that he implemented at its headquarters. That wall acts as part inspiration and part reminder of the importance of thinking creatively.

Creative Thinking begs each of us to be inventive. We must not hide from it either. If we literally or figuratively display the art of the possible, it just may enliven you and others to think more creatively. At a minimum, it may embolden your Open Thinking habits.

CREATIVE THINKING TIPS
FOR THE INDIVIDUAL

- Stop over-programming your every minute. Creative Thinking requires space *and* time. Find ways that permit your mind to wander. At a minimum, stop filling up every spare minute by staring at your smartphone or constantly attending meetings. Allow yourself to "marinate in the moment."

- Listen, pay attention, and observe. Each day presents itself with new chances to learn and remark on what is directly in front of you. Open your eyes and ears to your surroundings. Let random thoughts transport you elsewhere.

- Write it down. Devise a method of composing notes to yourself as reminders of what pops into your mind through-out the day. You cannot remember everything that crosses your path, yet creative thoughts can pop up at any moment.

CREATIVE THINKING TIPS FOR THE ORGANIZATION

- Analyze employee mental and physical loads. If the organi-zation (and its leaders) has no idea how much time or effort employees are applying to their work, they ought to find out, addressing any issues. Cognitive overload hampers thinking. It also affects productivity. You need to allow the space for Creative Thinking to occur if you desire sustainable, long-term success.

- A collaborative culture fosters Creative Thinking. An organization that knows how to work together—eliminat-ing the fiefdoms and silos across employees—is one that will more easily unleash Creative Thinking. Analyze your organization's culture. If it is closed and non-collaborative, take measures to get employees and teams to work better together.

- The Creative Thinking mindset of the organization cannot be rushed. It takes time. Build in brainstorming or ideation phases as part of a project plan. Ensure that the organization does not pay lip service to Creative Thinking. Encourage employees to allow their minds to wander, to think up inno-vative ways to support new ideas or existing objectives.

III

critical thinking

4

Think Hole

It is only in our decisions that we are important.

JEAN-PAUL SARTRE

DISCUSSED CRITICAL THINKING inhibitors with most of the people I interviewed for this book. Everyone was generally in agreement. There is something happening in society, and it's not good.

We have become too distracted.

The temptation for the next dopamine hit that accompanies a notification or the successful sending of a text or email has grown significantly. Many of the interviewees share similar concerns. In addition, we have become overly quick decision-makers. Furthermore, cognitive dissonance is more prevalent than it should be. Cognitive dissonance is a state in which people feel mental anguish when holding two or more contradictory beliefs or ideas at the same time. We will come back to this inhibitor later in the chapter.

We also possess a penchant to jump to conclusions by skimming headlines instead of understanding the long-term trend lines. All of this is affecting our Critical Thinking. Of course, it comes back to time. How are we spending our time, and how does that affect our Critical Thinking? It is this aspect of time and its relationship to our distractedness and technology addiction that should be our greatest concern.

Joel Plaskett, the musician we met in the previous chapter, recognized that his own Critical Thinking was affected by the lure of his device. He decided to remove all social media applications from his iPhone. "I realized I had become addicted to it on my phone," he said, "and it had shattered my ability to focus." Joel went even further. "The constant barrage of technology has fucked everything up. We're at a really weird, critical moment in human, technological development."

He described the difference between touring in the 1990s and today as an example. "I remember touring with a box of maps under the seat. I remember calling the clubs to find out where they were located. None of it was done over the Internet. None of it was done over a phone, or email, or texts. You had to call a club and find out where it was physically located. You had to actually talk to someone, spend some time thinking, and then use your maps to get to the gig on time." Joel believes technology has caused us to stop thinking critically about some of our simple, day-to-day actions.

The successful launch of the first-ever Invictus Games required a good dose of Critical Thinking and time management. This is exactly what Dominic Reid, the event director, was responsible for. Prince Harry is the inspiration behind the Games, an international sporting event for wounded, ill, and injured active duty and veteran service members. The first Games, held in London in 2014, saw hundreds of people participate. Subsequent events have been hosted to global acclaim in Orlando and Toronto. Another is planned for Sydney in October 2018.

The Invictus Games consists of sporting events run over the course of a week. Dominic was the event director for the inaugural Games in London, which ended up being a runaway success. It led to the creation of the Invictus Games Foundation, of which Dominic was appointed CEO. The purpose of the foundation is to ensure the future of the Games. Dominic's career spans the roles of soldier, architect, and producer of major events. It was his observations over the course of his career that shed further light on Critical Thinking inhibitors and reinforces my concern about time.

"These days, there are colossal time pressures on everybody because of the way the world works," said Dominic. "Electronic communication—the culture that expects an instant response—puts a lot of strain on people. It causes them to react to things because they have to be seen to be reacting to things. Technology causes people to behave in ways that they otherwise might not." Dominic works in an industry in which the large-scale events that he runs are only successful if they are collaborative endeavors. This goes back to the previous chapter and my point of building a collaborative culture if Open Thinking is to stand a chance. The magnitude of Dominic's projects is massive but the only way they can prosper is if his entire team buys into and invests in them. To reach a positive outcome is to employ Open Thinking in unison. Dominic has discovered that success often comes down to having the time to employ Critical Thinking.

Aside from the Invictus Games, Dominic has also run other significant events such as the 350th anniversary of the Royal Society and the Queen's Golden Jubilee. If that was not enough, Dominic is pageantmaster of The Lord Mayor's Show, the world's largest unrehearsed procession spanning three and a half miles across London, replete with "people, horses, vehicles, soldiers, bands, bicycles, and giant fish." It's a role he has held for over 25 years.

"In the old days, we used to do things by telephone and by having face-to-face conversations," Dominic said. It was much like how Joel Plaskett used to find the clubs for his concert shows with live telephone conversations and physical maps. "You would trust the others on the team because of the relationships you had built up face-to-face. You would end up building a sense of collaboration out of the process of relationship building. You remembered things because you spoke those words to another human being. You almost took it for granted. But it worked. Now it's all done by email and by technology. Email acts as an audit trail for failure. And it's becoming a big problem." Dominic made one thing clear: Technology affects time, and that in turn has been detrimentally affecting Critical Thinking.

Dominic was also insistent on a trend that is picking up speed, further affecting Critical Thinking. He feels as though email is simply an opportunity to shift blame. Being constantly on technology changes the culture of a team, a project, and, in his case, the requirements to successfully put together massive events. "Email and technology tightens up everyone's thinking, and not in a good way. Technology has created new constraints almost at a stroke eliminating the chance to hold two opposing views at the same time. To keep the relationships productive in my business, you need to have an obsessively detailed plan, but you have to be able to say 'we need to change this now.' A lot of people find this quite infuriating if buried by technology."

When Dominic began to highlight the need to simultaneously hold two opposing views to improve Critical Thinking, again I thought about the work of Roger L. Martin and his Integrative Thinking model. But what Dominic was getting at is important to consider. He believes that due to the influx of technology and the "always on" mindset, we are losing the ability to even debate two opposing views. To formulate a new idea that is made up of the good bits from each opposing view, leaders ought to be helping team members to manage their time. If people make decisions more hastily as a result of the "always on" mindset, there is no chance to consider opposing views. If time is the enemy and technology the weapon, everyone ends up as a battle victim. To counter this predicament, Dominic introduced a Critical Thinking tip: "We need the ability to create space for other people and yourself to be both creative and critical."

Dominic believes leaders should be giving team members "top cover" for their ideas to come to fruition and their decisions to be solid. He admits it has become a difficult task to teach, yet he remains steadfast in his efforts to help his teams with their Critical Thinking. He introduced a concept he calls "purposeful procrastination," a way to be bone idle. "What I have observed," he continued, "is that by not responding to stuff—by leaving things on the to-do list—a wide variety of benefits accrue. Some things just naturally go away. Sometimes there is more time for a measured response, or some other bits and pieces move underneath you. If you leave it for a few days, you eventually come up with the right answer. And this is what I am teaching my teams."

Dominic insisted that the "purposeful procrastination" tactic teaches a culture of pausing, one that allows opposable thoughts to co-exist. This technique ultimately leads to better decision-making. He is not deliberately missing deadlines. No, Dominic builds in a time buffer to enable improved decisions and Critical Thinking. Dominic admits, however, that the concept of purposeful procrastination is both difficult and never finished. "Email and texting creates work for the sake of work," he said. "It creates more work than needs to be done. Unfortunately, it's really hard to teach that culture of pausing. If you look at the way people work, the pace is insane. But the benefits are truly great once everyone gets it."

Critical Thinking, according to the American Philosophical Association, is "the process of purposeful, self-regulatory judgment." If we do not create the time in which to affect better Critical Thinking, we are merely operating in a culture of constant action, full of individuals possessed by Inflexible, Indecisive, and Indifferent Thinking.

Section III of *Open to Think* is devoted to Critical Thinking. For the remainder of this chapter we will continue to explore various inhibitors that affect Critical Thinking. In Chapter 5 we will add to Dominic's "purposeful procrastination" tip and discover additional ways to improve our Critical Thinking.

Socrates Meets Netflix

In 1997, Reed Hastings sold his company Pure Software to Rational Software for $750 million. Shortly thereafter—using the proceeds of the sale—he co-founded Netflix. Back then it was not the online streaming media empire that it has become today. Anachronistic as it may seem now, Netflix was originally a mail-order DVD rental company. Hastings was inspired to establish Netflix when he was fined $40 for the late return of a DVD to Blockbuster. Entering 2018, the company employed nearly 4,000 people, earned revenues close to $9 billion, and had morphed not only into an online streaming media service, but a successful entertainment studio producing hit shows such as *The Crown*, *Master of None*, and *Orange is the New Black*. Blockbuster, incidentally, filed for bankruptcy protection in 2010 and in 2011 it sold its remaining 1,700 stores to satellite television provider Dish Network.

Netflix is also known for its progressive people and culture practices. For example, its expense policy comprises a mere five words: "Act in Netflix's best interests." Annual performance reviews are non-existent. The company prefers frequent coaching conversations. Salaried team members have limitless vacation days, if they so choose. Stock options issued to employees contain no vesting period. Perhaps what I appreciate most about Netflix, however, can be found within its values and the way they shape behaviors and skills at the company.

There are nine Netflix values. The first is concerned with Critical Thinking. Netflix refers to this as "Judgment" and defines it as follows:

- You make wise decisions (people, technical, business, and creative) despite ambiguity.

- You identify root causes, and get beyond treating symptoms.

- You think strategically, and can articulate what you are, *and are not*, trying to do.

- You smartly separate what must be done well now, and what can be improved later.

These four lines act as an important signal to get Critical Thinking right. Netflix asks its employees to balance the near and the far, the easy and the hard, the known and the unknown. The company does not want its team members judging ignorantly, but openly. It implores them to seek out the truth—the facts—through reflection and interaction. It also wants them to act, not to sit on the fence of indecision. Judgment is so important to Netflix that it is their first value.

Netflix teaches its employees not simply to identify today's information, but to look ahead to the needs of tomorrow. Balance is further enabled by not only saying yes but no as well. This is the Netflix way. Exercise judgment in both action *and* reflection. It sounds very philosophical yet practical.

Socrates—whom many consider to be the father of western philosophy—was a man in search of the truth. Ancient Athens was where he honed his Critical Thinking habits. Northwest of the Acropolis was the Athens *agora*. Most Greek cities had one. These agoras were gathering places found near the city's center where spiritual, academic, athletic, artistic, and political events took place.

Inside the Athens *agora* and to the south of Panathenaic Way was the Enneakrounos, the public well. Just over 300 yards away and to the left was a portico known as the Stoa of Zeus. Socrates was often to be found just past the Monument of the Eponymous Heroes and inside the portico, standing on a wooden crate, thoroughly engaged in a discussion with a gaggle of people. It sounded like they were at odds with one another. It was loud. It seemed like bickering. But that is entirely the point.

Socrates, among other things, was renowned for introducing what is referred to in Greek as *elenchus*, a method of eliciting truth by question and answer. The argumentative dialogue spilling over among the people gathered at the Stoa of Zeus was *elenchus* in action, a dialectical method of Critical Thinking. It requires the constant asking and answering of questions. With *elenchus*, biases can be overcome, presumptions debunked, and points of view both defended and challenged. Dialectical discourse occurs between two or more people who hold differing viewpoints. The aim is to draw out their opinions on a subject, not only to establish the truth but ideally to create a new common ground between the two perspectives.

Back in the Athens *agora*, according to the writings of Plato, Socrates would invoke *elenchus* frequently. As he sought out the truth, Socrates felt cooperative debate was the way it would materialize. More specifically for Socrates, the *elenchus* allowed him to ascertain if humans were capable of living the good life while simultaneously probing if we knew *how* we ought to live the good life. This was his quest, the pursuit of truth. The purpose was to expose himself to the unknown and to contrary opinion.

Socrates never once believed he possessed all the answers. Rather, the *elenchus* would provide the singular truth imparted by the many opinions he came across. Vulnerability was always key. By being vulnerable, Socrates did not reach conclusions on his own. He used the immense power of other people's belief to define a new truth. The Socratic method of Critical Thinking creates an endpoint from multiple viewpoints to eventually make an informed decision that moves an idea forward.

Which brings us back to Netflix. When you reread those four lines defining Netflix's "Judgment" value, picture yourself at the company's headquarters. Might it be a modern-day *agora*, where employees are encouraged to invoke *elenchus* every day? At a minimum, Netflix and Socrates provide good food for thought when it comes to assessing your Critical Thinking habits.

Cognitive Dissonance

Netflix's definition of its Judgment value is designed to prevent cognitive dissonance, the term I promised I'd come back to. Leon Festinger published his theory about cognitive dissonance in 1957, with far-reaching implications for Critical Thinking. Festinger argued that when people possess conflicting beliefs or ideas, it can lead to disharmony. It is this disharmony that people try to avoid—which, ironically, eventually ends up causing them the most harm. Festinger wrote, "When dissonance is present, in addition to trying to reduce it, the person will actively avoid situations and information which would likely increase the dissonance." In the case of Netflix, the company truly wants its team members to embrace a multiplicity of perspectives.

Cognitive dissonance can be a significant source of stress in the workplace. If you run across situations that may be counter to your beliefs or goals, it can easily shift you into an Indecisive Thinking mindset. Instead of doing anything about it, you end up paralyzed, unable to make a better decision. Any sort of deep conflict with a task or action that you are asked to investigate may also push you into a state of paralysis, preventing Critical Thinking from ever happening.

Dropping out of her freshman year from Stanford University, Elizabeth Holmes founded Palo Alto–based Theranos in 2003, aged 19. At the time, Theranos was an incredible idea. During her schooling at Stanford, Holmes thought there could be a market for a state-of-the-art, handheld medical device. The contraption would be able to produce real-time assessments showing how your body might interact with certain drugs, based on a trace amount of blood drawn and inserted into the device. Imagine if lives could be saved or ailments prevented.

Holmes was certainly of that mindset. Theranos was an attractive option for several Silicon Valley investors. By 2014, financial backers had invested so much that the privately held company was valued at $9 billion. Holmes herself was worth $4.5 billion. In 2015, Forbes named Holmes the youngest self-made female billionaire.

But something alarming was happening behind those Palo Alto corporate walls. While Theranos was focused on building out Wellness Centers that customers could walk into—as well as partnering with the likes of Walgreens and Capital BlueCross to sell the handheld devices—the company was simultaneously acting unethically. Not only was it substituting its own blood-testing device with one developed by Siemens, its lab results were proving to be erroneous as well. Some of the results were tampered with.

According to the Centers for Medicare and Medicaid Services (CMS), it stated that their Newark, California testing lab "did not comply with certificate requirements and performance standards," which caused an "immediate jeopardy to patient health and safety." Thanks to the investigative work of reporters like John Carreyrou of The Wall Street Journal, Holmes and Theranos were exposed. The Securities and Exchange Commission (SEC) began a criminal investigation in 2016. The $9 billion valuation quickly dissipated. By 2016, the company had been pegged down to an $800 million valuation, a drop of more than 90 percent. Due to the structure of shares, Holmes's net worth in Theranos tumbled close to nothing. In late 2017 the company secured a $100 million loan from Fortress Investment Group LLC. In 2018, Holmes asked shareholders for more money to stay afloat.

There are two pertinent observations about the Theranos case and Critical Thinking. The first relates to Holmes and other senior leaders who were aware of the misdeeds. Were they blinded by the lure of those investment dollars and the glowing media attention the company was receiving? Instead of being forthright about their laboratory failures, they covered them up and pretended nothing was wrong. Not only did that end up causing much harm to their brand and operations, it changed the entire makeup and purpose of the company. In the end, Theranos laid off over 500 people—more than 70 percent of the workforce—and by 2017 the company was focusing solely on the production of portable medical devices, after closing all its blood-testing labs and Wellness Centers.

The second observation comes from a whistleblower. Tyler Shultz had been working at Theranos for roughly eight months when he had finally seen enough. Instead of sitting on the fence and not doing anything about what he was witnessing, he acted. Convinced that the company was operating unethically in several ways, Shultz first wrote a letter to Holmes outlining his concerns. That failed to produce the desired response. Even though his grandfather, George Shultz— President Richard Nixon's treasury and labor secretary and President Ronald Reagan's secretary of state—was a member of the Theranos board of directors, he pressed on.

The younger Shultz would not let the situation go. He was determined not only to right the wrong, but to exercise better judgment. He eventually contacted *The Wall Street Journal* and exposed the corporate malpractice. His courage potentially saved lives, despite leading to the loss of hundreds of jobs at the company. Shultz had this to say about the situation: "Fraud is not a trade secret. I refuse to allow bullying, intimidation, and threat of legal action to take away my First Amendment right to speak out against wrongdoing."

In the end, the downfall of Holmes and Theranos can be partially pinpointed to cognitive dissonance, and Holmes's refusal to use Critical Thinking to avoid it. Unfortunately, it ended up causing unnecessary harm to many stakeholders.

Bank On It

There is another corporate example I would like to detail that highlights the importance of Critical Thinking. In this case over 5,000 employees were implicated.

Wells Fargo & Company is an American bank headquartered in San Francisco, which earned revenues of close to $90 billion in 2017. In September of 2016, the bank was embroiled in a massive public relations crisis. If you thought it was bad in 2008 when the CEOs of Detroit's automakers arrived in Washington by private jet to request a $25 billion bailout, the situation at Wells Fargo might make your head spin.

The Consumer Financial Protection Bureau (CFPB) discovered that Wells Fargo employees had created over two million phony customer banking accounts. Not only did this independent body determine that Wells Fargo falsely generated the accounts over a five-year period, it also found that not a single customer had authorized the bank to do so on their behalf. Over 5,000 Wells Fargo employees were held responsible for the scheme. Illegally enrolling thousands of customers in financial services without their knowledge or consent is a significant breach of trust. The CFPB concluded that bonuses and other financial incentives tied to sales targets were the reason so many Wells Fargo employees took such reprehensible actions. In 2017 the CFPB revised the total number of affected customers to over 3.5 million.

Unsurprisingly, the CFPB issued a $185 million fine to Wells Fargo in response to the bank's fraudulent behavior. CFPB director Richard Cordray observed, "Because of the severity of these violations, Wells Fargo is paying the largest penalty the CFPB has ever imposed." In July of 2017, a federal judge in San Francisco ruled that the proposed settlement of a class-action lawsuit put forward by customers was "fair, reasonable and adequate." The settlement was for $142 million. Between the class-action lawsuit and the CFPB fine, Wells Fargo lost over $325 million. Furthermore, the company reported at the end of 2017 that it had set aside more than $1 billion toward associated legal fees.

With millions of customers affected by these unethical acts, it should come as no surprise that customer satisfaction took a toll as well. Just a few months after the crisis erupted, Wells Fargo reported that many of its key performance indicators had been negatively affected. In January of 2017, for example, the number of customers opening new checking accounts was down 31 percent from the previous year. Credit card applications had also dropped, by 47 percent. Furthermore, many customers were avoiding the bank altogether, with branch visits dropping by 14 percent.

In an interview during the fall of 2016 with *The Wall Street Journal*, Wells Fargo CEO John Stumpf laid blame specifically on rogue employees, not the organization's culture or ethics. Stumpf suggested that the 5,300 employees who were ultimately terminated as a result of the scandal failed to put customers first or honor the vision and values of the bank. "If they're not going to do the thing that we ask them to do—put customers first, honor our vision and values—I don't want them here," Stumpf said. Weeks later, Stumpf vacated his own role as CEO, taking with him $133.1 million into retirement, and was replaced by Tim Sloan. A few months earlier, Wells Fargo's consumer banking chief, Carrie Tolstedt—an individual whom Stumpf described as "a standard-bearer of our culture" and "a champion for our customers"—also retired abruptly from the company. She was the executive in charge of the business unit at Wells Fargo where the false accounts were opened. Tolstedt walked away with a $124 million payout, leaving well before the CFPB investigation published its findings.

Although thousands of employees lost their jobs because of what they had done, there were tens of thousands more left to wonder how and why these actions happened in the first place. After all, didn't Stumpf state he wanted employees working at the bank who honored its values? This is precisely where a lack of Critical Thinking can detrimentally impact the Open Thinking model. It can also run counter to operating with a higher purpose.

Wells Fargo advocated for a workplace in which sound decision-making was based on an engaged and ethical culture. The bank maintained that its ethics were "the sum of all the decisions each of us [its employees] makes every day." The leadership culture at this unit of the bank was one motivated by aggressive growth and profits. When spurious incentives are woven into any organization's operating ethos, there are bound to be adverse effects on Critical Thinking.

Was the company merely paying lip service to its values? What of those complicit employees? In Chapter 1, I defined Critical Thinking as *the thorough analysis of ideas and facts to make an ethical and timely decision.* Did the company display Critical Thinking when servicing its customers? That is, was it ethical when making decisions?

Wells Fargo defines its values as follows:

- People as a competitive advantage
- Ethics
- What's right for customers
- Diversity and inclusion
- Leadership

The Wells Fargo values help to drive three additional behaviors the company expects of its employees: conversation, interaction, and decision-making, all of them essential to Critical Thinking. It states, "If we can't link what we do to one of our values, we should ask ourselves why we're doing it. It's that simple." The organization infers further that its culture is defined by a "pattern of thinking and acting with the customer in mind."

For several years, many Wells Fargo employees consciously chose to skip past the company's values. Being ethical and doing what's right were imperative to putting the company's customers first, according to its values and expected behaviors. But these Wells Fargo employees somehow looked past these attributes. The implicated employees acted without concern for the potential ramifications. Perhaps some were pressured into such crimes. Others may have felt compelled to disregard the organization's values altogether for fear of losing their job and the paycheck that went with it. Regardless, the Wells Fargo story ought to really make us stop and think.

For Critical Thinking to be successful, individuals should be willing to converse openly with the facts, data, and all relevant information.

As Socrates demonstrated, having conversations with others and keeping your mind open to new ideas and opportunities is a good practice. The truth matters. Interaction with data can be as important as interacting with people. Time should be allowed for reflection and an assessment of options, before an ethical and timely decision is made. These steps are as relevant to the individual as to the organization as a whole. For Critical Thinking to work across multiple teams and business units, all team members should be conversing and interacting with one another to make better decisions.

Clearly, the actions of Wells Fargo employees were unethical. How many of them fell into a state of cognitive dissonance? How many understood that their behavior was wrong, yet they continued to deceive customer after customer? To harken back to our Greek metaphor, how many stepped into the *agora* and championed their own dialectical thinking path, invoking an *elenchus*? One would be hard-pressed to suggest these sorts of behaviors would occur at a company that practices sound Critical Thinking.

At Wells Fargo—or at least in the division that was under the leadership of Carrie Tolstedt—there was an utter failure to abide by its own values. It is a clear example of a concept known as Espoused Theory versus Theory-in-Use, conceived by professor of management Chris Argyris of Harvard University in 1974 and his colleague Donald Schön. Espoused Theory is defined as: "The world view and values people believe their behavior is based on." Theory-in-Use is defined by Argyris and Schön as: "The world view and values implied by their behavior, or the maps they use to take action." In essence, Wells Fargo defined itself by its five Wells Fargo values. In reality, the company's Theory-in-Use was antithetical to its Espoused Theory. It talked a good game about values such as ethics, what's right for the customers, and leadership, but in reality it did not put them into practice. All talk no action.

Many Wells Fargo employees ignored not only its ethics but the company's stated culture of "thinking and acting with the customer in mind." Simply put, they failed to use sound judgment in a time that desperately required it. They ended up getting caught in the trap of choosing action over reflection, profits over purpose, Theory-in-Action versus Espoused Theory. Thousands of Wells Fargo employees lost their jobs as a result. Hundreds of thousands of customers were impacted, too. Of course, millions of dollars were also paid out due to Wells Fargo's lack of Critical Thinking. It goes to show how costly bad (or a lack of) Critical Thinking can be.

The Pope Weighs In on Trump

Critical Thinking is further inhibited by an individual's grip on technology. That computer in your pocket masquerading as a mobile phone has made you not only more anxious and stressed, it has become an outsourcing tool. Research by Nathaniel Barr, Gordon Pennycook, Jennifer A. Stolz, and Jonathan A. Fugelsang in 2015 at the University of Waterloo has proven that we are becoming increasingly dependent on technology, so much so that it is acting as a substitute for Critical Thinking. The jury is still out on the long-term impact, but there are some alarming short-term signs.

The researchers found that people defined as intuitive thinkers have, as a result, morphed into lazy thinkers due to a growing reliance on readily accessible fingertip technology like smartphones. On the contrary, if you are or want to become someone with a Critical Thinking mindset, you will analyze problems more logically, often questioning and second-guessing yourself before making a final decision. That is, you do not outsource your analytical thinking solely to a device or technology. You understand the need to think through all the facts before making an informed decision. Technology may assist, but it does not supplant your thinking and decision-making. The academics from the University of Waterloo claim that highly intelligent people are more logical and less intuitive when solving problems. Furthermore, they employ Critical Thinking skills and refrain from over-relying on technology.

Nathaniel Barr, one of the researchers from the University of Waterloo study, said this about the findings on devices and thinking:

"Decades of research have revealed that humans are eager to avoid expending effort when problem-solving and it seems likely that people will increasingly use their smartphones as an extended mind." Barr and his colleagues suggest that "people typically forgo effortful analytic thinking in lieu of fast and easy intuition." This not only indicates that we may be allowing mobile devices to do Critical Thinking for us, it means that *if* we are more prone to relying on gut feelings and our own convictions to make decisions, we may be more likely to use a device than our own brainpower to arrive at such a decision.

Such thinking has consequences. Take, for instance, the 2016 U.S. presidential election campaign. During the summer months of the race for the White House, voters may have stumbled upon the following headline in one or more of their various digital news feeds: "Pope Francis Shocks World, Endorses Donald Trump for President, Releases Statement." Quite a headline, particularly so given that Pope Francis had become the first pope ever to endorse a political candidate from any country. It was utterly breathtaking. If anyone went the extra mile and read the full article, his statement included the following line: "I ask, not as the Holy Father, but as a concerned citizen of the world that Americans vote for Donald Trump for President of the United States." More than 100,000 people shared the link on Facebook. Thousands more discovered it through other social media outlets.

But there is one slight problem with the pope's endorsement. It never happened. Published by the now-defunct satirical news website WTOE 5 News, the post—and of course the pope's endorsement—was a complete fabrication. The editors who once worked at WTOE 5 News claimed their material to be fantasy news. But fantasy news is now "fake news" and fake news is as good an example of outsourcing our Critical Thinking to devices as there ever was. While fake news and alternate forms of propaganda have been with us for as long as we have had media, access to modern technologies has accelerated and amplified the reach much more than was the case with newspapers, flyers, radio, and television. We need to be more discerning about how we access, filter, and share information. Our actions affect others. If we fail to be critical thinkers, we might be inadvertently (or purposefully) infecting others with the click of a button.

Before thousands of people believed and then shared the story about the pope's endorsement, did they ever consider pausing for a moment and reflecting on how unusual it was for a pope to endorse a political candidate? Pope Francis himself declared later, "I never say a word about electoral campaigns. The people are sovereign. I will only say: Study the proposals well, pray, and choose in conscience." The entire episode reminded me of a 1710 passage in *The Examiner* from literary figure Jonathan Swift: "Falsehood flies, and the Truth comes limping after it; so that when Men come to be undeceiv'd, it is too late; the Jest is over, and the Tale hath had its Effect."

Even the pope was asking U.S. citizens to "study the proposals well," to take all the time that was needed to analyze the pros and cons of the presidential candidates. But because people were influenced by the electronic headline—and it was so easy to redistribute from whatever technology they were using—they felt the urge to share before stopping to think if it was true or not. That is an excellent example of how we outsource our thinking to technology in an effort to expedite action. "Pope Francis endorsed Donald Trump," some will mutter to themselves. "I had better share this with my network as quickly as possible." It matters not which way you lean politically; the harsh truth of the example is that many of us are acting in this manner. When we subcontract our Critical Thinking and decision-making to technology, we succumb to Inflexible Thinking.

Being Overly Busy

When Socrates held court at the *agora*, he relied wholly on the spoken word. He not only refused to write any of his thoughts down, he was distrustful of such action. Socrates believed that books would "introduce forgetfulness into the soul." Ironically, though, our awareness of his ideas has been dependent on others documenting them and their works enduring into the modern era. In *Phaedrus*, Plato records a warning from Socrates about books: "You have not discovered a potion for remembering, but for reminding; you provide your students with the appearance of wisdom, not with its reality. Your invention will enable them to hear many things without being properly taught, and they will imagine that they have come to know much while for the most part they will know nothing."

We know that writing, either on paper or electronically, can be an aid to rather than a replacement of memory. Making notes and reflecting on them is an important aspect of Creative Thinking, despite the concerns of Socrates. Dare I state it, but Socrates was wrong. Writing can assist problem-solving and decision-making, as well as serve as a catalyst to creativity. But the written notes themselves do not achieve this; we do not rely wholly on what has been outsourced to a page or a digital repository. In this sense, we can sympathize with Socrates's point of view. We cannot excise people and their mental faculties. We cannot completely abdicate responsibility to technologies, whether that takes the form of pen and paper, the printing press, or the latest mobile device. There is always a danger that the speed and volume each technological advance introduces has an adverse effect on our need for time and reflection. Always fast, rarely slow. There is a constant flurry of fragmentary information inducing the forgetfulness and lack of attention that Socrates feared.

Take, for instance, the Sparks Street location of the Bier Markt or D'Arcy McGee's pub in Canada's capital city, Ottawa. Enter either establishment midweek between 5 p.m. and 8 p.m., and you will be greeted by a sea of Canada's federal politicians, bureaucrats, and aides, many of them glued to their devices. I have witnessed the same behavior in Washington, D.C., at political networking establishments such as Bullfeathers and Johnny's Half Shell. Isn't the point of these pubs and restaurants to unwind, network, and build relationships? The same can be said of trips to the cinema. Before the main attraction, you are presented with a lengthy warning asking you to refrain from using your device. That warning never used to exist. Pass by a bus stop or watch people on the subway, tube, or metro and more often than not you will discover an army of faces glowing from the blue light emitted by a sea of mobile devices.

How many times have you witnessed, or been guilty of, answering a text or email during a dinner with friends or family, because you were jolted by the vibration of a mobile device? How often did you feel a sense of duty to respond right away? I have been in countless meetings where attendees have said, "Can you repeat the question?" usually as the result of being distracted by their device or an urge to respond to whatever request has come their digital way. It is now commonplace (and disheartening) to watch families out for dinner, each of the members staring into a mobile device. Next time you are near a children's soccer match take a look at the sidelines and count how many parents are actually watching the game as opposed to the device in their hand.

It would be immoral of me to go any further in this book without acknowledging that I owe Nicholas Carr an apology. When Carr published his 2010 book, *The Shallows: What the Internet Is Doing to Our Brains*, I reacted strongly against his thesis. In my 2013 book *Flat Army*, I wrote: "He single-handedly shreds the usefulness of easy and quick access to information and knowledge. Carr is, well, a tad cataclysmic in his thinking about the web, people, and quicker access to information."

Five years later, I realize that I was at least partially wrong. I have learned and revisited my thinking. Perhaps it's an example of my own Open Thinking maturation. The web and constantly accessible mobile devices are indeed tinkering with the brains of professionals, "remapping the neural circuitry, reprogramming the memory." Access to information is clearly helpful, but not if it thwarts our Critical Thinking and not if it causes us to become distracted or, worse, poor decision-makers.

Have the proliferation of personal technology and the correlated aftereffect of increased busyness introduced forgetfulness in our souls? I imagine that Socrates would be seething if he were still alive. At a minimum, people's stress levels have increased because they are constantly tethered to technology that persistently fosters constant busyness.

The American Psychological Association (APA) provides some context. It states, "Stress runs higher, on average, for constant [device] checkers than for those who do not engage with technology as frequently." Lynn Bufka, APA's associate executive director for practice research and policy, said, "What these individuals don't consider is that while technology helps us in many ways, being constantly connected can have a negative impact on both their physical and mental health."

In another research study conducted in 2015 by Kostadin Kushlev and Elizabeth W. Dunn, when people were assigned to limit the number of times they checked their email they ended up experiencing lower overall day-to-day stress, higher well-being, higher mindfulness, better self-perceived productivity, and improved sleep quality. Imagine what changing these behaviors could do to improve your Critical Thinking.

The Unfocused Self

In a 1930 paper titled "Economic Possibilities for our Grandchildren," economist John Maynard Keynes made a bold prediction. He claimed that early in the 21st century the workday would be no more than three hours. Keynes felt living a life of leisure would be far more enticing for all of us. Because our material desires would be satisfied by technological advances and much higher standards of living, we would be able to free up our time to laze in a life of reflection. Not only was Keynes fantastically wrong about this, but we are, if anything, experiencing a mounting sense of busyness. This busyness is itself affected by our increasing lack of focus. The busier and more distracted we get, the more unfocused we become. Research carried out by Microsoft in 2015 indicates that in the year 2000 we could focus our attention span for 12 seconds. Now it's 8 seconds. This equates to a 33 percent drop in our ability to focus. For perspective, the attention span of a goldfish is 9 seconds. As T.S. Eliot phrases it in his 1943 poem "Burnt Norton:"

> Only a flicker
> Over the strained time-ridden faces
> Distracted from distraction by distraction
> Filled with fancies and empty of meaning
> Tumid apathy with no concentration.

When author and Georgetown University professor Cal Newport was researching his book *Deep Work*, he decided to interview Adam Grant. Grant is a tenured professor at The Wharton School, part of the University of Pennsylvania. Moreover, Grant is a best-selling author of two books, *Give and Take* and *Originals*, and the co-author of another, *Option B*. Newport's curiosity about Grant grew when he discovered the volume of his academic paper production. In 2012, Grant had seven articles published in leading academic journals—a much higher number than the average scholar—and in 2013 he published five more, in addition to the publication of his first *New York Times* bestseller, *Give and Take*. By 2014, Grant had written 60 peer-reviewed publications and was in the throes of writing his second book. He was only 33 years old. Newport wondered what Grant was doing to be so productive *and* successful.

What it boiled down to be was focus. Newport discovered that Grant possesses the ability to batch together the "hard but important intellectual work into long, uninterrupted stretches." In other words, Grant does not get distracted. He remains focused and performs "deep work." From a Critical Thinking perspective, Newport's assessment of Grant is important. If you want to make solid decisions and if you want to see through the veneer of the status quo, you must improve your attention span. If you want to select right from wrong *and* successfully act on your decision, you will take the necessary steps to employ Critical Thinking in a distraction-free manner. You will fully concentrate on evaluating all facts and data to make the best decision possible.

On the concept of attention residue—the inability to remain deeply focused—Newport writes, "It might seem harmless to take a quick glance at your inbox every ten minutes or so. That quick check introduces a new target for your attention. The attention residue left by such unresolved switches dampens your performance. If you're not comfortable going deep for extended periods of time, it'll be difficult to get your performance to the peak levels of quality and quantity increasingly necessary to thrive professionally."

After I finished reading *Deep Work*, I reflected on my own Critical Thinking. In particular, I was interested in my book-writing habits. As

I have argued, Open Thinking occurs when we continuously dream, decide, and do. This is how all of my books are written, too. Any author must be constantly dreaming, deciding, and doing while developing a manuscript. In my case, as a non-fiction leadership/management writer, over the course of a book project I am frequently researching, interviewing, writing, rewriting, and making decisions about content and story sequences. After self-reflecting, I concluded that I may have done a minor disservice to the quality of my writing through my first two books. How?

While I may occasionally write on an iPhone or iPad when I am out and about, 90 percent of my writing is done on a laptop. I realized that I was subject to constant distractions that were completely avoidable. My attention was frequently interrupted by pop-up social media notifications from my LinkedIn, Twitter, Facebook, and Instagram accounts. In mid-thought—as I was making decisions over a story, or a theory, or the sequence of content for the book—I was distracted by something that had nothing to do with my original thinking, reflection, or decision-making. At least in part, I had become unfocused. Although I rarely acted on the pop-up browser or operating system notifications that encroached on my screen, I recognized that they were interfering with my train of thought. I could do better. I could easily achieve an improved form of "deep work" simply by shutting down all laptop notifications. Unsurprisingly, during the development of *Open to Think* I have felt far less writing stress or pressure than was the case on *The Purpose Effect* or *Flat Army*.

Author Daniel Goleman explains in his 2013 book, *Focus: The Hidden Driver of Excellence*, that improving executive function can assist attention control, self-discipline, and temptation. "The power to direct our focus onto one thing and ignore others lies at the core of willpower," Goleman argues. Indeed, there is a relationship between the unfocused self and the difficulty in developing Critical Thinking. It is very likely that your executive function needs improving if you are feeling stressed, distracted, and overly busy.

In the case of Adam Grant, his executive function is elevated. He has a heightened willpower. Executive function is controlled by an area of the brain called the frontal lobe. It is divided into two areas:

regulation and organization. If you can regulate, in effect you can take stock of a given situation and change your behavior and respond accordingly. You take proactive measures to cut off any distractions, as I did with the notifications on my laptop. The organization side of your frontal lobe collects information and then puts it together in such a way that you can properly evaluate what to do with it. Think of it as your mental processing engine. This was Socrates's sweet spot. An improved executive function ultimately aids your ability to focus while mitigating any potential attention residue or distractions.

Hat Tip to the Millinery

When I asked Karyn Ruiz about Critical Thinking, she put herself in the shoes of her customers. "I find that people who come into Lilliput are longing for the old days when things were made," she said. "So many people are now influenced by Amazon, Starbucks, and the like that their lives have become cheap, dirty, and quick." Karyn felt as though her customers have become loyal because they are the sorts of people who "yearn for the attachment of an establishment like Lilliput, where they get to see the traditional cycle of hat-making." She was referring to the time she and the team take to produce a hat.

"Good hats take time to make," she said, "and so our creativity and our decision-making may take longer than you expect. But you can't cut corners when making a hat. Likewise, you can't cut corners with our process." The metaphor of hat-making with Open Thinking is really starting to "take shape," isn't it?

CRITICAL THINKING QUESTIONS
FOR THE INDIVIDUAL

- Have you done everything possible to ensure all the facts are known before deciding? Are you willing to revisit a decision if additional information is presented that alters your thinking?

- Are you comfortable with cognitive dissonance, and are you capable of considering two opposing views to make a more informed decision?

- How much time are you spending distracted by technology? Is this distractedness causing you to be overly busy and less focused on the opportunity to be an Open Thinker?

CRITICAL THINKING QUESTIONS
FOR THE ORGANIZATION

- Where does Critical Thinking sit in your values or leadership model? Is it there at all?

- How is Critical Thinking woven into the organization's leadership development programs? Is it a part of your onboarding or new hire orientation program?

- Does the organization possess a decision-making model, one that is both collaborative and purposeful? How does this Critical Thinking model get used by senior leaders when coaching team members?

5

Great Minds Don't Think Alike

It is, in fact, far easier to act under conditions
of tyranny than it is to think.

HANNAH ARENDT

THERE IS ONE topic that has become a significant concern for many in the teaching profession. That topic is Critical Thinking.

I have been fortunate to attend and speak at the Learning Forward Annual Conference on multiple occasions. Learning Forward itself is a North American-based professional association "devoted exclusively to those who work in educator professional development." Its aim is to help administrators and staff plan, implement, and measure high-quality learning.

When I joined several educators for lunch at the 2012 Learning Forward conference in Boston, I asked a question I often ask when I am lucky enough to spend time with them. "What is stopping students from becoming better students?" While there were several opinions offered in response, one was unanimously held: Critical Thinking skills. Four years later the conference shifted to Vancouver. Once more I posed the question to a group of strangers, and again I discovered consensus regarding the need for Critical Thinking.

Many parallels can be drawn between the education space and the work world. If graduates continue to enter the professional ranks lacking Critical Thinking abilities it begins to impact not only their own engagement and purpose, it affects levels of productivity, innovation, growth, and customer service levels in the organizations where they work. Young people must be exposed to and practice Critical Thinking skills from an early age. If this does not happen, they progress from formal education to the workplace quick to judge and eager to act but ill-equipped to reflect and make informed decisions. The next time I visit a Learning Forward conference I would like the educators to tell me Critical Thinking is no longer a major concern.

But educators *are* professionals. Responsible as they are for educating students, they are also beholden to the organizations they work for. Teachers are thus quite capable of demonstrating Critical Thinking in two unique ways: with fellow colleagues, and by working with students in the classroom. It is in this unique combination of teacher and professional that I will unearth some of the key behaviors that make up Critical Thinking. Let's meet a couple of professional educators and learn how they demonstrate Critical Thinking.

Sage on the Critical Thinking Stage

"I am constantly evaluating and adjusting my teaching based on observations and feedback." These are the words of Alison Galloway, a grade three teacher at St. Michaels University School (SMUS) in Victoria, British Columbia, since 2007. "I try to put myself in the shoes of the students by listening to them and finding engaging ways to meet them at their interests and passions."

I first met Alison in September 2011. She was my middle child's grade one teacher. I was immediately struck by her curiosity, her compassion, and the collaborative way she practiced her profession. For Alison, teaching was not an individual-only act, it was the combined responsibility of the pupil, parents, community, classmates, and her. Her holistic views not only assisted the student's education, she unleashed their passions and interests through some unique teaching tactics.

But it was Alison's Critical Thinking mindset that really interested me. She was an educator who was happy to try new things while being completely at ease with making mistakes. Not prone to mistakes, but untroubled by them. Critical Thinking demands a relationship with both Creative Thinking and Applied Thinking. That is, if we are not open to new ideas or we refuse to return to Critical Thinking after having made a mistake, there is little chance of demonstrating Open Thinking. "Being open to new ideas and experimenting with new ways of teaching is key to my job satisfaction," she revealed. Indeed, Alison's teaching style is interconnected with the purpose she feels in her role as an educator at SMUS.

James Stewart is based at Toronto's Bishop Strachan School (BSS), where he has been a history teacher since 2001. Renowned for being an enlightening and thoughtful storyteller, James also honors the importance of flexibility in Critical Thinking. "My teaching framework is always structured," he said, "yet flexible enough to leave room for emerging ideas. Some of the best ideas for a unit come from my students, so part of my information-gathering involves asking them what they would like to learn."

In fact, James engages in the profession of teaching using five Critical Thinking guidelines:

- Ongoing professional training
- Reflection on practice
- Consultation with colleagues
- Flexibility in practice
- Desire to make the teaching better each time

"Things can change on the fly as well and this is usually skill-based," James remarked. If his students need extra time for research or additional instruction on a skill, James has to make a call right in the moment of action. That is, he is constantly evaluating the situation. "These decisions are based on my professional judgment as I watch my lesson progress or not," he said.

Teaching is not a solitary activity. It involves many others. Every school is an organization made up of a variety of professionals. "In a teaching team," said James, "these kinds of decisions would be discussed with my colleagues to see that we are on the same wavelength or to consult their views. Many small but important interjections are made by teachers every class as they observe what is happening. It's one of the things that can distinguish an expert teacher from a novice—that ability to notice what is going on." By continually observing the situation with his students—analyzing what is working, what is not, and collaborating with other teachers on the resulting scenario— James is assessing how to make the biggest impact in his role as a teacher. He often employs an evaluation loop to make each lesson that much better. In turn, this makes him an eminently effective and admired professional.

Alison wants her Critical Thinking philosophy to be used for the benefit of the child's long-term development. "I like to think in the long term. I try to see how my behaviors today will influence future events and how they will impact my students. Specifically, when I am planning lessons I try to figure out ways to make the learning relevant to the lives of my students and to find ways that tie into their prior knowledge and future needs."

Her approach to teaching and remaining flexible is, in part, due to her passion for the Reggio Emilia approach to teaching. Inspired by psychologist Loris Malaguzzi after World War II, this educational approach suggests that learning ought to be based on the values of responsibility, community, exploration, discovery, and respect through a child's self-guided curriculum of passions and interests. To carry this out in her classroom, Alison not only has to be diligent at Critical Thinking, she must consistently demonstrate Open Thinking.

Alison is a quintessential *Open to Think* role model. She often thinks about the idea, and then decides what the relevant steps and skills are to accomplish the task inside the classroom with the students. From there, she puts it into action. Yet Alison remains flexible to returning to Critical Thinking (or even Creative Thinking) to make additional improvements. "I draw out a mind map of sorts connecting the ideas, subject areas, and content. As the unit progresses, I monitor engagement levels and achievement in the required skills. If I feel that something hasn't clicked I will try a new way of teaching a topic or spend extra time re-teaching a concept. I trust my gut instinct and read my audience for ongoing feedback." Alison has come to the conclusion that teaching really is first about listening and then making sound decisions. By sitting back, observing, and watching students, she is best placed to be an even more effective teacher, aiding the development of her young learners.

While every teacher has a curriculum to follow—just as there are specific duties and responsibilities in any role, in any organization—James keeps his ear to the ground about current events in today's changing world, to make on-the-fly decisions that end up improving what he is currently teaching. For example, when President Donald Trump delivered his inaugural address in 2017, James spent more time reviewing President Abraham Lincoln's second inaugural address and used his words inside the classroom instead of what he had originally planned. "If I can tie in any history content with current events, it gives that topic a bit more time in the spotlight," he said. But it takes a continuously attentive professional to take such measures.

James provided another example. "2017 is the 100th anniversary of the Battle of Vimy Ridge in the First World War, fought near Arras, France, so more attention will be paid to it in my classroom." James believes that any news about historical events can play a role in his teaching, hence he is constantly in an information-gathering and fact-finding mode. "I read a great memoir, *The Education of Augie Merasty*," he continued, "and thought we should teach it." The book details the life journey of Joseph Auguste Merasty, one of an estimated 150,000 First Nations, Inuit, and Métis children in Canada who were taken from their families and sent to government-funded, church-run residential schools. "I brought the book to the attention of my colleagues and now we will teach it this year in class," James confirmed. It is yet another example of how Critical Thinking requires us to be alert, fact-based, information gatherers, and ready to make sound decisions as the situation warrants.

Both Alison's and James's approach to Critical Thinking reminded me of what investor Warren Buffett once said: "A checklist is no substitute for thinking." For certain, Critical Thinking is not a checklist. It is the ability to come to conclusions that positively affect an outcome by being proactive, flexible, participatory, mindful of others, and factual. Just like Alison and James.

Critical Thinking Components

According to the American Philosophical Association (APA), Critical Thinking is "the process of purposeful, self-regulatory judgment." A study performed by Professor Edward Glaser of Columbia University in 1941 defines Critical Thinking through three characteristics: (1) an attitude of being disposed to consider in a thoughtful way the problems and subjects that come within the range of one's experiences, (2) knowledge of the methods of logical inquiry and reasoning, and (3) some skill in applying those methods. The University of Waterloo defines it as being able to "examine an issue by breaking it down, and evaluating it in a conscious manner, while providing arguments/evidence to support the evaluation." Many academics and associations have come up with numerous definitions of Critical Thinking.

But if ever there was a piece of research that thoroughly investigated what makes up the key behaviors of Critical Thinking, it was the Delphi Report. Commissioned by the APA in 1987, its aim was to provide a systematic inquiry into the state of Critical Thinking so that the results could be used to improve America's elementary, secondary, and post-secondary curricula. Published in 1990 and led by Dr. Peter A. Facione—at the time, dean of the College of Arts and Sciences at Santa Clara University—the research showed that the ideal critical thinker is, among other things, habitually inquisitive, well-informed, trustful of reason, open-minded, flexible, honest in facing personal biases, prudent in making judgments, willing to reconsider, diligent in seeking relevant information, reasonable in the selection of criteria, focused in inquiry, and persistent in seeking results. Sadly, over a quarter of a century later it is difficult to confirm that the Delphi Report has made any difference.

Now, more than ever, we ought to pay closer attention to the importance of Critical Thinking as we live among the waves of societal uncertainty. For example, a study in 2010 by consulting and research firm McKinsey & Company found that 72 percent of senior executives thought bad decision-making was as frequent as good decision-making. This does not bode well for any of us if both societal and organizational complexities continue to grow.

As we know, *Open to Think* comprises three key elements: Creative Thinking, Critical Thinking, and Applied Thinking. Of these, Critical Thinking is arguably the model's most important category. It is where we converge on the ideas, facts, and knowledge to resolve a way forward. To recap, we have defined Critical Thinking in simple terms:

> The thorough analysis of ideas and facts to make an ethical and timely decision.

Without Critical Thinking, we end up making ineffectual decisions or no decisions at all. Sound Critical Thinking is what ensures that educators like Alison and James are as good as they are in their chosen profession.

Truppenführung

When one person or group possesses the logic or rationale for doing something, and another does not, it can prevent Open Thinking from coming to fruition. If we employ entrenched ideological partisanship with our Critical Thinking, it will be impossible for us to realize the dreams and ideas that were hatched in Creative Thinking.

Long before Martin Luther King, Jr., the sociologist, writer, and activist W.E.B. Du Bois fought for the equality of African Americans, opposing the notion of biological white superiority. Du Bois's prolific writing and thoughts on racial inadequacies—based on fact-based research, collaboration with others, and his acceptance of revisiting decisions—was criticized by many during the time he was writing, the first few decades of the 20th century.

For example, Du Bois felt that differing education levels and opportunities promoted racial inequality during the Reconstruction period in America between 1860 and 1880. At the time, his thoughts were ignored—even scoffed at—by many. By the 1960s and 1970s, most mainstream historians and academics had come to accept his conclusions. It makes one wonder where the United States might be today were it not for the entrenched political bias of the influential American leaders of the time. What level of societal harmony might there be across America if leaders had listened to Du Bois's opinions on racial injustice and discrimination? It is this entrenched type of thinking that can affect the Open Thinker, inhibiting Critical Thinking altogether.

In Chapter 3, I introduced the story about the Maginot Line involving the French and German military. Again, while I hope not to be considered a sympathizer of the Nazi regime or comfortable with its mission, there is something to learn from its historical application of Critical Thinking across the whole of the German military. As with the Du Bois example, it is incumbent upon us to remain open as we further define the attributes that make up sound and reasonable Critical Thinking.

In 1933, the Germans introduced a concept known as *Truppenführung*, the 20th century equivalent of Sun Tzu's *Art of War*. *Truppenführung* was a manual issued to every German soldier across all ranks. It was made up of intellectual tools and methodologies to be applied by soldiers in the ever-changing conditions of war. Of course, World War II had not yet broken out at that time, but Germany's plotting to invade other nations was well underway. *Truppenführung* was not a step-by-step manual. It was more philosophy and psychology than a tactical handbook. In hindsight, *Truppenführung* effectively provided insight into the social values of the German army and how it dealt with certain battle situations. It even contained the doctrinal framework for inducing a blitzkrieg, the method used at the Maginot Line. I first bumped into the concept of *Truppenführung* while reading

Stephen Bungay's wonderful 2012 book, *The Art of Action: How Leaders Close the Gaps Between Plans, Actions and Results*.

Truppenführung includes several behaviors the German military expected of its soldiers that relate to Critical Thinking. The following snippets illustrate the point.

- The mission and the situation form the basis of the action. The mission designates the objective to be attained. The leader must never forget his mission. The first demand in war is decisive action. Everyone, the highest commander to the most junior soldier, must be aware that omissions and neglects incriminate him more severely than the mistake of choice of means.

- The decision arises from the mission and the situation. Should the mission no longer suffice as the fundamental of conduct or it is changed by events, the decision must take these considerations into account. He who changes his mission or does not execute the one given must report his actions at once and assumes all responsibility for the consequences. He must always keep in mind the whole situation.

- Obscurity of the situation is the rule. Seldom will one have exact information of the enemy. However, to wait in tense situations for information is seldom a token of strong leadership, often of weakness.

- Without very good reason, a decision once made should not be abandoned. However, in the vicissitudes of war an inflexible maintenance of the original decision may lead to great mistakes. Timely recognition of the conditions and the time which call for a new decision is an attribute of the art of leadership. The commander must permit freedom of action to his subordinates insofar that this does not endanger the whole scheme.

- An estimate of the situation precedes each decision.

The territorial advances of the German military between the launch of *Truppenführung* and up until D-Day are unquestionable. Horrific, but unquestionable. Hitler's decision to invade the Rhineland on March 7, 1936—in violation of the Treaty of Versailles—began the official field enactment of *Truppenführung* and Hitler's goal to conquer Europe. By 1938, Germany had crossed the border of Austria and later Czechoslovakia, Poland, Denmark, Norway, Belgium, and eventually France. Ultimately, the *Truppenführung* field manual acted as a Critical Thinking philosophy to carry out Hitler's long-term plan. It empowered German soldiers to be critical thinkers.

For a six-year period, the German military was almost unstoppable. Why? How? Arguably, the *Truppenführung* manual helped to create the Open Thinking framework for such success. The manual informed soldiers that Critical Thinking was for everyone, not the few. Furthermore, *Truppenführung* showed that the decisions of soldiers were to be fact-based, collaborative, and timely but also flexible. Germany's success can, in part, be pinpointed to a philosophy that promoted adaptability alongside well-timed decision-making. Critical Thinking was pervasive across the German military, not simply the high commanders.

Germany's initial success and the relationship between Critical Thinking and *Truppenführung* can be summed up by this one line from the manual: "The emptiness of the battlefield requires soldiers who can think and act independently, who can make calculated, decisive and daring use of every situation, and who understand that victory depends on each individual."

How did Germany end up losing World War II after having made such inroads toward its overarching mission? Myriad reasons account for the combined failure of Hitler's regime and ambitions, but there is one that relates to *Truppenführung*. Hitler and his senior leaders abandoned it. Instead of continuing to trust the troops and allowing flexibility with on-the-ground and in-the-moment decision-making, Hitler ignored what had brought Germany its previous triumphs. He completely disregarded its Critical Thinking philosophy.

Whether it was the Battle of Moscow in December of 1941 or the Battle of the Bulge in December of 1944, Hitler took over Critical Thinking for the whole of the German military. He became the sole decision-maker. Not only did Hitler refuse to listen to the facts emanating from the field, he became a poor collaborator, made untimely decisions, and was terribly rigid with his judgments. By discounting *Truppenführung* entirely—neglecting the use of field-based Critical Thinking—Hitler ended up defeated.

Clearly, the world is better off with the fall of the Third Reich. But the abandonment of *Truppenführung* and the centralization of Critical Thinking to a single man is nonetheless a lesson in what *not* to do.

For the remainder of this chapter we will investigate five behavioral attributes that make up Critical Thinking. They are:

- Deciphering
- Collaborating
- Time
- Decisions
- Flexibility

Deciphering

Allen Devine is the Chief Dreamer at TELUS, a Canadian telecommunications company, and he helps us begin to unpack the first of the five key attributes that make up good Critical Thinking: deciphering. Working in the business unit known as Tech Strategy, Allen's role is to find creative ways to use existing technology to solve future problems. One of his passions is digital healthcare. Walk into the technologically advanced Innovation Centre that Allen has built for the company and you quickly come to grips with his purpose. The door you just came through to enter the Centre has already assessed your heart rate. You haven't even touched anything yet.

Now you find yourself in a typical kitchen. But what's different is that it has been set up to assume you have a critical ailment of some sort. Alzheimer's disease or osteoarthritis, perhaps. Through biometric indicators, artificial intelligence, and other communicative wizardry, sensor lights remind you where the cutlery is located. There are also audio cues—with robotic arms at-the-ready—to manage and disperse pills and other medicines at the appropriate time of day. It is a world Allen sees as necessary for today's rapidly aging population.

You would think that bearing the title Chief Dreamer would require a lot of dreaming, an inordinate amount of Creative Thinking. It is true, Allen does indulge in these activities, but not at the expense of Critical Thinking. "My number one objective is to take the lessons from the past, the information of today, and apply it to new trends that I see coming," he said. Allen reminds us that to employ Critical Thinking, we must constantly be deciphering facts and information if we want to improve tomorrow's world.

"Information, information, information," said Allen rather emphatically, referring to the importance of continually deconstructing his findings. "I spend at least 20 percent of my day reading as broadly as possible about trends affecting our world. I spend another 20 percent of my time learning about new solutions and what they are designed to do. The ones of interest to me I spend another 40 percent trying to sort out what they actually do, what their limits may be, and how they might affect my future thinking and projects. The remaining 20 percent is spent listening and watching people, trying to learn about their needs and issues."

Allen provides an important Critical Thinking lesson. Data is ubiquitous. Time *and* attention must be spent deciphering the lies from the truths, the good from the bad, and the misinformation from the facts. It is our responsibility to constantly sift through all forms of data and information—analyzing what is both credible and useful—to make better decisions and demonstrate Open Thinking.

It is the same point that Dion Hinchcliffe made during our interview. Dion is the chief strategy officer at 7 Summits—an online communities solutions provider—and a veteran of more than two decades in the enterprise information technology space. He is the author of several books and an expert in next-generation technologies. Dion observed, "To be an effective thinker and strategist these days you have to immerse yourself." He believes things change every two to three years in the high-tech industry, and it is incumbent upon everyone, regardless of their industry, to continually expand their current knowledge with additional information and ideas. "I collect notes every day, all year long," he said, "dedicating time to the collection of information." It's this relentless pursuit of information that fuels Dion and his Critical Thinking.

"If I look at the practice side of my work, I have become far more adaptable because I am constantly challenging my own hypothesis," he continued. "Data and information is plentiful but most of it is wrong. Our role is to continue to expand on the data and to ensure it is correct. We need to build an open-ended model of hypothesis if we are to be successful."

One of the easiest ways to bolster your deciphering skills is to learn Google's advanced search operators. Much of our data and information comes from the web, and the world's most popular search engine can be both a help and a hindrance to your Critical Thinking abilities. If you rely on a simply worded search and the first page of results, you may be provided with half-truths or falsities. But if you were to use search operators, you might unearth better information. For example, if you put the term "cache:" in front of the site address you will be presented with Google's cached version of the site leading to data or insights from an original version. Further, if you add the * symbol to a word or phrase you might find an answer quicker and with more citations. There are plenty more Google search operators to consider. I also use the Internet Archive's "Way Back Machine" as a tool to test what was written on the web long ago.

Allen and Dion do a lot of reading to aid their Critical Thinking. Google Books is another Google service that you might want to use to fact-check. With over 30 million books scanned, Google Books contains a plethora of written words to validate your assumptions.

WorldCat, the world's largest network of library content and services, is another invaluable online resource. As its mission states, "WorldCat libraries are dedicated to providing access to their resources on the Web, where most people start their search for information." The service enables you to search various library collections from around the world, where you can use the results to either fuel your hunt for information or use it to substantiate your existing evidence.

The most important tactic, however, is to continue asking questions while seeking proof. Resist the temptation to believe the information out of laziness. Do not solely operate in a homogenous digital ecosystem resistant to the actual facts either. Work harder at sourcing the truth. As Pope Francis wrote in his 2018 World Communications Day Message, "Disinformation thus thrives on the absence of healthy confrontation with other sources of information that could effectively challenge prejudices and generate constructive dialogue." For example, take a moment and look at the Chinese characters below:

危機
危机

If you had trusted the words of President John F. Kennedy and other American politicians, like former Vice President Al Gore and former Secretary of State Condoleezza Rice, you would have been led to believe that this symbol represents the word "crisis" in Mandarin. These three politicians defined this ideogram to mean both a danger and opportunity. Gore even used it in his 2007 Nobel Peace Prize acceptance speech.

As with the Frost poem with which we started this book, here we are confronted with another example of misinterpretation and misunderstanding. The ideogram does not mean *danger and opportunity*. Three different high-ranking politicians from three different U.S. administrations have used an incorrect translation and millions are now fooled by it. Like all words in Mandarin, characters and syllables matter. The word for crisis in Mandarin (wēijī) consists of two syllables that contain two separate written characters, wēi (危) and jī (機/机), as identified in the graphic above.

Unless you had done your homework and questioned the validity of the aforementioned politicians' statements, you would never have known that the wēi syllable of wēijī does in fact convey the notion of danger. However, the second component to the word, jī, refers more to a critical point when something begins to change. The Mandarin word and symbol for wēijī thus depicts a risky and potentially dangerous situation where one should be especially wary. It does not reflect both danger *and* opportunity.

Critical Thinking requires you to continually ask questions such as:

- Is this claim true?

- Can a second or even a third source back up the point?

- Where is the research or citations to prove the information truthful?

- What other data or facts are required to make an informed decision?

- Was this too easy to prove? Did I gloss over the information?

- How quickly did I make my final decision?

- Who else might I collaborate with on the facts? Can I trust them?

In the next section, we will tackle the concept of collaboration in more detail.

Collaborating

Makerspaces are an idea that has everything to do with collaboration and trust, key attributes of Critical Thinking. According to the *Makerspace Playbook*, makerspaces "serve as a gathering point for tools, projects, mentors and expertise." They come in all shapes and sizes. There are makerspaces in hospitals, libraries, museums, churches, garages, and community centers. The goal of a makerspace is to provide a physical space for people to come together to explore ideas and potential innovations. They use the confines of the space—and the availability of tools and technology—to explore, test, ideate, dream up, build, fail, and build some more.

I have witnessed makerspaces in action at the elementary-school level as well as with adults. At the school, the tools and technologies made available included LEGO, KEVA Planks, circuitry, 3D printers, computers, straws, glue, wiring, and lights, among a host of other options. At the adult level, the gear and hardware were slightly more advanced, including drills, lathes, soldering guns, and so on.

But the beauty of the makerspaces was a consequence not of the tools or technologies, but of the impressive interaction between people of all ages. It was evident in how the students interacted with one another, the way the teachers acted as guides and supported one another. In the makerspaces, Critical Thinking and Creative Thinking combined, the problem-solving and decision-making founded on mutual trust, equality, and collaboration.

The 2015 New Media Consortium (NMC) Horizon Report states, "Makerspaces are increasingly being looked to as a method for engaging learners in creative, higher-order problem-solving through hands-on design, construction, and iteration." John Burke of Miami University suggests, "What is made may not matter at all; it can still influence the thought process, vision, and ability to connect of a learning maker. These abilities can enhance a person's thinking and work in many different fields."

Alison Galloway—the elementary school teacher we met earlier—is a big fan of makerspaces. She also admires another collaborative and trust mechanism with her students called genius hour. It's a time provided to her students that allows them to follow their passions and learn about topics or ideas that really interest them. In this case the trust and collaboration is between student and teacher. As each student takes the lead in their own learning, Alison acts as a trusty resource, listening and collaborating with the students as necessary, and helping to problem-solve and sort through information. Often students are scattered across the school cooking, creating mini-robots, making movies, sewing, or coding but it is the trust and collaboration between Alison and her pupils that permits their Critical Thinking to take shape.

Whether through makerspaces or genius hour, Alison and other educators just may be on to something. Research conducted by Anuradha Gokhale of Western Illinois University in 1995 suggests learning that is more collaborative and trustworthy ends up developing graduates with higher levels of Critical Thinking. This is precisely what Stocksy knows. As we discovered in Chapter 3, the photo and video platform cooperative company has crafted a collaborative culture. Egos are checked at the door, with trust and respect fundamental to how work gets done. The integration of feedback is more important than simply being right.

Critical Thinking is not an "us-versus-them" mindset. Participants in makerspaces or genius hour sessions—or employees at Stocksy—do not feel superior to one another. There is no competitive lens or alienation. It does not harken back to medieval times when conquerors conquered. In these situations, students and adults alike are trustworthy and collaborative with one another through their respective Critical Thinking processes. In essence, they are working with one another to ensure their final decisions are sound. They work together and in so doing they move forward. Indeed, they are a modern-day *agora* and *elenchus*.

Being collaborative ensures we break the shackles of rigid thinking, helping us to make unbiased judgments. Doing so with others in a trusting manner—using the opinions and ideas of others to form a new one—will undoubtedly assist us in the quest to become Open Thinkers. Perhaps consider collaboration as a series of conversations where we "turn with" one another. As the etymology of the word *conversation* informs us, *versare* means to turn and *con* with.

To collaborate is to have a series of conversations. To turn with. Those conversations take *time*, the subject of our next Critical Thinking attribute.

Time After Time

In 1861, President Abraham Lincoln's first inaugural address contained the following lines:

Nothing valuable can be lost by taking time. If there be an object to hurry any of you in hot haste to a step which you would never take deliberately, that object will be frustrated by taking time; but no good object can be frustrated by it.

Time plays an important part in Critical Thinking. Wait too long to make a decision and you run the risk of demonstrating Indifferent or Indecisive Thinking. Rush to judgment too quickly and you end up exhibiting Inflexible Thinking. There is a fine line between delaying too much and acting too fleetingly, but both can dramatically affect the desired result.

We may think we have a lot of time at our disposal, but an over-abundance of information, people, actions, and distractions will eventually and detrimentally affect Critical Thinking. Your email inbox is not suddenly going to empty itself. Text messages will not magically disappear—nor will they stop arriving—on your mobile phone. Meeting requests will continue to be sent. People will continue to ask for your opinion *and* your time. Tasks will be assigned to you. Time will have to be budgeted to complete them. Reports will need to be written. They also beckon to be read. Life is an endless encroachment on your time. Unless you are an independent contractor who has mastered reducing distractions and related infringements, *time* is an important attribute of Critical Thinking to dissect.

Many of these time infractions continue to swell, too. For example, research conducted by consulting firm Bain & Company found that "15 percent of an organization's collective time is spent in meetings, a number that has increased steadily since 2008." Furthermore, the firm discovered that leaders are now receiving over 30,000 external communications per year, up from 1,000 in the 1970s. The Radicati Group's annual *Email Statistics Report* is a sobering reminder that each year we witness email growth of nearly 5 percent. By 2021, 320 billion emails will be sent every day, according to the group's 2017 report. Companies such as Volkswagen, Daimler, and Deutsche Telekom have subsequently implemented organization-wide policies that place limits on after-hours email. But is that enough to help Critical Thinking?

On the related topic of interruptions, according to a 2008 University of California, Irvine study, employees average 11 minutes of work before being interrupted. It takes an additional 23 minutes to return to the previous point of productivity.

But time thieving—as we have previously outlined—is not solely the fault of others. We are as much to blame for poor time use as those who infringe upon our calendars and devices. In turn, this affects our Critical Thinking abilities. In 2013, Julian Birkenshaw of London Business School and Jordan Cohen, head of Organizational Effectiveness, Learning and Development and Talent at Weight Watchers International, studied the productivity of knowledge workers. They discovered that people waste more than 41 percent of their time on tasks that offer little to help them get work done. High-tech firm Atlassian found in 2014 that we check our email 36 times an hour and we attend 62 meetings every month. Sadly, we consider half of all meetings we attend an utter waste of time. The bottom line is that we are bound to harm our ability to perform Critical Thinking as our time is sucked into so many different mismanagement vortexes.

The trick with managing your time more effectively in the Critical Thinking spectrum is related to both reflection and action. Spend no time reflecting and acting, and you are exhibiting Indifferent Thinking. Reflect too long, and you demonstrate Indecisive Thinking. Rush to action, and you are displaying Inflexible Thinking.

Having a knack to recognize how much time we ought to spend collecting and then deciphering information and data is crucial. We should also be aware of how many people we need to involve in the Critical Thinking phase. It is important that we determine how much time we might require of others when we need them to be involved in a given situation. Failing to do so implicates you as an accomplice in time theft.

Regardless, if we spend too much time in either the reflection or action phases, we wind up being trapped. Open Thinking becomes an unreachable destination. If we analyze a situation in perpetuity, we won't make any decision and we end up as fence-sitters. We will suffer from "paralysis by analysis." The flip side, of course, relates to action. We cannot jump to a rash judgment, negatively affecting what we have analyzed or built thus far. Indeed, the fraternal twins of reflection and action can cause quite an issue to Critical Thinking.

There are ways to combat various time-related problems that plague Critical Thinking. In no particular order, I have discovered four ways to mitigate these concerns:

- **Time Cushioning**: To avoid overcommitting yourself—and to negate any chance of not handling the interruptions or distractions that are bound to surface—build additional time for both reflection *and* action into your calendar. This is the easiest tactic to administer. It is also the most common habit of successful Open Thinkers that I have come across. For example, instead of 60-minute meetings, why not schedule (or only accept) 45-minute meetings so reflection and/ or action can occur during those precious extra 15 minutes of each hour? Build in 30-minute buffers at the start and end of your day as well to reflect and act.

- **Situational Capacity**: Devise a scheme to earmark situations by level of reflection and/or action. For example, a four-star system might suggest that one-star problems require more reflection before action is required. On the other hand, a four-star insignia means immediate action is imperative, with low reflection. Whatever your mechanism, "situational capacity" is the means by which you self-analyze an appropriate level of reflection and action for any given predicament. It is proactive versus reactive.

- **Outsourcing**: If you can outsource the minutiae of your daily life, you may be able to free up time to better reflect and take action. For example, the drug company Pfizer cultivated an internal program for employees called PfizerWorks. It permits people the chance to disburden various non-core tasks—including report writing, Power-Point file creation, statistical analysis, and publishing—to free up their time. The company claims it saves months of time per year, allowing employees the opportunity to complete other important activities instead of trivial ones.

- **Realism**: Far too often, Critical Thinking is treated like the all-you-can-eat buffet. We pile as much food onto our plates as we can just because it's there. However, we must be realistic with our reflections and our actions. Time is of the essence. We cannot be swayed by fancy reports and sexy data. We must know the difference between eating healthily and gorging. Furthermore, the allure of getting something done "just because" is not the goal either. Fast food is neither mindful nor nutritious. Realism must be aligned with good judgment. Realism is anchored by knowing how to differentiate when to reflect and when to take action. It is not about piling on the empty calories just because they taste good or eating fast food because it is quicker. It is also knowing when to say no.

Decisions

Once you have gathered and deciphered all facts and information, collaborated with the right people, and taken the necessary amount of time (a little or a lot) to ponder the situation, you then need a verdict. If you are employing sound Critical Thinking skills, the decision should be the easiest maneuver that you take. Daniel Levitin speaks of a unique post-decision-making technique he refers to as "satisficing." The term was invented by social scientist Herbert A. Simon to describe decision-makers who settle for the first alternative to meet the minimum requirements rather than the optimal solution. The purpose of satisficing is to help you seamlessly move into the next stage of Open to Think, Applied Thinking. As a bonus, it can also prevent Indecisive Thinking from appearing.

"Satisficing occurs when we preserve time and energy by not revisiting every little decision when things are good enough," said Daniel. In some cases, he believes we need to let go and move on. The decision we make may not be as good as it can get, but it just might be good enough. He reminds us that no decision is ever going to be 100 percent ideal, nor can decisions be completely error-proof. Effort can ultimately be saved, however, by eliminating the perfectionist decision-maker persona. "I probably don't have the very best dry cleaner in my city," he added, "but it's good enough and I don't want to expend time doing a thorough study that could eat into time I could use more productively in other ways."

In part, Daniel learned to be this way from Warren Buffett, the famous investor and CEO of Berkshire Hathaway. Buffett has lived in the same modest house for decades. No need to make additional decisions if what has worked in the past does not require a change. "The house I live in," Daniel continued, after referring to Buffett, "isn't perfect nor does it meet all my needs, but it is functional, and looking for a new place to live is very time-consuming." He finished his point with the following: "I know very wealthy people who still drive older model cars, not because they're cheapskates, but because there's no compelling reason to spend the time replacing them." Daniel makes a sound point. If you trust your reflection and action skills, you need not spend oodles of time agonizing over a decision as long as it is fact-based.

While "satisficing" is compelling when it comes to making decisions more efficiently—disarming potential perfectionist tendencies—another strategy to employ also comes from Warren Buffett. It is known as the "Circle of Competence." Management expert Peter Drucker once wrote, "Decisions are made at every level of the organization, beginning with individual professional contributors and frontline supervisors. Making good decisions is a crucial skill at every level." Drucker was right. Decision-making and Critical Thinking are for all, not the few, and that is why the Circle of Competence is something everyone ought to consider.

First mentioned in the 1996 annual letter to "Shareholders of Berkshire Hathaway Inc.," the Circle of Competence has been occasionally used by Buffett as a way of reminding investors that they should focus their efforts on their areas of expertise. But in its simplest form, the Circle of Competence is actually a handy decision-making tool. It has been used by several practitioners, including Shane Parrish of Farnam Street, an Ottawa firm devoted to helping people make better decisions.

Central to Buffett's theory are two areas of know-how that you should be mindful of when making an investment decision. Buffett claims good investors need to be aware of their Circle of Competence before acting. They need to know whether they are in it or outside of it. I have captured the salient points of Buffett's model as follows:

1. You sit inside your Circle of Competence (and you know it).
2. You sit outside your Circle of Competence (and you know it).
3. You sit outside your Circle of Competence (and you have no idea that you are there).

Based on the Critical Thinking attributes we have discussed thus far in Section III, the best of the three scenarios, rather obviously, is the first one. When you are the subject matter expert, decision-making should feel flawless if not straightforward. It's your *Open to Think* "sweet spot." It is the reason you have been hired, which was for your expertise, skills, talents, and decision-making capabilities. That does not mean you act in isolation or are quick to conclude. Sitting inside the Circle of Competence is a result of your acumen and proficiency, but it does not mean you should avoid gathering, deciphering, collaborating, or making good use of your time. It simply means you are proficient and that things may go more smoothly.

But when you sit outside your Circle of Competence (and you know it), how you handle decision-making becomes even more critical. This is the point at which you will want to ensure that you have properly gathered and deciphered the information and collaborated with the right people to help inform your opinion, while using your time wisely to make the decision itself. The key, of course, is to be proactive and to recognize that you are in a decision-making situation outside your Circle of Competence. If so, the quicker you get into the gather, decipher, collaborate, and time-management stages of Critical Thinking, the more successful your decision-making will be. If you sit outside your Circle of Competence and are blissfully unaware of such a predicament, you might wind up second-guessing the final result.

Major events producer Dominic Reid insists that the personal accretion of experience is invaluable. He also states that every team member has an equal opportunity to deliver such mastery. In his mind, having and using a team of highly competent individuals mitigates the times you sit outside the Circle of Competence. "Having a team of experts, knowing who to turn to when you don't have the answer, this allows you to be even more of an expert," he said. "The thing about experts is that they can see the problems coming much earlier than you." Dominic was suggesting that as the managing director of these events, many of the decisions may be his responsibility but he is often outside his Circle of Competence. "I have learned," he continued, "that I have gained in my decision-making confidence by being more comfortable with other people being experts. I used to enjoy being around people who knew what they were doing, but now I enjoy it even more. It makes my job not only easier but more gratifying."

Dominic demonstrates intellectual humility. In doing so, he is fully aware when he is inside or outside his Circle of Competence. He knows when to involve others—and to what depth—to make the most effective decision. It is Dominic's Critical Thinking modesty that helps illustrate his exemplary Open Thinking repertoire.

Flexibility

Demonstrating flexibility increases your chances of success with Critical Thinking. It is the fifth of five Critical Thinking attributes we will discuss.

If we are not open to revising our decisions after Applied Thinking has started—or revisiting Creative Thinking while we are collecting and verifying information—we end up falling into the trap of Inflexible and Indifferent Thinking. This may seem counter to Daniel Levitin's point about satisficing, however flexibility is not about decision-making efficiency.

Being malleable is important. Some decisions simply end up being wrong. Circumstances change and unexpected situations pop up. In reality, change is to be expected. But pigheadedness is not the antidote to Open Thinking. On the other hand, flexibility ought to be considered an important attribute if you want to sustain sound and consistent Critical Thinking. I believe the best way to illustrate the importance of flexibility in Critical Thinking is by introducing a story from the ER.

James Perry is the head of neurology at Sunnybrook Health Sciences Centre, a professor of medicine at the University of Toronto, and a neuro-oncologist at the Odette Cancer Centre and Hurvitz Brain Sciences program. He is also chair of the Canadian Brain Tumour Consortium (CBTC), a national not-for-profit investigator network of over 40 brain tumor specialists and researchers that treats both pediatric and adult patients afflicted with brain tumors. James is interested in the design, conduct, and analysis of clinical trials, where he focuses on testing innovative therapies for primary brain tumors.

Suffice it to say, James is an educated man, but he is also an Open Thinker. He is constantly demonstrating Creative, Critical, and Applied Thinking, whether conducting clinical trials or conferring with colleagues on ways to conquer cancers of the brain. But it was an example he shared with me from the emergency room (ER) that demonstrated his proclivity for Critical Thinking flexibility.

"The critical thing with an acute stroke is the time between the stroke and getting that person lifesaving medicine," said James. "For years, the standard has been three hours. If the patient received the tissue plasminogen activator (TPA) drug within a three-hour period it was potentially lifesaving to the patient."

Ever the inquisitive scientist, James started asking questions and rethinking why the norm had always been three hours. Buried within reams of data and research lay a startling piece of evidence. TPA worked well at the three-hour mark, but it was considerably better at the two-hour mark and, to a greater extent, at the one-hour mark. If TPA were to be administered earlier than three hours, perhaps more lives could be saved or side effects reduced. James was willing to revisit a healthcare norm. He was demonstrating flexibility with his Critical Thinking.

The three-hour mark had been in existence for years. Nobody refuted it. Nobody across the entire global profession of medical practitioners seriously questioned it. "What we found based on the regional system of Emergency Rooms is that every person involved in the process seemed to be fine with filling up those three hours," added James. "Because it was a recommended best practice, nobody was concerned about reducing it. 'Time is brain,' we often say in the ER. But we realized it was in our human behavior to fill up the tasks and the time allotted. We were conditioned to fill up those three hours and so we did."

Being flexible within Critical Thinking means revisiting decisions to see if improvements can be made. This is precisely what James decided to do. His next step was to discuss the opportunity with his colleague, Dr. Rick Swartz, who then began in earnest the hard work of finding an improved solution. "Rick began investigating the three-hour mark in the ER. As soon as a potential stroke patient came through the door, the analysis of what was happening began. In the ER we call it 'door to needle' time. Everyone was professional, doing their jobs, but Rick discovered that people were simply filling up the time."

James further elaborated. "For example, the imaging would get done and maybe the doctor would look at the scan one too many times. Maybe the radiologist was called in and that took extra time. It might take too long to call the patient's spouse." All of these incremental tasks that James alluded to added up to three hours. Yet the research suggested that stroke patients might have a greater chance of survival—or reduced adverse effects—if the time to administer the life-saving TPA drug was narrowed.

"Next, a randomized study with colleagues was administered," James continued. "A large stopwatch was set up so everyone could see it in the ER. The clock timed how long it was taking to perform the 'door to needle' actions, from the front door of the ER to the needle into the patient. For some groups, the target time was less than an hour. In these groups, everyone found a way to be more efficient. They managed to shave more than 50 percent off the old standard. The best part? Patient outcomes were much better in terms of residual abilities for stroke patients." Put simply, more lives were being saved and the detrimental effects that might occur after a stroke were significantly reduced.

If James had been unwilling to revisit a decision that had stood for many years—if he had deliberately ignored the facts and research he unearthed—things would have remained unchanged. If he had failed to discuss the opportunity with his colleague Rick, no action might have been taken. Ultimately the original time marker would still have been aligned within the standard operating procedure of a stroke patient. But through the demonstration of flexible Critical Thinking and the involvement of employees across the hospital, the old standard was dramatically enhanced.

"Everyone on the team responded to the need to improve," he said. "The porter wondered why the ER door was locked at night. He thought it could save valuable seconds if it were unlocked, and it did." In the end, as James illustrated how important a flexible mindset is in Critical Thinking, thousands of people are now benefiting from his malleable mindset. He added, "Quality-based funding is where health-care is heading. Hospitals will receive more funding from the Ministry of Health if quality indicators improve. If we improve, more budget will be granted for nursing, technology, and other factors. Everyone feels good when there is a positive outcome like this. Most importantly, the patients benefit."

Nowadays, a clock is commonplace in stroke centers across Canada and the world so that patients are administered the TPA drug by the 60-minute mark. But make no mistake, it was James's Critical Thinking flexibility to readdress an older decision that began the process of change.

During a Stanford University keynote lecture in 2016, former eBay CEO John Donahoe said, "There wasn't one moment during the last 30 years where I was certain I was doing the right thing. There wasn't one moment when I was in the middle of it that I felt, 'Great, I've got this all figured out.' I still don't."

In essence, Donahoe is alluding to one of human nature's greatest fallibilities. We truly do not know if every decision we make is going to be 100 percent correct. To be an Open Thinker—to demonstrate Critical Thinking in its highest form—we can learn from James and his willingness to revisit past decisions. Flexibility is key. It may even save a life.

Hat Tip to the Millinery

After I made another visit to Lilliput Hats, I did not expect to hear Karyn Ruiz utter these words: "What takes its toll is that I don't let enough of the decisions to be made on my behalf." Successful, famous, and creative, Karyn admitted that she might even be more at peace with herself if she could delegate more of her Critical Thinking to the loyal and trustworthy team members that make up the team. "Everyone has a good amount of independence, but they generally wait for or follow my decisions. They come to me seeking approval."

At that exact moment, I observed her sentiment in action. Karyn was in mid-sentence when a team member approached. Although respectful, it was evident she was looking for an answer.

"Karyn, what do you think of this feather?" asked the employee. Knowing the drill, Karyn seamlessly refocused her eyes from me to her colleague and quickly replied, "I think a red one would be better." It was uncanny. As we were discussing decision-making—and Karyn's wishes to take more time in which to make them *and* to empower other employees in her shop to make more decisions themselves— she was electing to jump to action versus reflection; taking control versus empowering.

It reminded me that regardless of our individual success, Critical Thinking might also potentially be a hinge between what we know is right and what our default behavior might be.

CRITICAL THINKING TIPS FOR THE INDIVIDUAL

- Take control of your time. It is arguably the most precious commodity of an Open Thinker. Avoid overcommitting yourself, develop situational capacity by defining your reflection/action scale, outsource the minutiae, and be realistic with what you can actually take on. Do whatever you can to take control of your time.

- Challenge yourself. Whether by seeking out new information, contrary opinions, or additional time, do not let your cognitive biases get the best of your decision-making. Arm yourself with as much evidence as is possible.

- Collaborate with others. Asking people for their advice on an important decision is not a weakness but rather a strength of Open Thinkers. Involving others in the lead-up to a decision will ultimately improve the decision itself.

CRITICAL THINKING TIPS
FOR THE ORGANIZATION

- Build a Critical Thinking guidebook. An organization that defines its Critical Thinking expectations and attributes—and makes them available to all employees through learning, coaching, and other methods—will be setting the tone for individual, team, and organization-wide decision-making.

- Focus on failure. Failures or mishaps can provide invaluable lessons about Critical Thinking. An organization would be wise to catalogue and share its failures. Others gain insights when you highlight where Critical Thinking may have gone wrong.

- Create a Critical Thinking leadership attribute. Netflix sets the bar when it comes to the importance of Critical Thinking and its organizational culture. Consider defining and adding a Critical Thinking attribute to your leadership model or philosophy, but make sure you put it into practice and it's not simply an "Espoused Theory."

IV

applied thinking

6

Sooner Than You Think

Beware the barrenness of a busy life.

SOCRATES

RENCH PHILOSOPHER, mathematician, and inventor Blaise Pascal once wrote, "All of humanity's problems stem from man's inability to sit quietly in a room alone." Pascal's observation begins our exploration into the third component of Open Thinking. I call it Applied Thinking, *the commitment to execute a decision.* So far, we have investigated both the inhibitors and the strategies of Creative Thinking and Critical Thinking. Applied Thinking is arguably the most difficult to understand and improve. Why?

For many, completing things is how they demonstrate their worth. Looking busy, ticking off items on their checklist, reporting accomplishments to their boss at meetings, endlessly answering emails and texts are all examples of how this is done. This is the "what" of action, the purpose to Applied Thinking. You are completing *what* you have decided to do, *what* you have dreamed up. But then there is the *how.* The manner in which you are actually completing your tasks is as important as the decision.

Pascal's observation is a clue. As we begin to produce, can we do so with simultaneous thoughtfulness, calmly completing what is required? Our performance is often subject to working with others.

Not only may we not be able to sit in a room alone, we must leave it in order to get things done. We have to work with others, and in different arenas, to complete our tasks. This is where some of our problems begin to surface. Perhaps the Roman philosopher Seneca said it best: "To be everywhere is to be nowhere." This is the crux of Section IV. To sustain Open Thinking—as we shift from dreaming and deciding to doing—we need to rethink and improve the "how" of thinking.

As with the previous two sections, we will start with what handicaps Applied Thinking. In line with Chapter 2 and the category of Creative Thinking, we will begin by using a film as a metaphor.

Charlie Chaplin's classic film *Modern Times* begins with a short introduction:

> *Modern Times*: A story of industry, or individual enterprise—humanity crusading in the pursuit of happiness.

The film may have been released in 1936—well before our *Cast Away* example with Tom Hanks from Chapter 2—but its contents remain relevant to today's "modern times." Chaplin's opening 10 minutes of the film aligns with the concerns of Applied Thinking. Our default habits and strategies to complete tasks have become brisk and short-sighted. In fact, Chaplin's film aligns nicely to each of my three books as it touches on issues related to organizational culture, purpose, *and* thinking.

The plot begins as hundreds of workers emerge from a subway stop en route to the shop floor of a steel company. This is their place of work. The people are characterized by their unenthusiastic body language and facial expressions. They are automatons. As each employee punches his or her time card, we are provided a glimpse of what ails many in today's modern organizations. Rigidity and disengagement remains pervasive while purpose is fleeting. Advanced technologies continue to be introduced in hopes of increasing productivity and efficiencies out of the workers. There is no room or time for Open Thinking. There is no encouragement for imagination. There is no use for creativity or criticality. The underlying tone is to get the job done as fast as you can. The routine is mechanistic, and any fluctuation is considered blasphemous. Open Thinking is as fleeting as happiness at the dentist's office.

Moviegoers are introduced to Charlie Chaplin—an employee at Electro Steel Corporation—who is busily trying to put widgets together on a conveyor belt. The scene can only be described as manic. Chaplin is failing miserably at his responsibilities, but so too is the technology. Chaplin's boss sets a goal to dramatically increase production. Chaplin begins to panic and then starts to lose his mind. The chance to rethink how the goal might be achieved differently at the factory is squashed. Why think differently when this is how things have always been done? Why change when the only requirement is to work faster? Why ask employees for their opinion? Just do it, as the saying goes.

Chaplin's foreman is none too pleased at what he sees unfolding. He begins to bark new orders while demonstrating the proper way to perform on the assembly line. Apparently, Chaplin was "thinking outside the box" in his attempt to rethink how to complete the tasks. Production becomes even more frenetic due to Chaplin's misguided interpretations. Chaos ensues. The technology that was supposed to increase productivity is conspicuously causing additional stress and serious delays. Workers begin to slowly go crazy. A foreman decides to halt things. Blame is quickly apportioned to the workers. There is tension oozing in every nook and cranny of the shop floor. Once again, the level of Open Thinking from all parties is shallow at best while everyone continues to push old habits of poor Applied Thinking.

Meanwhile, upstairs where the president of Electro Steel Corporation oversees his operations through video camera surveillance, things are not going well either. Ever the optimist, the president believes even more speed is needed in Chaplin's area of the factory. The pressure is clearly getting to him to produce superior results, to complete things more quickly. The stress has finally got to Chaplin so he escapes to the bathroom to smoke a cigarette, ostensibly to release some of the anxiety that is inherent within his role.

But there again, the president emerges from a giant video screen in the bathroom barking instructions to immediately return to the assembly line. Nonplussed, Chaplin returns to the shop floor and decides to perform a manicure of sorts on his nails. Like so many in today's organizations, Chaplin has now become so disengaged that his thinking mindset has turned apathetic. "This is how it will always be," he thinks to himself. No one bothers to ask for his opinion. Although the film is fictional, it reminds me of the enormous opportunity sitting in front of people who contemplate doing things differently and are willing to think openly.

Those first 10 minutes of the film are truly painful to watch if you aspire to be an Open Thinker in an engaged, purpose-driven organization. But they also provide a sublime illustration of today's state of Applied Thinking. Far too many of us spend too much time focusing on getting things done as fast as possible. Our desire to perform for the sake of performance has overtaken the need to perform with the correct behavior.

But we have to take action. Tasks *must* be completed. It is not the *what* that becomes the problem after effective Creative and Critical Thinking has been applied, it is the *how*. As pressures mount in the organization to "do more with less," as budgets and resources are diminished, as leaders demand more from employees, as we scramble or fixate on being busy, the manner in which we complete our actions is what we need to ameliorate. That is the aim of the next two chapters.

It is my hope that *Modern Times* will not become our modern times. Ultimately, it is the way we execute our actions—the *how*—that needs to improve.

The Backfire Effect

Our penchant to spend more time on completing things rather than on Creative or Critical Thinking is because of the "backfire effect." First coined by academics Brendan Nyhan and Jason Reifler in 2010, author David McRaney delved deep into the concept of the backfire effect in his book *You Are Now Less Dumb*. The backfire effect suggests that when your deepest convictions are challenged by contradictory evidence, your beliefs will actually get stronger. You double-down and exhibit even greater resolve to get things done. McRaney writes in his book, "Just as confirmation bias shields you when you actively seek information, the backfire effect defends you when the information seeks you, when it blindsides you. Coming or going, you stick to your beliefs instead of questioning them. When someone tries to correct you, tries to dilute your misconceptions, it backfires and strengthens those misconceptions instead. Over time, the backfire effect makes you less skeptical of those things that allow you to continue seeing your beliefs and attitudes as true and proper."

In the face of comfortable routine and myopia, have we become so blasé that we are unwilling to question what is wrong in a given situation? We ought to be constantly asking ourselves about the appropriateness of our action. When we exhibit the backfire effect, it prevents us from questioning the *why* of our *how*. Ignoring how we complete an action can have dire consequences. You might reflect, "I have always acted this way, so why change now?" Charlie Chaplin's character in *Modern Times* tries to do things differently but he is eventually overrun by his bosses. In a comedic way, he wants to make changes to his Applied Thinking but the backfire effect demonstrated by his bosses prevents a new way of doing things from ever materializing. Accordingly, mishaps ensue and the production facility at Electro Steel Corporation goes haywire.

I have previously suggested that the only true form of genuine productivity is to consistently demonstrate Open Thinking. Getting things done, as quickly as possible, is not the only way we can demonstrate success. If someone were to approach you to offer an alternative during Applied Thinking, would you reinforce your position and forgo the change in plans? Is being busy and locked into the backfire effect the only proof of progress?

Earlier in Chapter 2, I mentioned the tower activity I performed with my BCIT students. The team and department I was a part of at

BCIT was referred to as "cost recovery." In short, there were no public funds. To remain operational, we depended on the tuition fees paid by students. We had to be creative but we also had to make decisions and put them into action. I recall one personal situation, however, when I exhibited a bias to Applied Thinking, forgetting the acute importance of Creative and Critical Thinking.

In 1998, we launched four academic programs. One consisted of a six-month, full-time technology support curriculum targeted at people interested in call-center or tech-support careers. A second program was part-time, offered at night and geared toward those looking to improve their skills in network administration. The third focused on various software development languages such as C++ and Visual Basic, run full-time over six months. A fourth program—12 months long, full-time, and extremely intense—was aimed at students with a bachelor's degree who were looking to become business leaders in the high-tech networking, administration, or consulting space. It's this latter program, called Information Technology Professional (ITP) where I performed those paper tower experiments. But ITP also demonstrates how I personally used the backfire effect, and how my rush to complete the launch of an entirely new program failed miserably.

In 2001, it had been roughly three years since ITP first launched. Each year saw three different cohorts of 30 students begin their studies. Those students were paying a hefty tuition fee as well. For their year of immersive and intense education, each student paid approximately $17,000. The program was a mix of leadership development and concentrated technology education. The technology learning focused on concepts such as networking, web commerce, and business intelligence, among other technical topics. Simple web development was also taught, though the aim was not to make the graduates coders or programmers.

After three years of successfully running the ITP program, my mind began to wander. I had re-entered the Creative Thinking stage and was looking at ways to build upon the success of the ITP program model. This was the good news. The bad news is that the backfire effect was lurking, lying dormant in the Applied Thinking stage. I mused aloud to the team at BCIT, "What if we took the general concept of ITP—12 months, simulated business model, combination of technical and leadership development, three-month work term, highly interactive and intensive education experience—and substituted the technology curriculum with serious web development?" It was not so much a question as it was me insisting the idea would work.

Because we had an existing blueprint with the ITP model, I figured it would be easy to replicate the success we were having with the program simply by replacing one technology stream with another. Instead of information technology and networking, we would teach web development. We could keep all other facets of the program intact and everything would be fine. We even had on-site facilities to expand the new version of the program. It was going to be so straightforward, you could already picture students smiling from ear to ear on graduation day a year later. Without doing proper due diligence, market analysis, or program evaluation, I convinced both myself and the BCIT team that this new program would be a smashing success. While the Creative Thinking was noble, I overlooked Critical Thinking entirely. As we rushed into Applied Thinking, the entire plan was met at the door by the backfire effect.

We called the new program Professional Web Developer (PWD). Suffice it to say, in the lead-up to the launch it was an extremely difficult task trying to convince potential students of its merits. It was 2001 and the "dot com" bust was now in full swing. But I was oblivious to the issues. I remained steadfast—ignoring the news, facts, and data with the backfire effect now in motion—that PWD would be even more successful than ITP. The first cohort launched with only 18 students, compared to 30 with ITP. It was a sign. This was after roughly a year of marketing and promotions. I shrugged off the low numbers. I was "managing up" to the dean and associate dean, too, convincing them the first cohort numbers were merely a blip. I continued with my sub-par Applied Thinking, pushing everyone on the team to proceed as planned. I was locked in on the goal despite the reality of the situation.

There were further examples of my zest to enter Applied Thinking. While in theory it made sense to swap out one type of education stream for another, it was a perilous error. Network administration is very different from web development. To compound matters, we were accepting the same types of students as in the ITP program. As long as students had a degree, I felt we could teach anyone to code. It was a colossal mistake. I was so convinced that it could work I did not once stop to consider potential pitfalls with the students and their aptitude for programming. Consequently, I kept motoring along, instructing the team to continue building out the PWD curriculum.

Problems popped up the first week of the PWD launch. Some of the students were doing fine while several others were experiencing incredible difficulties with the basic logic of coding. We had to spend more time on the technology side of the curriculum than we planned. That is, instead of blending professional development with web development—as the program was set up to do—we spent far too much time on the rudimentary skills needed to code. There was a large gap in coding ability in the classroom. The simulated business that students had to run to practice management skills also suffered, as less time could be spent on it. To add insult to injury, finding paid co-op placements with the business community was a nightmare. No one was willing to take on web development students, let alone pay them. Yet a three-month work term was a key component of the program.

In the ITP program, almost all positions for the work term period that commenced at the halfway point of the program were paid. As we rolled out the PWD program, less than a handful were paid. As you can imagine, the level of stress was very high with the students *and* the BCIT faculty team. By the fourth and final term, several students were demanding partial refunds on their tuition. The PWD program had backfired, so to say.

Authors Rasmus Hougaard, Jacqueline Carter, and Gillian Coutts investigated the addiction to action in their book *One Second Ahead: Enhance Your Performance at Work with Mindfulness*. The authors write, "When we're addicted to action, we do things not because they're important, but because we want to feel important. The tasks are in front of us, and we want to be useful and productive. The problem is, when we don't step back to ensure we're spending time on tasks aligned with our main goals, we end up wasting a lot of time on immediate—though often inessential—tasks." My personal story here—although painful—highlights how important it is not to become addicted to getting something done just for the sake of it. Applied Thinking requires you to overcome your own ego. It requires you to become aware of the backfire effect and the potential consequences of plowing ahead "just because."

Executive Dysfunctions

Because part of my career was dedicated to teaching at both high school and higher education levels before entering the corporate world as a chief learning officer, I have a natural curiosity for research and issues in the learning profession. I also married an educator. My wife, Denise, is director of academics at a kindergarten through grade 12 school in Victoria. Dinner-table discussions and date nights can often segue to challenges and opportunities in the education space.

One evening over dinner, we were discussing the progress I was making on this book. Since I straddle both the education and corporate worlds, I tend to use academic rather than corporate jargon when we start chatting about our professional situations. "It's as though people have become dysfunctional with their thinking," I blurted out. The bottle of red wine was not quite finished but getting perilously close for another to be opened. "They become so fixated on 'doing,' it's a wonder their prefrontal cortex is even working. Everyone seems either stressed or distracted or both."

My nod to the brain's prefrontal cortex region was, in part, due to vast amounts of literature that suggests it does not fully develop until your early 20s. As a result, educators in the kindergarten to grade 12 span are well aware that children do not possess the same capacity as adults when it comes to the relationship between Critical Thinking and Applied Thinking. The prefrontal cortex is the brain's rational part. But children and teenagers tend to use their amygdala. This is the emotional region of the brain and, unfortunately for those younger than 20, it is where they make most decisions. If you ask a teenager

"What were you thinking?" after they have taken your car for a joy-ride, they would probably answer "I have no idea, I wasn't thinking." It was the amygdala making that emotional, irrational decision, not the prefrontal cortex.

Back at the dinner table, Denise responded to my exasperation with utter precision. "It seems as though adults are struggling with their executive functions in your model, don't you think?"

She was right. To successfully change our Applied Thinking, we need to spend some time defining, understanding, and resetting the importance of executive functions. It is a concept prevalent in the education of young people, but seems lost or forgotten (or never learned) in the professional ranks.

The link? The prefrontal cortex controls our executive functions.

The irony? *Executive functions* is a term based on a business metaphor.

A CEO is expected to help a company move forward with its goals, overseeing all functions. The executive functions of the prefrontal cortex act in the same way for each of us as adults. It is our executive functions that enable us to properly and consistently administer Applied Thinking.

Philip David Zelazo of the University of Minnesota has spent his entire professional career devoted to studying executive functions. He refers to them as "the business of making decisions and carrying them out, as when one is deliberately trying to solve a problem." Muriel Lezak of the Oregon Health Science University states that executive functions "comprise those mental capacities necessary for formulating goals, planning how to achieve them, and carrying out the plans effectively." Shintaro Funahashi of Kyoto University defines it as "a product of the co-ordinated operation of various processes to accomplish a particular goal in a flexible manner." You can see a pattern emerging. Executive functions are instrumental when we shift from decision to action, thus they are crucial to Applied Thinking.

Executive functions are thus extremely important to the way we take action. As a collection of integrated systems, EF—as it is often referred to in the medical community—acts to help us organize, time manage, restrain, recall, and perform. Executive functions are dependent on three brain processes: working memory, inhibition, and self-control. These brain functions must work in concert if we want to successfully accomplish our ideas or tasks. If we become imbalanced, forgetful, or overrun, we can be certain either that we will not meet the goal or that other adverse effects will ensue. Once we understand the importance of executive functions better, Applied Thinking has a far greater chance of succeeding.

Put yourself in a situation at work for a moment. You are part of a project team. You are not the project lead but a contributing team member. The team size is 10 people, made up of employees from different parts of your organization. The project has several milestones that eventually lead to the deadline date four weeks away. So far, the team is working well together—all sorts of ideas were bandied about through several meetings and the decision-making was rather seamless—and now efforts have shifted to completing the actual tasks of the project itself. You have shifted to action. You are feeling great. The camaraderie on the team is palpable.

This project is important. The final presentation will be given in front of three senior vice presidents, people with influence inside the organization. This could lead to a huge opportunity at work for you or, at a minimum, the chance to build up your network. However, the harsh reality is that you have already missed your first milestone deadline. Although you remember a fair bit of what is required from you, your note-taking during the initial project meetings is rather suspect. You have forgotten to be mindful of the relevant bits of information that will help you complete your tasks successfully. How you are tackling the tasks is questionable, too. You have employed a sporadic approach, often trying to tackle three or four tasks at the same time. You have become unfocused. The pressure mounts. Furthermore, you have failed to eliminate the distractions that buzz about. Peers keep coming to you to relay office gossip, your phone is beeping every 60 seconds, and you have been unable to keep to a committed schedule of completing tasks.

In a nutshell, you have missed your milestone deadline because you are failing to remember, focus, and block out distractions. A fog of ineptitude has affected your executive functions. Mindfulness, attentiveness, and ruthlessness are non-existent. What worked during the Creative and Critical Thinking stages is not the same for Applied Thinking. Your attention span seems murky and it has affected your ability to deliver results. Team members are questioning your competence. Attempts to multitask have left you feeling flustered. Your brain is suffering from sensory overload and, as a result, you are not finishing your tasks on time. You are no longer the CEO of your prefrontal cortex. In business parlance, you have been demoted. Soon you may even be fired.

Regulating our executive functions is at the heart of Applied Thinking. To complete our actions we must be able to first manage ourselves over the course of doing. Creative and Critical Thinking are of no use unless we can remember, focus, and block things out during the Applied Thinking stage. We will have confidence in our executive functions when we have set clear goals and stay committed but can withstand changing conditions. That is, we must be in control of ourselves if we want to be in control of completing our actions.

To Be (Busy) or Not to Be (Busy)

As a lifelong soccer fan, I have always been fascinated by penalty kicks. Personally, I find the penalty shoot-out one of the most merciless rules in all of sport. Just ask anyone on England's men's national soccer team. After a hard-fought match, if the scores remain level, the champion is determined by a contest between the goalkeepers and a group of penalty takers. Each penalty is itself a mini-contest: individual versus individual. But this is exactly where we pick up the scent of poor Applied Thinking habits in Open to Think.

Put yourself in the shoes of the goalkeeper. As you attempt to outwit your opponent before their kick, you might clap your hands or do jumping jacks. Your bid to distract them aside, the kick is on its way. As the last line of defense between your team winning or losing, you have to make a choice. The goal area that you protect is 24 feet by 8 feet, making you responsible for covering 192 square feet of space. The ball that you aim to stop is 36 feet away. A player will strike the ball from the penalty spot with an average speed of 70 miles per hour. That means you have 700 milliseconds to decide which way to dive— left or right—to stop the ball. But therein lies a clue with respect to Applied Thinking. Do we have to move? Do we have to be busy?

According to research conducted by Michael Bar-Eli and colleagues at the Ben-Gurion University of the Negev in Israel in 2007, goalkeepers who stay put and refrain from jumping either to the left or right have a 33.3 percent chance of stopping the penalty kick. Interestingly, the researchers discovered that goalkeepers move either to the left or the right 93.7 percent of the time. The researchers write, "The norm during penalty kicks is that the goalkeeper jumps to one of the sides and does not stay in the goal's center. The results are also compatible with our explanation for the tendency of goalkeepers to jump more than is optimal, which suggests that goalkeepers feel worse about a goal being scored when it follows from inaction (staying in the center) than from action (jumping)."

During what can only be described as a critical junction for the team's success or failure, goalkeepers almost unanimously choose to be busy. They dive either to the left or the right because it feels better to take action. Doing nothing and then watching the ball sail to their right or left into the net feels unnatural. Despite contrary evidence that shows they would be more successful if they stood in the middle of their net at least a third of the time, goalkeepers do not want to be seen as not having taken action. "This non-optimal behavior suggests that a bias in goalkeepers' decision-making might be present. According to our hypothesis, the reason for this non-optimal behavior is 'action bias.'"

Action bias refers to an individual's propensity to be busy. We discussed the inhibitor of busyness in both Creative and Critical Thinking, so why is it important to Applied Thinking? We need to analyze how we complete our most critical tasks. Although it seems counterintuitive, Applied Thinking is *not* about taking action all of the time. For example, just because Facebook, LinkedIn, Instagram, Snapchat, or Twitter has sent a notification does not mean you need to jump. Instead, stand still. Ignore it. Continue with your primary tasks, with what you were doing.

The phone that rings in your pocket or at your desk does not require you to answer it. Let it go to voicemail. Social reciprocity is a form of goalkeeping and immediately jumping to the left or right during a penalty kick. It is perfectly fine to refrain from engaging. John Medina is the author of *Brain Rules: 12 Principles for Surviving and Thriving at Work, Home, and School.* He discovered that "a person who is interrupted takes 50 percent longer to accomplish a task and makes up to 50 percent more errors." We must become mindful of our action decision-making.

The way you choose to be busy can affect your success. We were introduced to Sameer Patel, CEO of Kahuna, in Chapter 3. Sameer views execution habits as a potential trap that is often related to how people see themselves in context with the rest of the organization. "You come to work putting undue pressure on yourself that you know everything," he said. "You end up believing you were hired because you have the best answers and from there you spend all your time trying to live up to that expectation. You become overly busy trying to prove to people you know it all. This eats up a lot of your time. Today, there are large amounts of change happening. The reality is you need to have the agility to change, to be adaptive, versus spending all of your time proving to people you have all the answers." If your action bias is to constantly prove your worth, you will end up failing to complete any of the ideas or decisions that came out of Creative Thinking and/or Critical Thinking. It is this state of busyness that can lead to a litany of incomplete actions and an utter lack of Applied Thinking.

If you possess an inappropriate action bias, resulting in inefficient busyness and ineffectiveness, your actual behavior is inhibiting Applied Thinking. Picture for a moment an adolescent child at school. Energy oozes in almost every interaction. But are they effectively applying their energy to the right tasks, to the correct ways to complete what is actually due? The job of any school teacher is to help students turn their unbridled enthusiasm and energy into effective and task-specific Applied Thinking. Now imagine yourself as part of a project team at work. If some of your colleagues are representative of that adolescent child—off-task, inefficient, unfocused, or scatterbrained—will the project be completed on time? If behaviors seem frantic, Applied Thinking becomes stunted. When focus is not applied to the identified tasks, delays or failures will occur.

Edward de Bono, the Maltese physician, psychologist, and author of *Six Thinking Hats*, wrote, "Activity is not the same as effectiveness. A skilled sportsman seems to have more time and to do things more slowly than the less skilled one." Take Wayne Gretzky, the ice hockey great, for example. Gretzky broke every major National Hockey League scoring record—and captained four Stanley Cup championships—largely because of his sensational decision-making and performance on the ice. His Applied Thinking was both effective *and* efficient. Gretzky's activity on the ice was not wasted or overly onerous, it was potent.

As a young boy, Gretzky was implored by his father to "skate to where the puck is going, not where it has been." As Gretzky went from child prodigy to adult superstar, he consciously chose not to exert himself unnecessarily. His skating was never the fastest, his shot was never the hardest, and he rarely threw a body check. Ice hockey, like any team sport, is a sequence of actions that occur in the heat of competition. Despite the overuse of his father's quote in the business world, Gretzky's superiority was not just athletic—rather, it was his ability to be effective *and* efficient while taking action on the ice. This is the key to understanding the quote and appreciating Gretzky's performance. He did not misspend his energy. He nurtured the ability to be in the right spot at the right time. It was not luck. He eliminated any opportunity to be overly busy on the ice—refusing to be an inefficient and ineffective hockey player—and, as a result, he became the greatest hockey player ever.

As David Evans Macdonnell reminds us in the January 1, 1798 issue of *The Monthly Review*, "Duos qui sequitur lepores neutrum capit" (He who chases two rabbits catches neither). Getting actions completed is a crucial requirement of Applied Thinking. But being ineffective and inefficient while completing your actions is the type of busyness that fails to accomplish Open Thinking.

Saying Yes When You Should Really Say No

In a 2005 research paper, "Bottomless Bowls: Why Visual Cues of Portion Size May Influence Intake," Cornell professor Brian Wansink discovered people have a hard time saying no. By giving test subjects soup from a bowl that automatically but secretly continued to refill, people were unaware that they were eating more soup than the other test group who were using regular bowls. "Despite consuming 73 percent more, [the research subjects] did not believe they had consumed more, nor did they perceive themselves as more sated than those eating from normal bowls." Not only were people with the refilling bowls unaware that they were subconsciously saying yes to more soup, they underestimated how much they had overeaten. On average, the test subjects underestimated their caloric intake by 140 calories.

It is our ability to say no that can significantly aid Applied Thinking. When we say yes to too many things, we wind up overburdened, or in the case of the soup eaters, over-nourished. Properly determining how to say *no* can govern whether you are going to accomplish your goals and objectives. Of course, the opposite is true, too. If you say *yes* to everything, you negatively affect Applied Thinking. Constantly saying yes to people and new projects (or soup) can be a significant inhibitor to getting things done, and thus to Applied Thinking. As with executive functions, if we are not ruthless about how we take action—blocking out items that are irrelevant, destructive, or impulsive—we will fail.

Darren Entwistle is the CEO of TELUS, the telecommunications company I have worked at since late 2008. Darren has taught me and many leaders across the organization much about saying no. There are no bottomless bowls of soup at TELUS. In 2009 and 2010, I was part of the team developing the TELUS Leadership Philosophy (TLP), an organization-wide framework to help TELUS team members become more collaborative and open in the quest to put "Customers First," the company's number one corporate priority.

We included 10 leadership techniques that complemented other facets of the philosophy. The techniques were a combination of how-tos and what-ifs as they relate to leadership at TELUS. Darren suggested that the TLP should include the following line as part of the first leadership technique dedicated to strategy: "If you are not anxious about what you have purposely selected *not* to do, you are not sufficiently focused as a leader, which is critical to ensuring your team delivers on your vital priorities."

In other words, how you focus is related to your ability to say no, which in turn helps you prioritize getting things done. Conversely, the inability to say no leaves you subject to time-management and resource issues. Furthermore, it creates undue pressure to complete more than ought to be on your plate while your level of focus becomes suspect and tattered. In his book *Essentialism: The Disciplined Pursuit of Less*, Greg McKeown captures the point sublimely: "Only once you give yourself permission to stop trying to do it all, to stop saying yes to everyone, can you make your highest contribution towards the things that really matter."

But it really is hard to say *no*. Researchers Donald Sull, Rebecca Homkes, and Charles Sull discovered in 2015 that even senior leaders have difficulty doing so. For example, instead of closing businesses or initiatives that are clearly failing or under-performing, 80 percent of leaders said they would continue operating as is despite evidence to the contrary. Not only does this create impediments to Applied Thinking—undermining the ability to execute—it can severely affect existing resources. "Top executives devote a disproportionate amount of time and attention to businesses with limited upside and send in talented managers who often burn themselves out trying to save businesses that should have been shut down or sold years earlier." Even when we might have previously said yes and entered Applied Thinking, it is wise to constantly evaluate how things are performing. There is the potential that what was once a yes may have to become a no.

Steve Jobs, the co-founder of Apple, was famous for saying no. When he returned to the company in 1997, for example, it took him a matter of months to reduce the number of products Apple was churning out from 350 to 10. He even discussed the relationship between saying no and focus in his public keynotes. At the 1997 MacWorld Developers Conference in San Francisco, he said, "When you think about focusing, you think, 'Well, focusing is saying yes.' No! Focusing is about saying no." Kathy Bloomgarden, CEO of Ruder Finn, a public relations firm with headquarters in both the United States and China, believes saying no is the sign of a good leader. She states, "Sometimes saying no can serve as an opportunity to refocus the team or reprioritize deliverables and next steps."

There is an example at TELUS that illustrates the power of saying no from the onset, rather than saying yes without any idea how things might turn out. During the mid-to-late 2000s, telecommunications analysts and pundits often queried Darren and other senior leaders about the company's strategy. TELUS competitors like BCE, Rogers, and Shaw began (or continued) acquiring media content providers, yet TELUS stood on the acquisition sidelines. Instead of saying yes, it firmly and repeatedly said no to entering the media space. A decade later TELUS remains the only company of its main rivals in Canadian telecommunications not to enter the media content business. Why?

Whenever he was asked, Darren responded that owning media content is not a "core competency" for TELUS and that any attempt to enter the space would distract the organization from its mission to put "Customers First" in its wireless, wireline, television, and electronic healthcare businesses. The company's singular focus on its core competencies has seen some remarkable gains. Its wireless post-paid monthly churn rate—where customers leave for a competitor's offerings—dropped to under one percent, significantly lower than any telecommunications company in Canada. The company's lifetime revenue per customer rate of nearly $7,000 is 40 percent higher than its national peers. Finally, since the beginning of 2000 through to early 2018, TELUS has generated a total shareholder return of nearly 400 percent, a statistic that is the highest among any global telecom company. These are merely business metrics but, because the company said no to media, it has also been able to serve its higher purpose to "give where we live." TELUS has given $482 million to charitable and not-for-profit organizations and volunteered more than one million days to communities across the globe. Sometimes saying no goes beyond the bottom line.

Rigidity in Flight

In the previous chapter, we met James Perry, who helped us understand the importance of Critical Thinking flexibility in the healthcare space. As with Critical Thinking, when we become too rigid during Applied Thinking—jumping to action simply because we want to get things done—errors are likely to occur. Moreover, the people you are working with will become disengaged. Either way, rigidity can be a significant inhibitor to Open Thinking in general. To illustrate what can happen if we are too rigid with our Applied Thinking, let's visit NASA.

The Space Shuttle *Challenger* disaster was a terrible tragedy that exemplifies Applied Thinking rigidity. It was January of 1986 and much of the world was preoccupied by their television screens. For the first time, a regular citizen was going up into space. Christa McAuliffe, an American teacher from Concord, New Hampshire, was selected from over 11,000 applicants to join six NASA astronauts in a historic mission. *Challenger* was set to take off from Kennedy Space Center in Titusville, Florida, on a Tuesday morning, but questions were being asked about the outside temperature. It had become unseasonably cold on the eastern coast of Florida for that time of year—barely above the freezing mark—and some officials began to raise a few flags.

The concerns about the cold weather centered around the O-ring pressure seals on the shuttle at the joints of the *Challenger's* solid rocket boosters. If the O-rings failed, hot gas would end up leaking out of the joints. From there hot flames would breach the external fuel tank causing an explosion due to the ignition of liquid hydrogen and liquid oxygen. The pending scenario would take place in a matter of seconds soon after the solid rocket boosters had been cleared to light up for takeoff.

Anything that NASA launches into space is an exercise in Applied Thinking. There are procedures, rules, countdowns, and hundreds of people performing a variety of roles. It is nonstop action before, during, and after a launch. Naturally, there are loads of decisions to be made, too. It is a prime example of how Applied Thinking requires the back-and-forth of Critical Thinking to be successful. In the case of the *Challenger* disaster, instead of listening to the evidence and reading the hard facts that were right under their noses, senior NASA officials chose rigidity over flexibility. Inappropriately, they proceeded with the countdown.

Several months earlier, the Utah-based contractor that supplied the O-ring pressure seals, Morton-Thiokol, had distributed a warning about the pending issue. In a weekly activity report on October 1, 1985, Robert Ebeling of Morton-Thiokol tried to draw his senior management's attention to the O-ring pressure seals. The executive summary began with "HELP!" and ended with "This is a red flag." By the time of the launch, NASA had asked about the red flag. The O-rings had been tested to perform in 40-degree Fahrenheit or above weather conditions. On that fateful morning in Florida it was only 18 degrees.

With NASA pressing Morton-Thiokol for more information hours before the launch, Ebeling assembled his O-rings team in Utah to discuss the situation. Years later Ebeling remarked, "We discussed what might happen below our 40-degree qualification temperature and practically to a man we decided it would be catastrophic." But NASA officials pressed the company to green-light the O-rings.

It was the engineers at Morton-Thiokol who did not recommend launching the shuttle. At least not in temperatures that were near freezing. The engineers wanted NASA to wait until the afternoon when temperatures would be closer to 53 degrees Fahrenheit. Due to the pressure exerted by NASA—in addition to the capitulation of Morton-Thiokol senior managers—the company reversed its original decision and ended up giving the go-ahead for launch. As Ebeling and his entire team at Morton-Thiokol watched the launch, he said to himself, "Lord, make me and all these other engineers wrong, let it go." I was 14 years old at the time and watched the event unfold live in my classroom. For a member of GenX, it was a defining childhood moment. Before my very eyes I watched with my classmates as the *Challenger* disintegrated into thousands of pieces.

Almost immediately after the incident, President Reagan instituted a presidential commission to investigate the *Challenger* disaster. The main findings included an item that ought to give us all pause. NASA's rigidity with its launch schedule led managers to look past the seriousness of the situation. Instead of taking into account the facts about the potential O-ring issues, leaders held firm to the agenda of launching the *Challenger*. Had NASA not insisted on liftoff, seven people might have gone on to live full lives. Instead, the *Challenger* disaster acts as an unfortunate lesson for us all. We cannot remain rigid within Applied Thinking. Sticking to an agenda "just because" is a recipe for closed thinking, and unmitigated disaster.

Rigidity in Behavior

Tim Hockey is the CEO of TD Ameritrade. He recounts a story that provides another example of rigidity, of how our blind desire to complete things can have a detrimental effect on the people we work with on a daily basis. At the time of the events he relates, Tim was a senior vice president reporting to TD Bank's CEO Ed Clark. He was in a boardroom with the bank's senior-most executive team, making the case for an acquisition.

"The chief risk officer (CRO) at the time," said Tim, "did not want to do the deal." Tim and the CRO were disagreeing over the merits of the purchase of a financial services company that would add value and profitability to TD Bank's overall portfolio. "It's seldom that you disagree and go against your own chief risk officer, and I'd never done it before… or since. But I believed strongly in the deal," he continued. "Ed's brilliance as a leader, particularly from a process perspective, ensured that we went through a due diligence review of the acquisition with the entire senior leadership team with every deal we did." But on the day that the review was scheduled, the CRO was ill and could not make the meeting. "We went through the entire review despite the CRO not being there," said Tim. "I said to Ed, 'The CRO is not here, but he does not agree with the deal.'" At the conclusion of the meeting, Ed told the team that the review would be done again as soon as the CRO could take part.

The CRO was well enough to come into work the next week, so the due diligence review was scheduled again. The senior leaders met, including the CRO, and he had a chance to present his case. Tim, however, treated it as a perfunctory process. In his mind, the deal was sound—irrefutable in fact—and his mind was made up. "I thought to myself, 'OK, we need to go through this process again anyway, so let's just get it over with.' I wasn't really listening to the CRO in the meeting because I had already made up my mind."

At the end of this second meeting, Tim declared his support of the deal notwithstanding the CRO's reservations, and the executives agreed to proceed with the acquisition just as Tim had wished and expected. But Clark took Tim aside and said to him, "Let's go for a walk."

"Is that the best way you could have handled the situation, Tim?" the CEO asked. Ed Clark had become CEO of TD Bank in 2002 and retired in 2014. Tim reported to him for a good portion of those years. Clark's reputation as an open and thoughtful leader is legendary. He was Canada's Outstanding CEO of the Year in 2010 and named to the Order of Canada that same year. *Harvard Business Review* named Clark to its list of the 100 Top Performing CEOs in the World as well. When Clark pulled Tim aside to discuss how he handled the meeting, he was probing his rigid behavior. "You listened politely," said Clark to Tim, "but you also dismissed his points." Clark continued his coaching of Tim. "What would it have taken to thank him for his input, ask for some time to consider his views, leave the meeting without jumping to the decision, sleep on it, and come back the next day? What would it have taken to give that man honor?"

If you are a senior leader in an organization like TD, much of your Applied Thinking takes place in situations like this. You perform in meetings like Tim's due diligence review to make decisions that meet organizational objectives. The way you take action is often the feat of making decisions. As a result, if your behavior is too rigid, you may wind up either making bad decisions or you can bulldoze people's feelings in the process. Either way there may be adverse aftereffects downstream.

In essence, TD Bank's CEO had pulled Tim aside to teach him about honorable leadership in the midst of his Applied Thinking. In a 2011 public speech on leadership, Clark advised, "We all seek growth, but know that some forms of growth can kill. That's especially true in organizations like TD where our core business is taking risk. Being opportunistic is one thing. Going too far, too fast, is another. Knowing the difference can be a matter of life and death for organizations."

Tim was candid in his reflections. "Ed was completely right in the feedback he provided me. It was one of the biggest brain cramps I have ever had. How I was treating that situation with myopic closed thinking is something I will never forget. It was really good for Ed to share that with me, even though the outcome of the acquisition was the same. And thankfully, the deal turned out well, or I might not be around to tell you this story! Stylistically, I learned from Ed how to handle that situation better." The chief risk officer subsequently died some time later. "I never told him I was sorry," Tim concluded. "I wish I had."

Tim was especially generous to share this story with me. Heartbreaking as it is, it serves as a final piece of insight into Applied Thinking inhibitors. Even though each of us has to get things done—Applied Thinking is of course where the rubber meets the road—*how* we conduct ourselves during the act of completion is often as important as *what* we are trying to accomplish.

Hat Tip to the Millinery

"I have not taken off more than four days in a row over the last two years," Karyn Ruiz said with a twinge of exasperation in her tone. "I have to do a better job of not being 'on' all the time."

It was a stark reminder that it is somewhat effortless to get consumed by the act of doing. She continued, "Because I do all the bookkeeping, operations, promotions, and so on, I feel like I am always on."

While Karyn can fire on all cylinders—she can be highly engaged with a client, supplier, or a staff member—there are different moments of every day that require different types of Applied Thinking attention. "I have recognized that my days are one big continuous act of prioritization. Do I need to take that call? Should I help that staff member now? I have to write that blog post. Did the felt supplier call back? It's all a balancing act."

As we will explore in the next chapter, prioritizing our actions within Applied Thinking is as big a hat tip as there is to Open Thinking.

APPLIED THINKING QUESTIONS
FOR THE INDIVIDUAL

- Have you given any thought to *how* you are completing your actions? Is your goal simply to get things done as quickly as possible?

- Are you so locked into the completion of a goal that you disregard additional feedback, clues, or information to potentially alter course?

- Do you consistently manage your executive functions—to remember, focus, and block out distractions—so that your Applied Thinking is relatively stress free? Or are you so unnerved by being constantly busy that life feels like a pressure cooker?

APPLIED THINKING QUESTIONS
FOR THE ORGANIZATION

- If a situation warrants more time or additional input, does the organization provide the means in which to do so or is it so rigid that it continues as is?

- Is there difficulty in saying no, leaving the organization subject to time management, resourcing, or financial issues?

- Does the organization have a bias for action where employees are urged toward unhealthy levels of busyness, causing disengagement and/or health issues?

You Have Another Think Coming

Situation seems to be the mold in which men's characters are formed.
MARY WOLLSTONECRAFT

"THE BEST THING I can do as a conductor is to enable spontaneity, to allow art to emerge of its own source and accord."

Those are the words of Tania Miller, a prolific orchestral conductor. For well over two decades, she has been leading orchestras across the globe. Tania has appeared as a conductor in Canada, the United States, and Europe with such orchestras as the Toronto Symphony, Seattle Symphony, Bern Symphony, Oregon Symphony, Orchestre Métropolitain du Grand Montréal, Naples Philharmonic, Hartford Symphony, Chicago Symphony, and Wroclaw Philharmonic. Most recently, Tania was music director of the Victoria Symphony for 14 years.

Maestra Tania believes music is an extension of our humanity and personal creation. There is no right or wrong judgment. Rather, music is something for each of us to interpret through what she refers to as a "beauty scorecard." When conducting an orchestra, Tania knows it is her responsibility to help the audience reach such a place. The concert is the performance, an exercise in attaining the expectations of the patrons through the musicians. While a music director like Tania will exhibit Creative and Critical Thinking before, during, and after a concert, it is how she invokes Applied Thinking—conducting a live performance to a room full of high expectations—that helps us understand an important criterion. When in action, there is a time to push the throttle and a time to relax it.

"In performance, for example," she said, "as a conductor I might have reversed a tempo that is fast early on, but I'm saving a slightly faster tempo for later in the performance. I am being strategic in determining when a group can handle something. If I push them, the payoff can be extraordinary. Think of it as an explosion that simultaneously the group didn't know they were capable of. It becomes an electric spontaneous performance that everyone knows was a shock to the room. If you took everything 'as is' during the performance, that moment gets lost."

Tania's insights remind us that Applied Thinking requires malleability. There is an ebb and flow to getting things done, to completing our actions. One minute you will need to be increasing your pace, while another requires you to take the foot off the gas. "When we are rehearsing, the best strategy is to prepare our musicians so that there should be an element of the unknown," she added. It serves as a reminder that when we complete our tasks we should expect to encounter hiccups and curve balls. How we handle these deviations will determine whether Applied Thinking is successful or not.

According to Tania, "the most satisfying musical experiences for the conductor, audience, and orchestra is to let the music constantly change. The art changes us. We respond to the moment. We are responding to how the music flows. The audience changes the atmosphere whether there is frenetic energy, or boredom, or rapt attention. Nerves change us, too. We may be nervous and then calm and then nervous again. But we must react to what the situation calls for. This is the key."

When Tania used the word flows, I thought of research by psychologist Mihaly Csikszentmihalyi. In his flow model, individuals who portray apathetic behavior (lacking feelings, emotions, interests, or even meaning in their life) are said to be low in both challenging themselves and their skill level. Their Applied Thinking is suspect. When someone is "in the flow," however, they exhibit a high penchant for taking up challenging and rewarding tasks. Furthermore, they demonstrate a high aptitude for skill development. When "in the flow," the individual is responding to the nature of a situation, too. It looks effortless but behind the scenes they are continuously balancing effort versus output. They are examining the requirements to be a productive Applied Thinker.

Through the example of conducting an orchestra, Tania helps us recognize that Applied Thinking is, in part, about enacting the middle ground of action and resisting inhibiting forces. For example, too much preparation can become boring. Too much pace or freneticism can be risky. Too many nerves can detrimentally affect other members of your team, as well as your own performance. Conversely, being complacent about Applied Thinking sets you up for ego issues. "You want to ride on the side of responsiveness but close to the line, not so far away that you are out of control," Tania observed.

Tania confirms that an orchestral musician and conductor deliver their performance with this balance in mind. It is the basis of good Applied Thinking. She believes that a musician is most comfortable when they are focused on the technical aspects of what they're doing. This could be paying attention to rhythms or watching each other's body language or that of the conductor. But any technical aspect is countered by artistic expression. The balance between under-performing and over-performing is the point at which the orchestra arrives at a higher place, the release of the music, the art. "Ultimately we are so in control of the preparation—the left-brain part of our playing—but it submerges itself in favor of 'letting go' of what the music is," said Tania. "This is what we are after in our performance, a balance between preparation and exhilaration." In other words, optimal performance arrives when Applied Thinking can be thought of as balanced and "in the flow."

This chapter explores several scenarios and provides suggestions that will help you find your own flow for Applied Thinking. "People underestimate their own capabilities," said Tania. "But when pushed to the test, to perform, people actually can do it."

The Introduction of Execution Functions

In the previous chapter, I reviewed the psychology concept of executive functions. This special and integrated set of processes in our brain helps to establish our working memory, inhibitions, and self-control. Adele Diamond is the Canada Research Chair Professor of Developmental Cognitive Neuroscience at the University of British Columbia. She has spent much of her distinguished career researching executive functions. Among a host of other awards, in 2014 Adele was named one of the world's 15 most influential neuroscientists. It was Adele's research and responses to my queries about improvement recommendations that led me to conclude how important executive functions are to Applied Thinking. "At a general level," said Adele, "to improve Applied Thinking, activities that challenge executive functions and where difficulty can keep increasing are recommended."

To get better at Applied Thinking, we need to improve the behaviors associated with *how* we do things. To get better at doing, we also need to continually challenge ourselves. In a research paper published in 2014, Adele wrote, "The most fundamental principle is that whether executive function gains are seen depends on the amount of time spent practicing, working on these skills, and pushing oneself to improve. If participants are not challenged to keep improving, but simply continue doing what is easy, minimal benefit is seen."

For purposes of improving your Applied Thinking, I propose that we introduce something specific for Open Thinking loosely related to executive functions. To exhibit better Applied Thinking we need to take existing research on executive functions and differentiate it for today's work environments. In this day and age of distractedness, stress, exhaustion, disengagement, and "doing more with less," Applied Thinking can be advanced by challenging, honing, and improving four key attributes that I refer to as *execution functions*. Each of them can help us improve our performance and actions.

- **Be mindful**. Remember what is relevant and pivotal to completing the task.

- **Be attentive**. Stay flexible yet focused on specific actions.

- **Be ruthless**. Block out anything that is irrelevant, destructive, or impulsive.

- **Be humane**. Empathize with those you work with and those you serve.

As a conductor, whether in rehearsal or during the live orchestral performance, Tania is mindful, attentive, ruthless, and humane. She always remembers where she is in the piece, focuses on the right levers to elicit the appropriate responses from the orchestra, blocks out distractions—a crying child, an unexpected burnt light bulb on the stage, or a snapped violin string—while empathizing with the audience and the orchestra as the music progresses. Maybe it's a wink or a smile, but Tania is continuously compassionate to those she serves while conducting.

Another individual who exemplifies these four behaviors is Mark Mattson, the founder and president of Lake Ontario Water-keeper. After 10 years in the courtroom as a lawyer, Mark founded Waterkeeper, an organization that devotes its time to restoring and protecting watersheds for generations to come. Not only has he remained president since 2001, Mark also sits as a director on the board of four other Waterkeeper organizations in the U.S. and Canada.

To say that Mark is mindful, attentive, ruthless, and humane might be an understatement. "I started out as a criminal lawyer and very quickly I was asked to get involved in cases that had an environmental slant to them," said Mark. Landfill issues and nuclear power plants, among other environmentally related situations, were his introduction to a different way of Applied Thinking. As a lawyer, Mark came at the environmental issues he sought to litigate from a privileged position. In each of his cases, the onus of proof needed to be addressed. During various hearings and cross-examinations, he fought hard to beat down the groups that were poisoning the planet. In doing so, he had to constantly exhibit execution functions. "I really believed," said Mark, "that if we gave meaning and force to laws, we could have swimmable, drinkable water."

Mark left the law profession when he recognized his efforts as a lawyer, while fruitful, were not having the impact he desired. For every 15 or so cases that he successfully defended and won, there were another 300 that he could not get to. Worse, there were many more that he did not know about. Founding Lake Ontario Waterkeeper has allowed him the chance to build out a community of activists, individuals with like-minded goals to allow people the right to swim, drink, and fish. "At the end of the day, what are we fighting for?" asked Mark. "I'm constantly working on ways to help communities to think and act differently to use their water. I have to be flexible."

Approaching two decades of service in the Waterkeeper movement, Mark discussed the behaviors that have made him successful. "Be nimble and be different," he said. "You have to love what you're doing, be prepared to make mistakes—learn from them—remember where you're going and why you're doing it." Mark's disposition helps us recognize that Applied Thinking is not solely about doing. It requires not only the focus, flexibility, and attitude to complete an action, it needs the openness of a higher purpose. It requires empathy.

"As soon as you lose hope with what you're doing, and who you're doing it for, it's over. Our job at Waterkeeper is to keep people on the lakes fishing and swimming, drinking fresh water. We have to constantly inform naysayers why it's important. If we're not focused to carry out the mission—if we do not possess that commonality among ourselves—we're finished. It's a full-time fight but I remind myself every day why I'm doing it."

The rest of this chapter is devoted to the four execution functions of Applied Thinking that both Mark and Tania demonstrate. What follows is an investigation into the ways in which you can become more mindful, attentive, ruthless, and humane. These four behaviors are ultimately what will improve your Applied Thinking results, the final component to Open Thinking.

Be Mindful

The constant barrage of information from varying sources has made it difficult for many of us to successfully execute. Applied Thinking, however, requires our working memory to be sharp and observant. When we allow an overflow of data to flood our memory, the end result is circumspect. Ultimately, we have difficulty remembering and it affects our actions. Eric Kandel, the Nobel Prize–winning neuroscientist, wrote in his 2006 book, *In Search of Memory*, that if we are to be successful, we must be able to apply new information and associate it "meaningfully and systematically with knowledge already well established in memory." But if our brains are overloaded or taxed by information, the process becomes difficult.

Furthermore, to properly enact Applied Thinking, we not only have to recall what *has* happened, we must retrain ourselves to be receptive to what *may* happen. Put differently, to complete a task, our brains rely on information that is both previously stored and newly interpreted. This is the act of being *mindful*. When you ride an elevator, for example, you know you must push a button to go up or down. That's easy to remember. But if the elevator stops unexpectedly between floors, new information floods your brain and you must address the new circumstances. To complete your goal of arriving at the desired floor, you must change course. Your performance has to adjust. Your actions will need to deviate. When the elevator stalled—during the original moments of your action—you had to contend with the new situation and take a different path to complete the goal.

While the elevator example may seem obtuse, situations like this metaphorically help us understand what can happen when we enter the performance stage of Open Thinking. Simply put, to effectively enact Applied Thinking, we have to keep in mind how important working memory is to successfully complete our actions. Recalling what occurred earlier and being able to relate to what is happening "in the now" is key. Both are crucial to Applied Thinking. So, too, is prioritizing what to remember. But how?

Individuals cannot remember everything. This is rather obvious. It is impossible for an entire population of employees in the organization to recall what has previously happened either. In both cases, if valuable information has not been recorded, it becomes difficult to recall anything. It becomes equally difficult to adjust your Applied Thinking if you have no idea how to draw upon or learn from past experiences. Apple, for example, hired people to document its history, making it possible to learn from its various successes and mistakes. Taking the time to document your organization's history is an easy way to preserve the past.

Another opportunity to improve organizational memory is to conduct an after action review (AAR). Made famous by the U.S. military, an AAR allows a team to analyze how a previous project met or did not meet the intended goal. The team records the analysis, enabling the learnings to be applied by others in the organization for a different project at another time. Apple and the U.S. military examples are straightforward ways to help improve or at least maintain an organization's working memory.

At TELUS, annual corporate priorities and strategic imperatives are published across the entirety of the organization. The act of establishing them is one thing, but ensuring more than 50,000 team members are aware of them is another. The priorities and imperatives can be found on TELUS's own internal website, which anyone in the company can access. They can also be downloaded as a graphic, poster, or document. The priorities and imperatives are used in many internal communication messages, serving as reminders throughout the year of the company's organizational goals. Quarterly reviews with financial analysts also provide the chance to discuss the priorities and imperatives. The lesson at TELUS is that they are both created *and* constantly communicated. This aids the organization's working memory, lessening the burden of remembering what it is the company is trying to accomplish during a given fiscal year. When employees are able to tap into a handy job aid like this, it makes remembering that much easier.

From the perspective of an individual, the more we write down our thoughts, the better off our Applied Thinking will be. Journaling is an option that may be worth considering. Taking the time to regularly jot down impressions, observations, and analyses of actions and projects currently being worked on will serve as useful reminders at a future date. It's something we learned earlier from musicians Gord Downie and Joel Plaskett about how it assists their Creative Thinking. Naturally, to help remember what you have written down, you ought to occasionally review your notes to reinforce what has already taken place. General George Patton, instrumental in the liberation of Germany from the Nazis in World War II, was famous for his black leather notebook, where he would record thoughts and occurrences, spending time at night to review what he had written each day.

Many useful technologies can be used to assist remembering as well. One of my favorites is the use of Evernote, a cloud-based note-taking application where you can record thoughts or comments on any of your devices. Author Richard Martin tracks every book he reads in Evernote. He transcribes passages, records his own reflections, makes a note of related websites, and creates a network of hyperlinks to other files in his Evernote library. This serves as both research repository and inspiration for his own writing. Productivity applications such as Microsoft Office, Google Docs, or Apple iWork include a comment feature where you or your team members can insert notes and feedback into the application itself. This can be handy if you need to remember what more you need to address, or to recall certain feedback provided by the team.

Charlene Li is the founder and CEO of Altimeter Group and the author of *Open Leadership*. She is a sought-after consultant on topics such as leadership, strategy, social technologies, interactive media, and marketing. Before founding Altimeter Group, Charlene was vice president and principal analyst at Forrester Research. Her business is and has always been about people. Charlene was one of the leaders I featured in my first book, *Flat Army*. She has been in the unique situation of being able to analyze people and their thinking habits for more than two decades. She reminds us of the importance of setting deadlines when it comes to mindful Applied Thinking. "Deadlines serve as a wonderful forcing function. At some point, I have to 'ship' so the completion stage is refining the thinking to make sure that it's easy to understand, and that my points are clear. This is where crafting the language, the imagery, and especially the emotion to make my points stick. It's clearly anchored by keeping the audience that I'm trying to reach central to my efforts." When we set and then write down deadlines, they become a reminder of what is expected of us. Through the simple act of scribing, the written form of the deadline can act as a way to lessen the cognitive load on your brain. Rohan Light, an Auckland-based consultant, encourages people to "be prepared to summarize the heart of an idea at any time, knowing when to recognize cognitive deficit."

Think of the arrangements for a wedding day and the important personal deadline that it represents. If the soon-to-be-married couple decides to have a traditional wedding, they know that all actions associated with the big day—choosing a guest list, venue, food, first song, and so on—must be completed before the two exchange vows. Imagine if there is no actual date. How stressful would that be? How ludicrous does that sound? Imagine if due to cognitive deficit they had no idea of the actions required to pull off the event. The same can be said about your actions within Applied Thinking. If you don't set deadlines for the goals that you've defined, it will become absurdly difficult to remember what action is due at a given time. It is therefore wise to set deadlines and establish action lists for any project.

When you finally begin working on those actions for the wedding—or anything related to projects at work, of course—it is best to refrain from multitasking if you want to do a credible job of remembering. Multitasking has a detrimental effect on your memory capability and thus Applied Thinking. When we multitask, the production of the stress hormone cortisol has been proven to increase. Furthermore, adrenaline rises in your body, inducing the fight-or-flight phenomenon. Put together, increased levels of adrenaline and cortisol causes our brains to become cloudy. When this occurs, it becomes significantly more difficult to recall information. The ability to remember wanes. Multitasking also reduces our attempts at successful Applied Thinking because it introduces something known as cognitive load, the amount of mental effort required by our brains to process information. When cognitive load is high, it will negatively affect the ability to process information. When we cannot process information—combined with the fog that has now overtaken the brain—we cannot properly remember. We are no longer mindful.

To combat multitasking and to increase your ability to remember, we need to rethink *how* we perform our actions. In particular, patterns of concentration ought to be analyzed. Adam Grant says, "To produce at your peak level you need to work for extended periods with full concentration on a single task free from distraction." In Chapter 4, I introduced the research highlighted by Cal Newport. He recommends something he calls "Deep Work" where people ought to be dedicating long, concentrated periods of time to performing their actions. In part, this is to combat another term that affects remembering: "attention residue."

The term comes from a 2009 research paper written by Sophie Leroy in *Organizational Behavior and Human Decision Processes.* Attention residue refers to the residual negative effect of switching from task to task. In essence, multitasking. "People experiencing attention residue after switching tasks are likely to demonstrate poor performance on that next task," she wrote. When you operate by working on multiple tasks at a time—no matter what you say to yourself—your performance will worsen. Your Applied Thinking will ultimately suffer.

What to do? Dedicate the time necessary to perform a single action. Try as best as is possible to throw yourself fully into completing one task at a time. It behooves you to find ways in which to commit yourself to concentrated levels of effort. Whether by blocking off time on your calendar or by retraining your mind not to fall into the trap of succumbing to distractedness, to remember is to do "deep work." You owe it to your memory to be an anti-multitasking individual.

As an organization, leaders may want to consider implementing learning programs that help employees recognize the acute importance of remembering and the perils of multitasking. Other options include the enterprise-wide reduction of meetings, phone calls, emails, and text messages. The more an employee is expected to attend to communication interruptions, the more they will be forced to yield to multitasking. Permitting employees to block off time to direct their efforts to single tasks will also help. In the end, when employees can direct their attention to a single action, their ability to remember increases and they will be more likely to accomplish the action itself on time.

Be Attentive, Flexible, and Focused

When we take action, it is important to be attentive, flexible, and focused. In doing so, we are able to accomplish our tasks, but we will deviate or adjust as the situation warrants. Demands, priorities, and situations change. It is to be expected. As a result, and when necessary, our Applied Thinking will need to alter course quickly if we want to achieve the goal. Remaining dogmatic is as useful as shoveling snow with a dinner fork. Ignoring the need to change or remaining headstrong just to meet a deadline is of no use to anyone. If new information has surfaced, we are obliged to counteract. Put simply, as the sands shift, our Applied Thinking must shift too. The trick is to remain focused so that we can get back on track as quickly as possible.

Chris Myers is the co-founder and CEO of BodeTree, an American company that provides financial management solutions to small businesses. Chris recommends an approach called "reflective urgency," his personal take on remaining flexible and focused. He says that reflective urgency is the ability to both consciously and rapidly reflect on such things as resources, priorities, and needs of the moment. In trying to find the most "direct path to the most important priority of the moment," Chris uses his past experiences to assist his current actions. Furthermore, he remains flexible enough to adjust his Applied Thinking as the situation dictates. Author Jesse Sostrin refers to reflective urgency in a 2017 *Harvard Business Review* article as "the ability to bring conscious, rapid reflection to the priorities of the moment—to align your best thinking with the swiftest course of action." It is this balance between doing and staying malleable that can be of incredible benefit to Open Thinking.

For example, picture yourself alone near the top of Mount Logan, Canada's highest mountain, when a series of earthquakes hit. Your plan was to reach the summit, but the force of the earthquakes has triggered a slew of avalanches, making it dangerous to continue. You are now stuck at 12,139 feet, with your bag of supplies, a satellite phone, and whatever is left of your wits. You cannot climb to the 19,685-foot summit but, to make matters worse, you cannot descend the mountain either. The situation is grave. You are by yourself, hoping to be rescued.

This is precisely the scenario that unfolded for Argentine mountain climber Natalia Martínez. During a solo climb of Mount Logan in May of 2017, the 37-year-old was just past the halfway point when a series of earthquakes was triggered. As an experienced mountain climber, she knew she was not going to reach her goal. Instead, her objective shifted from ascent to survival. Without both flexibility *and* focus—without being attentive—Natalia would be putting her life at risk. She needed to put new ideas into action, switch from one form of problem-solving to another.

Visibility was limited due to a combination of snow and windstorms that prevented any helicopter from making the trip up Mount Logan. Natalia knew it could be several hours if not days before she might be saved. Survival mode kicked in. "I had to keep drinking, eating, changing my tent, making a wall for the wind," she said. Natalia knew if she did not remain focused on the new goal—surviving as long as it might take for a rescue team to appear—her life could end. At temperatures well below zero, and in a punishing wind that toppled trees, Natalia's cognitive flexibility was necessary more than at any other point in her life.

Her experiences also highlight the importance of perseverance. Being flexible yet focused during Applied Thinking requires persistence. Regardless of whether you have to change course—as Natalia did—or you remain on track as originally planned, Applied Thinking requires a sense of resolve for you to reach a successful conclusion. Author Angela Duckworth calls it *grit*. In her 2016 book of the same name, she writes, "To be gritty is to keep putting one foot in front of the other. To be gritty is to hold fast to an interesting and purposeful goal. To be gritty is to invest, day after week after year, in challenging practice. To be gritty is to fall down seven times, and rise eight."

Natalia had been on the mountain for three days when she began tapping into her perseverance and grit reservoirs. "The last day before the rescue, my mind was eating me," she said. "I wanted to show myself that I can do it. It was a personal challenge. I was more sensitive to every sound. I felt alert to every danger. I had to keep focused." It took four days for the rescue team to make it to Natalia's location on the mountain. The story has a happy ending, in part because Natalia demonstrated cognitive flexibility. Her adaptability—in combination with her determination—ensured that she would make it off Mount Logan. Quizzed about her survival skills after her rescue, she responded, "Now I know I can do it." It is a lesson for all of us when we enter into the Applied Thinking phase of Open Thinking. Be flexible, with grit, and remain focused. Be ever so attentive.

When it comes to being flexible yet focused, Dominic Reid insists we ought to be offsetting the need for on-time and on-budget project requirements with emotional investment. "If my events do not provide good entertainment, then it misses the point entirely," he said. "You have to have faith in your ability and that of your people to do the delivery—to know that you can complete things on time and on budget—but we also have to ask ourselves, 'What are we trying to achieve?'" Dominic looks for the bits and pieces that allow the balance between the action and emotion to come together. This ensures the tasks are completed, but that they are done in a way that is fueled by passion and team collaboration. This is what allows for flexibility to easily pair with continued focus. In his eyes, the flexibility to change course happens by virtue of the team's culture.

"The interplay is important between those two," he continued. "Whatever the plan was when you started, rest assured it will change as you go through the delivery. But when people get a sense of involvement, of collaborating and having fun—when they know they don't have to resist and they can be flexible in the moment—this is what you want to see as an outcome." Dominic believes the events that he runs see him playing the part of a conductor of an orchestra. Much like Tania Miller, Dominic recognizes that there are many "on the fly" moments during the events, but it is the relationships and trust that have been previously established that allow the outcome to be achieved. "You have to trust people to resolve any issue that may pop up," he said. "The power of those relationships is very strong. A lot of people will over-engineer things, staying too focused and not flexible. Sometimes you just have to let it wobble a bit and things will come to fruition."

Another powerful Applied Thinking attribute found within the flexible-yet-focused execution function is not only admitting you were wrong, but taking the steps to remedy the error as diligently as possible. This will eliminate the chance for Inflexible Thinking and cognitive bias, too. During the process of getting things done, not everything will go according to plan. How you handle the scenario is key. Belaboring the problem is a surefire way to miss a deadline. Ignoring a known mishap altogether is another. Blaming others can cause rifts in the team, leading to less buy-in and possible delays. Mistakes and errors happen. They are inevitable. Each of us needs to accept this fact. Remaining calm yet flexible will help ensure that Applied Thinking is successful. I am reminded of the words of Oliver Goldsmith, who in 1761 observed, "Our greatest glory is, not in never falling, but in rising every time we fall."

In his book *Adapt: Why Success Always Starts with Failure*, economist and journalist Tim Harford writes about the importance of failing and how correcting those mistakes can lead to a state of enfranchisement. "To embrace the idea of adapting in everyday life seems to be to accept blundering into a process of unremitting failure. So it's worth remembering once again why it is worth experimenting, even though so many experiments will, indeed, end in failure. It's because the process of correcting the mistakes can be more liberating than the mistakes themselves are crushing, even though at the time we so often feel that the reverse is true." Harford reminds us that even in the moment of performance, a mistake or error can lead to something superior. It might even bring Applied Thinking to a better end state.

Be Ruthless and Block Out

John Dalla Costa is the founder of the Centre for Ethical Orientation, a consultancy that fosters ethical excellence. He works with private, public, and non-profit organizations across the globe on projects involving governance innovation, cultural renewal, and trust. He is the author of five books on responsible management and personal integrity. John also teaches regularly in several university business schools as well as with the Conference Board of Canada. I heard John speak at a conference about the virtues of moral leadership and how it is good for business. I reached out to him to discuss Open Thinking, hoping he might assist my research. He did not disappoint.

My reasons for doing so were simple. John's thoughts on personal integrity resonated with me when he touched on the aspects of how we manage our day-to-day lives. As society continues to change, John had some intriguing insights from his research on our abilities—or lack thereof—to keep focused on what truly matters. "How much time do we give executives, managers, or front-line staff just to think?" he asked. "I don't believe it's possible to do serious thinking without ceasing the otherwise distracting doing. Busyness has become a badge of honor, more a feature of status than of perspicacity or even productivity. Socially, we usually are introduced to others by what we do. Ever more defined by profession or expertise, we therefore derive more personal worth from the busyness which suggests one's indispensability to those tasks."

How can we block out what is irrelevant or destructive if our busyness defines who we are? It becomes impossible to prioritize key actions if we allow any or all actions to invade our schedule. Put differently, how can we get things done if we become too consumed by the unimportant and non-urgent? Furthermore, if we do not possess inhibitory self-control—so that any inconsequential impulse is rejected—how can we remain focused to complete our actions? The previous execution function explored the concept of being attentive, flexible, and focused. If we do not possess self-control, however, the chance for attentiveness, flexibility, and focus becomes moot. We must block out the irrelevancies of life.

John believes that the lack of ruthlessness with our focus—based on the increase in our busyness—is partially a result of the technology that sits at our fingertips. "Our capabilities for involvement are 24/7," he described, "and the flow of information is instantaneous and growing exponentially." He believes the very notion of a set working day with defined hours for effective effort is anachronistic. "Just as this incredible technological capacity emerged in the early 1990s, companies also adopted new structures based on process reengineering. These efforts removed managerial layers and eliminated whole categories of work. Many of the work-life and mindfulness protocols businesses have adopted are intended as correctives. However, the emotional investment many of us make in busyness is such that turning off over-consuming activities can unleash long-avoided questions relating to identity, authenticity, meaning, and purposefulness." It is this pull toward busyness that becomes so powerful it eventually distracts us from life's existential questions. John suggests that we become so preoccupied with "What to do?" that we end up forgetting the bigger questions relating to "Why?" and "Is it worth it?"

John's insights, again, brought me back to my second book, *The Purpose Effect*. When we are unable to block out the distractions or the busyness, not only does it hamper our Applied Thinking, it can affect what I refer to as "personal purpose." With no time to truly develop our skills, passions, and interests, we wind up stuck in a rut. Unfocused and unable to decipher what is truly important, we forgo the opportunity to define our short- and long-term objectives. Too occupied with consuming mindless information we become incapable of deciding how we want to show up in a room, how we want people to feel when we leave it. In *The Purpose Effect*, I wrote that we must develop, define, and decide our personal purpose if we want to achieve meaning in our lives. As John states, if we are absorbed with the *what* we will ultimately miss out on the *why*. When we are trying to move forward with our Applied Thinking actions, we also need to be clear about our personal purpose. If we don't know what our personal purpose is, it's no wonder we aim to fill the void with vacuous content. We end up displacing the *why* with far too many things that are inappropriate.

Aside from the link with personal purpose, these busyness, distraction, and interruption issues are not new. In fact, management guru Peter Drucker wrote in his 1967 book *The Effective Executive*, "To be effective, every knowledge worker, and especially every executive, needs to be able to dispose of time in fairly large chunks. To have small dribs and drabs of time at his disposal will not be sufficient even if the total is an impressive number of hours." Pippi Longstocking might agree. Remember she was never exploited by time, she explored it on her own terms. She was in charge. Today, there are some who agree with Drucker and Pippi, too. Brad Smith, CEO of Intuit, for example, says, "Time is our most precious and limited resource, therefore managing my time is my most important priority."

Technologist and author Alexandra Samuel states, "Your goals should be to sort and limit the information you receive and to streamline the work of reading, responding to, and sharing what matters." Samuel is referring to the act of filtering. As with Smith's recognition of the importance of time, Samuel recommends filtering the endless and unavoidable amount of information, data, and content that inevitably finds its way to you. By filtering the information noise—through options such as rules, turning off notifications, and various automation techniques—you can build a reprieve from seemingly inescapable time encroachments.

When we cannot remain focused to complete our critical actions, we can lose sight of what has priority. The quest to be busy can exhaust our time to complete the important stuff. That is, if the allure of engaging in less than desirable action impedes our ability to enact Applied Thinking, there is no doubt failure will ensue. Through his research, John believes we have shifted toward valuing quantity over quality and "short-term gratification over longer-term investments in social and economic sustainability." With this intense penchant to be busy on matters that do not aid Applied Thinking, John thinks we are squandering the opportunity to realize greater potential in our own abilities. To be ruthless is to mercilessly separate relevance from irrelevance.

For individuals, the easiest and most common remedy that I have seen work with successful people is a comfort with saying no. The first person to say no to is in fact yourself. The more comfortable you are saying no to yourself, the more likely you will be successful with Applied Thinking. The types of questions to ask yourself include but are not limited to:

- Should I answer that call?
- Can I cancel or skip this meeting?
- Can that deadline slip?
- Should I check my social media streams right now?

Once you realize that you are the first line of defense when it comes to blocking distractions out, you will have more time for Applied Thinking. The second step is to say no to others, in particular to their requests for your time. Conversely, if you say yes to requests that end up putting your actions at risk, your busyness will have affected Applied Thinking. Busyness occurs when we say yes more often than we say no. Saying no to others can be difficult because we do not want to disappoint people. It reminds me of something I call the "soft shoulder."

A director approached me one day for some advice over a work issue. He worked in an open office. Most of the team members worked in and around his area. Some others worked from home in different cities. The office workers had a desk, chair, filing cabinet, and so on. Everyone could hear each other's conversations because the dividers between each workstation were made of thin, acrylic fabric. In the middle of the team's area was a common space with a large table and chairs. The director was looking for help because ever since the team had moved to the open-office environment—about six months before—he felt as though his work had been suffering. He had given up his four-walled office in favor of being with the team and he felt his leadership abilities were waning. In particular, his Applied Thinking was suffering.

We had a couple of conversations about the pros and cons of an open office. We discussed various strategies for improvement. But there was one issue he had failed to mention during our first two chats. His boss. During the transition to the new work area the director had also inherited a new direct manager, who worked in the same building but, as a vice president, had remained in his office. He did not give up what he had worked toward: a fancy corner office with an executive assistant parked outside.

While the director was having difficulties adjusting to his new environment, it paled in comparison to the true problem. His vice president had developed a pattern of showing up at the director's office pod area, sitting down on an adjacent chair, and letting loose with whatever was on his mind at the time. It might be early in the morning, right after lunch, or toward the end of the day. There was no real pattern, but it was clear the vice president was using the director as an impromptu sounding board. On the one hand, the behavior was positive. The vice president was comfortable reaching out to the director and discussing various matters. On the other hand, these spur-of-the-moment meetings were not only a source of stress for the director, they were negatively affecting his ability to get things done.

The director was demonstrating the "soft shoulder." Partly out of respect, partly out of curiosity, and partly out of guilt, the director did not have it in him to say no. He was allowing the meetings to continue and as a result he had increased his busyness. The soft shoulder of the director was permitting the vice president to get what he wanted—someone to listen to his mental meanderings. But it was clearly having a detrimental effect on the director's Applied Thinking. Upon this discovery, I asked the director, if he could change one thing with his situation—his desk location, the open-office environment, or these extemporaneous examples of avoidable busyness—what would it be. When it was put to him in this manner, he easily recognized what had become the issue. It was the director's inability to say no to his vice president.

We strategized some solutions, but the first step was about honesty. If we are not honest with ourselves about how we spend our time, Applied Thinking will be constrained. If we do not learn how to say no to requests for our time, we only have ourselves to blame. The director decided to have an honest conversation with the vice president about their working relationship. As I suspected, the vice president meant no harm and was not aware of the adverse effect he was having. They agreed to schedule these types of conversations into their calendars through breakfasts, coffee meetings, or lunches. This way, the vice president continued to get what he wanted and the director was able to properly schedule time for these meetings.

This example is a reminder that we must *take* control of our busyness if we want to *be* in control of our actions. We must own the process of blocking out interruptions by having the courage to say no. Organizations can assist by including such time-management or behavior enhancement tactics in development programs. Leaders should also be sympathetic to the demands they place on their colleagues' time. In the case of the vice president, if he had been more aware of how counterproductive his actions were, he might not have affected the director's behavior at all.

There is another way the organization can assist employees with execution functions of being ruthless and blocking out. It is helpful to set time aside to ensure employees are as aligned as possible, fully aware of the organization's mission and current status. When employees are left wondering why they are there or confused about the goals for the organization, it leaves room to be distracted. Of course, this ties in nicely with the "mindful" execution function we discussed earlier.

When trying to keep an entire team focused on the task at hand, Sameer Patel is a fan of blocking out distractions by reminding employees about the business's current and future state. Each of his all-hands meetings, for example, sees Sameer starting with the same presentation slide. "Here's where we are, here's where we want to be, and here is the nirvana state." In other words, Sameer's organizational focus pushes employees to recall *why* they are there, not just *what* they are doing. This ensures that everyone knows how they are moving, what is left to achieve in addition to the aspirational aspects of the company's goals. By doing so, Sameer is taking the proactive steps to block out any irrelevancies or distractions with their mission and objectives. The reinforced alignment negates questions about the company's position, permitting team members to stay on task.

Another CEO whom we met earlier in the book, Brian Scudamore, feels the same way as Sameer. "We have a lot of rigor around our meetings to ensure we stay on track as a company," said Brian. "Every month we have a five-person strategy meeting where there is a lot of discussion about our strategic direction, the issues at hand, and what actions we have to take. We also conduct a larger leadership team meeting weekly. These are also very focused meetings to ensure we are on track as an organization, that our Applied Thinking is not being impacted by other issues or distractions."

The O2E Brands group that Brian runs also conducts a daily seven-minute huddle at 11 a.m. with all employees. These get-together sessions aim to share what is working and what might not be working. The true purpose is to help everyone stay on task. "It's a way to bring all the brilliant minds into one room, to share our latest thinking and actions," said Brian, "and to, most importantly, make sure we are all aligned with the strategy and daily actions." Brian believes this sort of alignment is core to the organization's success. It creates an environment in which O2E Brands and its subsidiary companies are able to block out distractions, which in turn helps to meet the organization's objectives.

Be Humane and Empathize

In my 2013 book *Flat Army*, I introduced 15 "Connected Leader Attributes," behaviors that made up something I called Open Leadership. I defined the latter as "the act of engaging others to influence and execute a coordinated and harmonious conclusion." One of the 15 attributes that makes up Open Leadership is empathy. Through my research, interviews, and observations while writing *Open to Think*, it has become apparent that not only is empathy required for Open Leadership, it is critical to Open Thinking. Both Open Leadership and Open Thinking require a better understanding, appreciation, and sensitivity of others. When we are empathetic, we negate closed-mindedness. A lack of compassion can affect Applied Thinking. We must remember that the word human is firmly nested in humane.

Empathy and the act of being more humane is the final of four execution functions that make up Applied Thinking. When we demonstrate perspective or put ourselves in the shoes of others in the midst of execution, there is a greater possibility for success. By being empathetic, you are looking out for those you work with as well as those you might be serving while you are completing a goal. When we empathize, we are observant of patterns that may affect our desired result. An empathetic Applied Thinking individual is attentive not only to what is required by one's self to achieve the goal, but to the needs and feelings of related stakeholders.

In a 2001 *Harvard Business Review* article titled "Leadership in a Combat Zone," Lieutenant General William Pagonis observes, "Owning the facts is a prerequisite to leadership. But there are millions of technocrats out there with lots of facts in their quivers and little leadership potential. In many cases, what they are missing is empathy. No one is a leader who can't put himself or herself in the other person's shoes." Pagonis was the director of logistics during the 1991 Gulf War, responsible for Applied Thinking on an enormous scale. While Pagonis's point is well taken, empathy is far more than putting ourselves in the shoes of others. In fact, there are three key categories of empathy that can alter Applied Thinking.

In a 2012 paper published in *Nature Neuroscience*, Columbia University psychologists Jamil Zaki and Kevin Ochsner define empathy in three distinct ways. *Mentalizing* is how we explicitly consider and understand someone else's "states and sources." *Experience sharing* is when we vicariously share "targets' internal states." The third type of empathy, *prosocial concern*, is when we express "motivation to improve targets' experiences."

As you enter Applied Thinking, it is important to understand that the three types of empathy can assist you in reaching the desired goal. While Zaki and Ochsner's definitions are academically sound, we might take the liberty of refining them into layman's language: *rational empathy, emotional empathy, and sympathetic empathy.*

Rational empathy is the process by which you sense how others view the world, or how they may intellectually perceive something. In essence, it gets you into the head space of others. As opposed to trying to understand the feelings of someone else, you seek out their mental views, how they may be interpreting a situation. Imagine yourself on a team, entering Applied Thinking and initiating various tasks. When you are able to hypothesize how someone on the team may mentally react to new information—based on what they know or even what they may not know—you can anticipate how you might handle things. If a situation requires a pivot in direction, possessing the ability to envision the manner in which people will handle the change can greatly affect your success.

Emotional empathy occurs when we are able to feel the pain of others. This is perhaps the best known and used definition of empathy. It is your sensitivity to someone else's concerns. We are able to put ourselves in the shoes of the other person to vicariously feel their joy or pain. It differs from rational empathy because you are sensing how someone else feels, not how they think. Emotional empathy can also be thought of as the chance to build rapport with someone else. Often, the actions associated with Applied Thinking will require the assistance of others. If we do not possess the ability to create a rapport with those on our team or those we are aiming to serve, a smooth ride may be less likely.

Sympathetic empathy is when we observe enough in others that we become motivated to act. I believe it provides the key to the overarching concept of empathy itself and its relationship to Applied Thinking. Perhaps someone on your team seems to be under duress and their work is suffering. You have been observing both their behavior (how they are feeling) as well as their responses (how they are thinking). If you employ sympathetic empathy you will take action to help that individual with their plight. It is the difference between being aware—whether rational or emotional—and doing something about it.

All three types of empathy are important to Applied Thinking. Each of them can make you more humane as you carry out action. Behaviors that cover perspective-taking, an emotional understanding, and a willingness to act can enhance both our performance and our Applied Thinking. Whether you need the help of others during the execution of a current action or at some later point, your understanding of empathy can play a significant importance.

Take, for example, a situation that unfolded at Microsoft in 2016 when it launched Tay.ai, an artificial intelligence bot hosted on a Twitter account. Within hours of the launch, the bot became wickedly rude due to a coordinated attack by hackers. Tay began spewing profane and racist comments, including a denial that the Holocaust ever happened. The world was aghast at the vitriolic hate it began to disseminate. The company was forced to issue a public apology and the team responsible was left with a customer relations nightmare. Just 16 hours after launch, Tay was taken offline.

Tay was actually an offspring of XiaoIce, a Microsoft-developed chatbot with over 40 million users in China and Japan. Satya Nadella, CEO of Microsoft, entered the picture a few days after the Tay debacle. Instead of berating the team responsible for Tay, Nadella chose the empathetic route. In fact, he depended on all three types of empathy in his dealings with the situation. Nadella put himself in the shoes of developers, both how they were thinking and how they were feeling, and he took sympathetic action. He wrote directly to the group of developers responsible.

In an email he said, "Keep pushing, and know that I am with you." He went on to remind them that the "key is to keep learning and improving." In an interview with USA Today shortly after the incident, Nadella said, "It's so critical for leaders not to freak people out, but to give them air cover to solve the real problem. If people are doing things out of fear, it's hard or impossible to actually drive any innovation." Nadella cuts to the heart of the issue. If we do not exhibit the three types of empathy during Applied Thinking, inevitably our productivity will wane. Ever since the Tay issue, Microsoft has continued to press technological advancement through bots like Tay. The Microsoft Bot Framework, introduced in 2016 shortly after Tay, is now being used by more than 130,000 developers.

Jane Dutton, a professor in the CompassionLab at the University of Michigan, supports the way Nadella handled the situation at Microsoft. Dutton's research shows that when a leader demonstrates empathy to employees—being compassionate when things go sideways—the individuals will be more resilient during challenging times.

Objectives wind up getting fixed despite the setback. It is another example of how levels of empathy can positively impact Applied Thinking.

Additionally, a 2012 study published in *Leadership Quarterly* by professors Richard Boyatzis and Angela Passarelli, and Cleveland Clinic doctors Michael Phillips, Mark Lowe, Katherine Koenig, Blessy Matthews, and Jamie Stoller, proved that when people are not empathetic with one another, our brains tend to demonstrate negative emotion, leading to avoidance or apathetic behavior. In an accompanying 2012 *Ivey Business Journal* article, the lead researcher, Richard Boyatzis, writes:

> To build more effective leadership relationships and to help others feel motivated and inspired to change, learn and develop, leaders need to have empathy. Beyond feeling that they are understood, other people need to feel that the leader "cares" about them. A basic component of this process is likely to be a leader's ability to suspend his or her own issues and agenda and understand the other person's issues, thoughts, and feelings. That is, engage in a truer form of empathy.

Analyzing data from over 6,000 managers from 38 different countries, the Center for Creative Leadership (CCL) found in 2007 that "empathy is positively related to job performance. Managers who show more empathy toward direct reports are viewed as better performers in their job by their bosses." Another firm, Development Dimensions International (DDI), analyzed the behaviors of over 15,000 employees across 300 companies in 18 countries. Data spanned a 10-year period. The results, published in 2016, back up the need to exhibit the three types of empathy when in the Applied Thinking phase. DDI discovered that empathy is the most critical driver of overall performance. In fact, the research and development firm found that those who consistently employ empathy will perform 40 percent higher than those who do not. "The research shows there is no other single leadership skill that is more important and yet, in today's culture, empathy is near extinction. I believe it is one of the most dangerous global trends of our time," said Rich Wellins, senior research associate at DDI and co-author of the report.

I agree with Wellins. Alarm bells ought to be going off. Empathy is on the decline. When empathy declines, we should not be surprised that our Applied Thinking will be affected, too. University of Michigan researchers Sara Konrath, Edward O'Brien, and Courtney Hsing released a paper in 2011, titled "Changes in Dispositional Empathy in American College Students Over Time," that found that university students are 40 percent less likely to demonstrate empathy compared with three decades ago. DDI discovered that only 40 percent of front-line team members were proficient or strong in empathy. In my experience, I find that one of the leading reasons projects go off the rails is due to a lack of empathy, a lack of being humane. All too often, when leaders and team members alike miss out on the opportunity to put themselves in the shoes of others—with perspective, emotional, and sympathetic receptiveness—inhibitors begin to pile up. This pileup is what results in Applied Thinking issues.

Jonathan Becher, co-president of Sharks Sports & Entertainment which oversees the National Hockey League's San Jose Sharks, commented, "People and companies push a philosophy of 'bias for action.'" It is this bias Jonathan mentions—previously introduced in Chapter 6—that can impact empathy. It can also hurt Applied Thinking. Jonathan continued, "The mantra is: 'Speed matters in business. Many decisions and actions are reversible and do not need extensive study.' But undifferentiated bias for action can cause dysfunctional behavior. Author Liz Wiseman calls these accidental diminishers 'rapid responders.' By solving problems quickly, often problems they aren't directly responsible for, they limit the organization's ability to scale." Without rational, emotional, or sympathetic empathy, we may be subjecting ourselves and those we lead to Applied Thinking that is unnecessarily fast. Such a lack of empathy can jeopardize the overarching objective.

Daniel Lubetzky is the CEO of snack food company KIND. He is a Mexican immigrant to the United States and the son of a Holocaust survivor. Concerned for the state of his adopted nation on the night of Donald Trump's presidential election win, Lubetzky touched on the difficulty of empathy in an email he sent to all KIND employees:

I've highlighted in the past that empathy and kindness are often confused with weakness. That, actually, it takes strength to be kind, particularly when we feel most vulnerable. That empathizing with "the other" requires enormous amounts of self-confidence, to feel comfortable putting yourself in the shoes of someone that you deeply disagree with.

Empathy is hard. It takes significant effort to pause and look through someone else's lens before rushing to action. It is even more difficult to be nonjudgmental. In the midst of Applied Thinking, we have to be constantly viewing our complex situations through the eyes of those we are working with, or for. Those who are employing excellent Applied Thinking skills are continuously wondering what it is like to be their co-worker, boss, partner, customer, and so on. What are they thinking? What are they feeling? Should I jump in and change course because of it?

We will close out the concept of being more humane through empathy with a few sage words from author Daniel Pink in an interview he conducted with Oprah Winfrey. "Empathy is about standing in someone else's shoes, feeling with his or her heart, seeing with his or her eyes. Not only is empathy hard to outsource and automate but it makes the world a better place."

Hat Tip to the Millinery

"I'm always thinking on my feet," said Karyn. "It's a necessary quality to think on your feet but I'm constantly checking and rechecking my notes, every step of the way. It only gets done properly when I'm combining the two."

When I was observing Karyn and her team at Lilliput actually making the hats, her characterization of the production process was spot on. All too often during the Applied Thinking phase the milliners were not only remembering what was relevant to hat-making, they were referring to handwritten notes as well as to each other. In parallel there was an incredible amount of focus as the milliners were steaming, sewing, wetting, measuring, sketching, or sculpting.

You could also feel there was a sense of purpose in their craft, their chosen profession. It came out not only in their smiles, but in the way they were engaged. It was obvious to me that the shop was chock full of empathy. They were humane to one another. While each hat had a deadline—thereby necessitating a degree of ruthlessness with their actions—it was clear they also had each other's back. Whether it was suggestions for a ribbon or feather, or a query if someone else might need the steamer, the Lilliput team was always looking out for one another. By using their notes and each other, remaining flexible yet focused and blocking out the distractions while demonstrating empathy, the Lilliput team was able to meet the three-to-four-day deadlines for each hat. In my humble estimation, they were a wonderful example of exhibiting all facets of Applied Thinking.

APPLIED THINKING TIPS FOR THE INDIVIDUAL

- Conduct like the maestra. Rest assured that Applied Thinking will result in hiccups and curve balls. The more malleable and flexible you are, the more successful you will be at conducting. Try to be "in the flow."

- Be empathetic. Be humane. When you employ rational, emotional, and sympathetic empathy, you gain the trust and buy-in of others, which can be key to completing your objectives on time and devoid of stress. Being empathetic is proven to enhance your own personal performance, too.

- Get organized. Time is the most precious resource of any employee. You need to set up a time-management system that blocks out time for productivity as well as the means to capture thoughts and record progress.

APPLIED THINKING TIPS
FOR THE ORGANIZATION

- Be ruthless about the long term. Your organization must be more than a factory of actions and getting things done. Keep the long term in mind, asking questions about how today's actions might affect your overarching purpose and future.

- Be vigilant about the short term. The natural tendency of an organization is to fixate on short-term actions. In doing so, it needs to establish better guidelines at an organizational level, including meeting and calendar etiquette, prioritization recommendations, and time-management practices and procedures.

- Be pragmatic about mistakes. Things will go wrong. Failures will occur. Errors will be made. New information will surface. An organization's Applied Thinking mindset is dictated by how it reacts to the aforementioned. Create a culture that is flexible, tolerant, and always learning versus one that is rigid, intolerant, and operating with a fixed mindset.

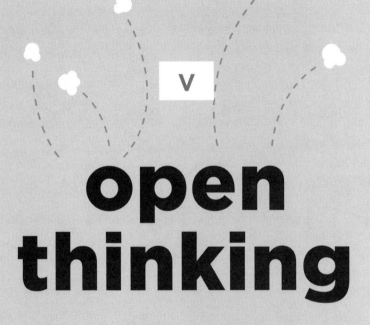

v

open
thinking

8

Think Again

Thought is the seed of action; but action is
as much its second form as thought is its first.
RALPH WALDO EMERSON

One of the troubles with our culture is we
do not respect and train the imagination.
It needs exercise. It needs practice.
URSULA K. LE GUIN

PETER GILMORE IS a world-renowned Australian executive
chef. He plies his trade at two of the country's most famous
restaurants: Quay Restaurant in Sydney's Circular Quay
and Bennelong at the Sydney Opera House. Both have won several national and international awards. From an early age Peter was
inspired to cook. He even started his first apprenticeship at the ten-
der age of 16 years old. Peter is a natural collaborator, often working
with small farmers and local fisherman to bring superior flavors to his
menus. As a passionate gardener himself, Peter ensures his plates are
full of diverse colors, tastes, and textures straight from the earth. He
refers to his cuisine as "food inspired by nature." Having visited both
restaurants on a few occasions, I wanted to know how Peter operated
between Creative, Critical, and Applied Thinking.

"My role as a chef is multifaceted, with lots of practical concerns as
well as the need and desire to be creative," he said. Peter recognized
early on in his career that to be successful he had to spend time in

all three categories of Open Thinking. But any chef is only as good as their dishes (the dreaming) and how they are presented to the customer (the deciding and the doing). Peter's insights shed further light on the need to be continuously cycling through the categories of Open Thinking. His story is a perfect way to start the final chapter of *Open to Think*.

"When it comes to creating a new dish, the starting point is always about creative visualization, dreaming up a new dish," Peter stated. His approach includes not wanting to constrain his thinking with certain practicalities. In essence, Peter does not want to get bogged down. But, in the midst of Creative Thinking, Peter also knows that the end result needs to be workable. "The thinking has to have some realistic guidelines." What I gathered from Peter is that Creative Thinking is important, but it must also be practical. As we discovered earlier in the book with the inhibitor known as Indecisive Thinking, if we spend too much time ideating and not being pragmatic, we end up getting nothing accomplished. The balance between reflection and action is key to Peter's success.

How does he come up with ideas for a new dish? "In general, the inspiration comes from many different sources. An idea can form from seeing a new raw product and wondering about its applications. Sometimes an idea will almost burst to life through my imagination. Its starting point may be a flavor combination, a visual construction, or an idea of combining or layering textures within a dish."

Unsurprisingly, Peter draws inspiration from his views and outlook on the world. Like others we have met in this book, including Karyn Ruiz, Joel Plaskett, Gord Downie, and Tania Miller, Peter is an artist. Together they share the knack of viewing the world in creative ways. "Sometimes there is a reference point to work from," Peter said. "This could be a piece of art, sculpture, or simply looking at a piece of curling bark on a tree." Most of his ideas start out visually. He finds that working with that initial visual spark creates the process to then begin assembling the ingredients. In turn, this leads to reviewing different cooking methods that end up achieving certain textures. He also uses his execution functions by recalling taste memories that can further enhance or change a menu item.

As he mentally maps out the new dish in his head or jots it down on paper, Peter enters another form of thinking. But what is extraordinary is how he admitted to continuously bouncing between all three categories of Open Thinking. "I find the process of actually doing then leads to new ideas, and down unexpected paths, often ending in a different result than I had originally imagined. At this point the creative process is reactionary and also intuitive. I would have to say that the initial spark and an open mind is what is important." Peter is open to creativity through the entire Open Thinking process, particularly as he enters the kitchen to start putting things together for guests. His creativity has no end point.

According to Anna Antinori, Olivia Carter, and Luke Smillie of the Melbourne School of Psychological Science at the University of Melbourne, "people who are 'open' see the world in a way that is different to the average person." They found in their 2017 *Journal of Research in Personality* paper, "Seeing It Both Ways: Openness to Experience and Binocular Rivalry Suppression," that openness positively assists both engagement in everyday creative pursuits and real-world achievements. They write, "Our findings suggest that the creative tendencies of open people extend all the way down to basic visual perception. Open people may have fundamentally different visual experiences to the average person."

In Peter's case, while much of the creativity for a new dish may originate from him, he often relies on his team to fine-tune the end result. This is where collaboration plays a part in his Open Thinking. "I find my team's input helpful and valuable in the practical application of reproducing my dish within a commercial kitchen." Another chef or team member will regularly suggest a more efficient method or technique to cook a particular aspect of a new dish. "There are often several components of a dish that need to be ready at the same time, so a suggestion of a way to create a more efficient workflow is welcomed as long as it doesn't compromise the integrity of the dish." As the idea of a new dish enters the kitchen and the next stage, Peter inserts another instance of Open Thinking, this time with his valued team members. In this case, everyone is working together on Creative, Critical, and Applied Thinking techniques.

"There are many practical concerns when implementing a new idea or dish to the menu," Peter added. "Ensuring continuity of supply of ingredients, being able to adjust a dish to enable dietary concerns, teaching of new skills to staff, and also how the flow of the kitchen relates to the implementation of a new menu item." It is in the execution of the new dish while in the kitchen that Peter must rely on the different skill sets of his team members to be successful. But it does not end there.

Any kitchen also requires a form of Open Thinking to deliver the dish to the customers. This is the third instance of Open Thinking in Peter's role as an executive chef. "There is also the documentation and costing of a new recipe, as well as the communication that needs to be relayed to the front-of-house team about the new dish, tasting notes, and translating the emotion and intent of the new dish. The reality of running a restaurant is that you need to rely on many people doing their job with passion and skill. Everyone needs to feel that they are doing something special within that process, with the ultimate goal of creating a great experience for people. Passion and the teaching of knowledge is what is most important here."

In his 2004 book *Organizational Culture and Leadership*, Edgar Schein argues, "Knowledge and skill are becoming more widely distributed, forcing leaders—whether they like it or not—to be more dependent on other people in their organizations. Under such circumstances a cynical attitude toward human nature is bound to create, at best, bureaucratic rigidity and, at the worst extreme, counter organizational subgroups." Schein's point applies to Open Thinking conceptually and specifically to Peter's application of it.

Thousands of people visit Peter's restaurants every year. They have come to expect wildly entertaining, mouth-watering, and diversified menus. The list of awards he has garnered over the years is too long to mention, a success underpinned by the Open Thinking that informs his own actions and those of his teams.

Active, Always Learning

I discovered another trait found in Open Thinkers that helped them continuously demonstrate Creative, Critical, and Applied Thinking. They were always learning. Their curiosity seemed almost infinite. They asked questions, usually a lot of them. Not only were they autodidacts—self-taught—they had an insatiable appetite to add to their intellectual reservoirs. Open Thinking individuals loathed the status quo. They needed new knowledge, new ideas, new relationships, and new information to fuel their Open Thinking.

Charlene Li, for example, divulged her thinking mantra: "Always be researching." She said, "Every time I meet someone new, no matter in what situation, I'm curious to see what I can learn. I strike up conversations with Uber drivers. I'll engage a receptionist while I'm waiting to go into a meeting. I'll ask a CEO about something she posted on Facebook. I never know where my next big 'aha' will come from, and inevitably the best examples I've come across have been because I've made myself open and available to new perspectives." It is very much in line with Kyna Leski's point about the passing glance, but aided by Charlene's natural penchant to learn.

Charlene also helps us recognize that learning is not a one-time event. Her comments make sense because thinking is not a one-time event, either. When the World Economic Forum released a research paper entitled "The Future of Jobs," it noted that a variety of skills needed to be improved upon if we are to be prepared for 2020 and beyond. In Chapter 2 I highlighted that the report placed Creative Thinking at the top, but the list of skills also included Critical Thinking, cognitive flexibility, decision-making, problem solving, and active learning. The combination of Open Thinking and active learning can be seen within the WEF recommendations. In the report, however, the authors also deliver a chilling warning. "Without urgent and targeted action today to manage the near-term transition and build a workforce with futureproof skills, governments will have to cope with ever-growing unemployment and inequality, and businesses with a shrinking consumer base."

In his role as a chief strategy officer, Dion Hinchcliffe has created a mental map that outlines his own link between Open Thinking and learning, bridging the gap between his near-term needs and the future. Dion has already futureproofed himself. He filled me in on a handy model he uses that ultimately demonstrates how he is flexible with his learning *and* his thinking. Dion's process is as follows:

1. Come up with an idea.

2. Experiment with it and fail as fast as possible.

3. Once you've made a decision of some sort, refine it and then double-down on further problem solving.

4. If you don't solve the problem, table the idea for another project— move on to something else.

5. Keep it cyclical and flexible—always maintain the option of returning again, learning throughout the process.

Dion insists that his flexibility and learning radar allows for "plenty of discoveries along the path of thinking." He added, "I use this type of thinking as the learning vehicle, the means to get the project or idea completed. Things become successful when we are cyclical and flexible, and always learning."

Jonathan Becher, whom we met in the previous chapter, contends there is a relationship between thinking, learning, and asking questions. "For some people, if they only think about a topic privately or with their normal trusted advisors, they suffer from groupthink. You need an environment with lots of different points of view to really be able to think critically about a topic." He believes that to receive the valuable learnings and insights from people with different points of view, people need to know how to ask good questions, seeking to avoid confirmation bias. "Before I ask a question, I try to examine what bias I already have and then ask myself what new facts would cause me to change my mind. Then my questions are often trying to uncover whether anyone has these facts." It is these questions that lead to Jonathan's continuous learning, which in turn helps him to demonstrate Open Thinking.

Thomas Edison was both an Open Thinking role model and a continuous learner. Edison's Menlo Park working lab in the 1870s and 1880s reflected his appreciation for different-minded individuals thinking collaboratively about new, inventive technologies. His team of inventors made up a working lab of innovation, building upon previous learning and past experiences. Not only were they learning from failure, they were learning from each other.

Harper's Magazine once reported this observation by Edison: "During all those years of experimentation and research, I never once made a discovery. All my work was deductive, and the results I achieved were those of invention, pure and simple. I would construct a theory and work on its lines until I found it was untenable. Then it would be discarded at once and another theory evolved. This was the only possible way for me to work out the problem." It is this relationship between learning, failing, asking questions, experimentation, and thinking that helped propel Edison and his team to glorious heights of innovation. It is a tactic that both Dion and Jonathan have employed for years.

But as much as Charlene, Dion, and Jonathan articulate the importance of learning with Open Thinking, there is also some concern that educators are not doing enough to introduce the concept in the adolescent years of development. Yong Zhao is the Foundation Distinguished Professor in the School of Education at the University of Kansas. He has published more than 100 articles and 30 books, including *Counting What Counts*, *Never Send a Human to Do a Machine's Job*, and *Catching Up or Leading the Way*. He is one of the foremost experts on today's education system, what ails it, and what can be done to help it. He minces no words when I ask about the state of learning and its relationship to Open Thinking. "Creative and Critical Thinking are extremely important in education, but unfortunately lacking. It is not only missing in the curriculum for students, but also missing from the entire process and environment."

Yong believes that students, teachers, and school leaders alike are often discouraged—either by someone else or themselves—to be creative and critical during the learning process. "Educators should practice becoming Open Thinkers themselves first," he said, "and then allow and eventually create a culture that values Open Thinking."

It was Yong's emphatic suggestion that reminded me of James Perry's philosophy at Sunnybrook Health Sciences Centre. The Centre also acts as a teaching hospital for up-and-coming neuro-oncologists, as well as a host of other medical roles. The overarching philosophy at Sunnybrook, "Research embedded in care," acts as a further lesson about the importance of learning and Open Thinking. "We are patient-person centered," said James, "and we always recognize the ability to learn from them. Patients are going to tell us where there are gaps, what is working, and how we can improve. This is the very essence of our philosophy."

James believes every patient that walks through the door is part of their research and, more important, a significant part of the Centre's learning and thinking. Whether through clinical trials or logging a case into a database where imaging scientists can tap into brain diagnoses to help another patient, anyone who enters Sunnybrook is a part of the learning and thinking regimen. "A key attribute of our work at Sunnybrook," continued James, "is to create more questions than what you originally started with." But there is a flaw in the system that James wishes to address to strengthen learning at the Centre.

"It is very important to answer the question, 'Why did the bad results happen too?'" According to James, scientists and doctors are pressured to have a bias for positive results. He believes medical practitioners across any field need to explain why something did not work just as easily as what did work. "Our universities judge the quality of our research by citations, not by what we learned between the positive and the negative results. It has to change. Our thinking has to change." The insights of James and Yong serve as reminders that we are better off when there is a positive link between learning and Open Thinking.

Opposites Can Attract

In *Liminal Thinking*, business consultant Dave Gray defines the core concept as "the art of creating change by understanding, shaping, and reframing beliefs." Dave suggests that "the most important material to understand is belief." Our beliefs shape us, but we are also in charge of their construction. When I quizzed Dave regarding *his* beliefs about Open Thinking, his initial response was telling. "The sad truth is that most organizations do not seem to value thinking," he said. "Thinking requires space and unstructured time in which to think, but most workplaces do not provide this space and time." Dave feels as though today's leaders talk up a good game when it comes to being creative and placing a strong emphasis on thinking. He believes that their actions demonstrate they do not actually value it.

His suggestions to invoke more creativity into the Open Thinking philosophy were crystal clear. "Even if your boss and family leave you little time for yourself, wherever you are and whatever you are doing, it's you who chooses where to spend that most precious resource, your attention. You choose what you pay attention to. To be more open to new ideas and beliefs, you need to pay attention to things you might normally ignore. Seek out alternative viewpoints. Read a newspaper whose slant is opposite to your views. Or subscribe to a blog from the other side of the world. If you feel stuck in an enterprise mindset, go to a start-up conference or a hackathon. Seek views that can help you triangulate among multiple perspectives." In a nutshell, do what might be considered diametrically opposed to your current way of thinking.

Daniel Levitin, whom we first met in Chapter 2, provided a unique personal example that reinforces this notion of adding some opposable thinking to your Open Thinking framework. "I once had to replace the roof of my house in Montreal, a city known for punishing winters. My home had a flat roof, so shingles were not possible, and the roofing contractors who worked my neighborhood did all the houses in hot tar and gravel. But on a trip outside of town, I had seen a roof with a smooth, white, rubbery-looking coating, and I started asking around about it. It's called elastomeric, and it has a number of properties that make it better than tar and gravel, and also cheaper over the long run because it also helps to insulate. It took several phone calls, but I found someone who could install it and I was very happy with the results. I consider that a somewhat creative solution, in that it went against the path of least resistance, was relatively unknown, and it took a bit of effort. It's not like I invented my own way of making a roof, but not all creative acts are completely *sui generis*."

As I have discovered, Open Thinkers not only continuously cycle through Creative, Critical, and Applied Thinking, they are unafraid to push their own thinking in a different direction. They see it as the healthier way to operate. When it comes to seeking out a different opinion or viewpoint, they are adventurous. Open Thinkers recognize that one of the easiest ways to fall into Inflexible Thinking is to accept or prove an existing bias. Successful people who employ Open Thinking are cognizant of the detrimental effect confirmation bias can have. It is one thing to be confident, but it is quite another to be ignorantly overconfident.

Dave's feedback and Daniel's story echoed sentiments shared by Marc Kielburger, whom we were first introduced to in Chapter 1. The social enterprise WE, which Marc co-founded with his brother, Craig, got its start in Canada. For several years it was a Canadian-only shop. In particular, its popular WE Day was hosted exclusively in Canadian cities. Marc and his brother felt the WE Day concept could also be successful in the United States. What to do?

"You need to be hands-on, in the trenches, and thinking differently," said Marc. "We had never put on WE Day in places like Minneapolis, Chicago, New York, Los Angeles, or Seattle. While the blueprint was the same, we had to think differently to overcome the obstacles of a different country. Whether it was sponsors, local politicians, the United Nations, and so on, we had to pitch and plan differently than our events in Canada." He also stated that different thinking had to be incorporated into the WE Day model when they decided to enter the United Kingdom, too.

"Our messaging, positioning, and our entire thought process has to be different in the U.S. and the U.K.," said Marc. "Because of different cultural norms, we have to be slightly different in each country. Messaging about credibility is a lot different. In the U.S., for example, we learned that we need to lead with 'As seen on *Oprah* and *60 Minutes*,' whereas in Canada we talk about our work, charities, and the purpose of giving back."

WE Day has had an incredible impact on today's youth. Since its inaugural 2007 extravaganza in Toronto, over 2 million young people have attended various events worldwide, including WE Day Canada on July 2, 2017, on Parliament Hill in Ottawa, celebrating the country's 150th year of Confederation. Tickets are not sold. Students have to earn their way to WE Day through demonstrable acts of giving and citizenship. As for an impact, Marc disclosed that over 80 percent of WE Day attendees go on to volunteer more than 150 hours of time per year. "Thinking differently is not wrong, it's necessary," he added. "We are always looking at the opportunity to collaborate and learn, to think differently, rather than simply to win."

Back to Dave. I asked if he could share an example where his contrarian, Open Thinking methodology helped. "We were pitching to a new client, one of the largest companies in the software business. We knew the problem they were trying to solve and we put our heads together as a team to really think through their problem. When they arrived at our office in St. Louis, we drew out our thinking on a whiteboard and engaged in a long discussion about ideas and options for directions they could take." What was so contrarian? Instead of rehashing what Dave's firm XPlane might have done in the past, they chose to take a look at the problem from square one. They won the business, and Dave had the wherewithal to ask the executive sponsor why they chose his firm over others. They responded, "Everyone else we met with used the time to show us the problems they had solved for others. The implication was that maybe they could do the same for us. But when we met with you, you were already providing value from the first minute, helping us think through and solve our problems. That's why we chose you."

As Dave, Daniel, and Marc help us understand, Open Thinkers are constantly pushing how to do things differently for any given situation. Not only are they open to learning and willing to revisit past decisions and beliefs, they seek out opposing ideologies to improve their overarching tendency. They are not afraid to eliminate any status quo thinking about what might have worked in the past.

Practical, Inclusive, and Open

Brian Scudamore, the CEO of O2E Brands we met earlier, believes many organizations and their employees become trapped by the allure of Applied Thinking. Brian considers an organization's fixation on "just doing" to be a key factor for its potential disengagement and lack of purpose. He also believes if senior leaders actively demonstrate a few key habits of Open Thinking, everyone in the organization will likely be better off. Brian has developed several Open Thinking practices that help him and the employees in his companies to be in a continuous flow of Creative, Critical, and Applied Thinking.

"Monday is my day out of the office," he said. "This is a day where I am thinking through problems, brainstorming on my own, writing notes to myself, ideating, and generally pondering new things." Brian said he might go to several coffee shops in a given day to change the environment so his creativity and decision-making improve. Between Tuesday and Thursday, Brian is back in the office. Friday, however, is treated as a "free day," with Brian off work entirely. It is a day when he is unencumbered by business thinking. "I refuse to check emails; I'm exercising, living life, and enjoying things outside of the office. I find that it gives me the rejuvenated energy needed to be at my best for the next week."

Conductor and music director Tania Miller believes Open Thinking comes down to inclusion. "In my world, I have a programming committee and I believe the orchestra should feel a part of the decision-making process with our programs," she said. "There is a strong hierarchy in the orchestra, a very successful aspect of how we operate. But I want to listen to their ideas, their new programming options, so that everyone feels as though they are leaders of the creativity and decision-making process. Not only is this very helpful to the final outcome, it builds trust." Despite the centuries-old hierarchical structure of an orchestra, Tania's preference is to banish any notion of rigidity. Her style is to include orchestra members in order that everyone has the opportunity to be a part of the Creative and Critical Thinking phases, not solely the playing of an instrument during Applied Thinking.

John Dalla Costa, the author and academic from the previous chapter, suggested the secret to Open Thinking lies in our ability to spend less time fixating on "what to do" than in investing time to understand "why we are doing what we do." John is adamant that Open Thinking is iterative, never complete, and as much a discovery of questions as a realization of answers. His point fits in neatly with the continuously active definition of Open Thinking. For John, it is the asking of questions that helps us to define the *why*. "To think is not to know or to own knowledge," he said, "but to participate in making meaning of what is being experienced and learned." Society's fixation on doing is creating the opposite of an Open Thinker. In John's estimation, we have enabled legions of closed thinkers because of our fixation on "what to do."

His biggest suggestion to improve Open Thinking—to move from solely focusing on the *what* to making more sense of the *why*—comes back to the importance of purpose as we think and take action with others. "Open Thinking begins on the inside, being open to one's humanity, heritage, and hopes. Such interior openness develops attentiveness to responsibility, but also the capacity to forgive one's self for mistakes, so as to extract wisdom and resolve for future growth." Echoing Tania's suggestion that Open Thinking requires the inclusion of others, John believes that Open Thinking requires mutual inclusion. "Open Thinking is not so much an intellectual or intelligence skill as a relational one," he said. "To think openly is to think with others, to be enriched by ideas from others, and to take the social satisfaction from having our ideas contribute to others."

John recommends Open Thinkers demonstrate the following three traits as they work with others throughout the Open Thinking cycle:

- **Courage:** to escape the timidity of what we know to bravely connect the new thinking of others to our own heart and insight.
- **Responsibility:** the ability to respond with integrity and care to new data when working with others.
- **Fairness:** to balance appreciation with critique, and to accept or forgive failures as the cost for the innovation and experimentation.

Mark Mattson, the head of Waterkeeper, also advocates Open Thinking as an inclusive, community-driven mindset. "Over the last few years, I have discovered it's the community that has fueled my learning, my thinking," said Mark. "Capturing their stories, listening to their issues, understanding how they are using the data to improve water quality, beaches, and so on, has paid enormous dividends. For me, Waterkeeper has become a focus where we now want to keep the structure of the community—the map, if you will—alive so that their stories and ideas are shared from one community to the next. Our thinking has become collective thinking." It was another example of how important it is for Open Thinking to be in a continuous cycle, always willing to use the thoughts and ideas of others to improve a future situation.

The Reality of Patience and of Continuous Open Thinking

How patient are you when it comes to Open Thinking? How willing are you to ensure your Open Thinking is continuous? The latter is distinct to multitasking, in that different situations may call for distinctive Open Thinking approaches. Peter Gilmore touched on this notion when he alluded to the different Open Thinking styles he uses when dreaming up a new dish in comparison with working out how to serve that same dish to restaurant patrons. Looked at in its entirety, Open Thinking is a natural part of Peter's culinary repertoire. The musician Kathryn Calder provides us with more insights into this partnership of patience and continuous Open Thinking.

Kathryn is a Canadian singer and songwriter, known for her work as a solo artist, founding the alternative band Immaculate Machine, and being a member of the popular indie band The New Pornographers. "The inspiration for my creativity often comes from hearing something," she said. "The more I listen to music, the more creative I feel. I have also learned to tap into the 'little voice,' a voice in my brain that guides me. Somehow, I subconsciously know that I have to let the process play itself out. I let the voice pass by, letting my brain make decisions. If I stop to think about things too much during the writing or recording process, it can negatively affect the outcome."

When it comes to Open Thinking, Kathryn believes we should heed the advice of actor John Cleese, who is celebrated for his work with the comedy group Monty Python and the British television series *Fawlty Towers*. Cleese argues that people need to be extremely patient if they want to be more creative. He suggests that his own work was more creative and prolific than some of his comic peers because he was often prepared to stick with a problem longer. Citing the 1970s work of psychologist Donald MacKinnon of the University of California at Berkeley, Cleese encourages people to tolerate the discomfort of being idle and letting the thinking process play itself out for much longer periods than might be considered normal. MacKinnon's research shows that Creative Thinking is more fruitful when we are prepared to stomach the discomfort and anxiety of not having solved a problem. Cleese once said, "The most creative people have learned to tolerate that discomfort for much longer. And so, just because they put in more pondering time, their solutions are more creative."

Kathryn believes her Open Thinking mindset is guided by her patience with the process. "It's one of the reasons creativity is hard to unlock for some people," she added. "Half the time you come up with things you don't like, but you should keep going until you get something you do like. It is really uncomfortable sitting still, but it is far more worthwhile—at least for me—to not push through for the sake of completion." As a musician, Kathryn cannot live without the constant cycle of Creative, Critical, and Applied Thinking. Without creativity, there are no songs. Without decision-making, the lyrics and melodies never see the light of day. Without Applied Thinking, the songs are never recorded.

"Writing is a subconscious thing for me," she continued. "When I'm writing a new song, it's typically that I'm trying to work something out, or address something that is bothering me. That is why it works better to be comfortable with being patient. I can only write when I feel the emotion of the situation. My entire creative process allows me to attach to my emotional connectedness, to guide the way through the entire process. And that only happens if I am patient with myself." Kathryn's feedback is akin to the difference between a 100-yard sprint and a marathon. You cannot finish a marathon in the time it takes to run a short sprint. Your mindset must be shaped so that you are patient and prepared to run for hours at a time. A marathon cannot be completed in a handful of seconds. You will reach the finish line, as long as you invest patience into the process.

With her busy schedule, Kathryn's time-management skills are vitally important to her success and her sanity. We are far more successful when we come to grips with the idea that our thinking is ever changing, always in flux. Musicians like Kathryn illustrate this by virtue of their need to be constantly dreaming up new songs, making decisions on their various melodies and musical arrangements, getting into the studio to record them, and then going out and playing them live in front of audiences. Each of these are in fact examples of how Open Thinking is a cycle. Kathryn sheds some light on this with a song of hers called "New Millennium."

"I had written this song that I thought was finished. But after I had played it a few times live, I recognized I was not completely happy with it." Later, she went back into the studio, dreamed up a few different arrangements and lyrics, and re-recorded the song for inclusion as a new single. It was a realization during the live performance— Applied Thinking—that sent her back into another cycle of Creative and Critical Thinking.

"The live part of playing, of getting a song 'concert ready,' sees me change my thinking," she acknowledged. "Although the same general process applies as it does with my writing where I have to try and listen to my inner voice when I'm playing live, I also involve more people. I have to be a different kind of patient. I am involving other musicians during a live show. Although every musician is different, I try to be open to the ideas and opinions of others when playing live. It's more fun."

There is one aspect that Kathryn advises against, something that can affect even the best Open Thinkers. "Even if no one is there,

I am not as open to trying things if I feel I am being judged. I like to be relaxed with the freedom to try something ridiculous. The studio allows me to enter into a place where I can go wherever and whenever I choose. It's a place that is private. I can work through my wacky ideas with absolutely no pressure."

Kathryn teaches us that Open Thinking requires patience and a high level of personal trust, but that we must be comfortable revisiting our ideas even if we are in the midst of Applied Thinking. Furthermore, if we believe we are being constantly scrutinized or judged, it may affect our creativity or our decisions. Put bluntly, being patient, possessing the willingness to cycle through Open Thinking multiple times, and operating in a stress-free environment are some of the most important habits of Open Thinking. The best Open Thinkers really are more mindful than those who are not.

Kathryn captures things ever so well in her song "Take a Little Time:"

> Take a little time, take a little time to find
> Toss me around, feeling the sound
> To see what else there's to find
> Watch a little change, nothing will come to mind
> Though we can't breathe, we could still be
> Silhouettes amplifier.

The Nisga'a Thinking Common Bowl

The Nisga'a people are a First Nations community that has lived in the Nass River Valley of northwestern British Columbia "since time immemorial." There are approximately 2,500 citizens who inhabit this 772-square-mile region, with another 3,500 Nisga'a people living in other parts of Canada. The Nass River Valley region became Nisga'a property as a result of a momentous April 13, 2000, land-claim settlement between the Nisga'a Nation, the Government of British Columbia, and the Government of Canada. The agreement has allowed the Nisga'a to self-govern, the first of its kind in Canada. The Nisga'a

Lisims Government governs the Nisga'a nation, looking out for its traditional and historical roots while paving a path toward the future.

Eva Clayton is the president of the Nisga'a Lisims Government, the first female to ever hold the post. I was curious to see how the Nisga'a, a culture of people who have passed on traditions and customs for centuries, conducted Creative, Critical, and Applied Thinking. "Decision-making is made from a holistic point of view and considers all aspects of the world we live in," she explained. Eva divulged that Ayuuk—the time-honored Nisga'a code that has guided their thinking and actions for years—is what has allowed it to thrive. Ayuuk defines the ancient laws and customs of the Nisga'a people. It informs, guides, and inspires the learning of Nisga'a culture. All decisions of the Nisga'a move forward under the premise of Sayt-K'ilim-Goot, the Nisga'a common bowl philosophy. "We believe we are bound together as one people in all that we do, thus our official branded identity is anchored by the positioning line, 'one heart, one path, one nation.'"

I learned of the Nisga'a in the late 1990s when they were negotiating their land claim. I mentioned the Nisga'a common bowl philosophy in my first book, Flat Army. I believe that any organization operating under the rally cry of "one heart, one path, one nation" must be doing something right. Eva not only referenced Sayt-K'ilim-Goot, she insisted that their way of being is, in fact, tied to their patient and long-term thinking. "Implementation of decisions affects many as relationships are all tied together. Because we are grounded in our Ayuuk, governance and leadership is guided by the philosophy and values of our Ayuuk. There is an ability to find a balance between the philosophy and values of our Ayuuk and the decisions that are needed to be made so action can occur. Decisions are made and disagreements are resolved in a manner that allows consensus to be reached as based on the teachings of the Ayuuk."

I was struck by her use of the word holistic. By definition, holism relates to complete systems as opposed to the analysis or dissection of wholes into parts. The very survival of the Nisga'a Nation requires it to be holistic, to be contemplating itself in totality rather than in fragments. What was truly enlightening, however, was how Eva noted that the Nisga'a's thinking and actions takes into account, well, everything. "Nisga'a are cognizant of the fact that the decisions we make not only affect the lives of Nisga'a citizens but also have an impact on the environment in which we live," she said. "It is recognized that as a Nation under treaty, Nisga'a will continue to evolve and grow and that the effects of decisions have an impact on the whole. It is this holistic approach that lays the foundation for the balance between the cultural values and the advancement the Nation faces. It is the obligation of the individual to determine what their responsibility is, through their lifelong training, and contribute to the Nation. It is through each individual's uniqueness and the collective contributions that the Nation continues to thrive."

The survival of an entire culture rests on its ability to think *and* act holistically. This is the precise definition of Open Thinking. It also nicely encapsulates the Nisga'a, a culture of people who have persevered for centuries. If they are not holistic, they are no more. If they spend too much time—or not enough time—in the three phases of Open Thinking, their people might have been lost. Again, there is a delicate balance between reflection *and* action.

In the first chapter of this book I defined three components that make up Open Thinking: Creative, Critical, and Applied Thinking. We then wove our way through each stage to get to this point. I purposefully left out a definition for Open Thinking until this moment. Why? The Nisga'a Nation helps us put Open Thinking into context.

Open Thinking: a holistic approach of reflection, decision-making, and action to secure an ethical outcome.

In Chapter 1, I urged you to consider three questions as you progressed through the book.

- Do I spend enough time reflecting and dreaming?
- Do I make thorough decisions based on facts and evidence?
- Do I rush to complete an action?

Indeed, these three questions help form the definition of Open Thinking. It took the Nisga'a 113 years to finally settle their land claim. A land claim based on the fact that the Nisga'a were the first owners of the Nass Valley River region. Since time immemorial. The principles of *Sayt-K'ilim-Goot* and of *Ayuuk* have always been at the core of their identity, even as generations came and went. Being of "one heart, one path, one nation" and unified with their holistic thinking habits, the Nisga'a's pursuit of a just, patient, and honorable settlement was testament not only to their culture, but to their Open Thinking. They were undeterred *and* continuously willing to adapt. They were whole. It can be argued that the Nisga'a remained steadfast with their Open Thinking in the quest to finish their objective.

They continued to deal with successive colonial governments to ensure a settlement that would be in the best interest of the Nisga'a Nation. There were over 40 annual conventions that saw the Nation test its patience, its holistic thinking. By 2000, it had broken through, and the Nisga'a Final Agreement was enacted. It had fought, but it had also remained resolute in its Open Thinking. The Nisga'a were unafraid to cycle through Creative, Critical, and Applied Thinking many times over to achieve its goal. "As a modern government we are a teenager," Eva added, "and like our culture, we will continue to evolve to meet the needs of our people."

Sayt-K'ilim-Goot and *Ayuuk* demonstrate that the Nisga'a—and every citizen in its Nation—have a rightful and meaningful place in society. The Nisga'a people believe they are all interdependent, that they need one another in order to thrive and survive. The Nisga'a *are* holistic. Indeed, they *are* a Nation of Open Thinkers. In conclusion, they are an Open Thinking role model for all of us to look up to and learn from.

The Kernel of Open Thinking

The book is nearly complete and I have one final question to ask. Have you wondered why I used a popcorn theme for the front and back covers? This isn't a cookbook, or a snack book for that matter.

Maybe I'm old fashioned but when at home with the family and it happens to be movie night, I like to make popcorn on the stove by using a giant pot full of oil. It may not be the healthiest way to enjoy popcorn, but enjoy it the Pontefracts do!

The process is the same each time I make it. Grab the gigantic "popcorn" pot from the drawer. Drizzle the bottom of it with oil. Turn on the stove and heat up the oil with a couple of kernels placed in the pot to signify when the oil is hot. Once those kernels start to sizzle, dump as many kernels into the pot that will satisfy your audience. Get some bowls ready. When the kernels start to madly pop, dexterity and patience become key. You have to carefully lift open the lid and dump the popped popcorn into the bowls while keeping the unpopped kernels in the pot. Then put the lid back on and place the pot on the stove for a second or even a third round of popping. It can be quite stressful if you lose control, I assure you.

What does my personal example of popcorn have to do with Open Thinking? It's a final metaphor for you to consider.

If you were to eat popcorn kernels right out of the bag or jar, we might liken this to someone rushing to judgment or speeding to action. This is the antithesis of an Open Thinker. We are Inflexible Thinkers. When we lack patience—when we go straight for the kernel—we are doing a disservice to our thinking. It's definitely not recommended for your digestive system either.

If, however, we spend too long cooking the kernels on the stove, something dreadful occurs. Burnt popcorn. When we devote too much time debating our options or never making a decision, the end result is equally as bad as eating kernels straight out of the bag. This too is the antithesis of Open Thinking. It's the mark of Indecisive Thinkers. (And it's simply awful to eat.)

But what if we manage to stir up the energy to put oil and kernels in the pot, only to walk away from the stove out of disinterest? What eventually happens? Fire. Perhaps the kitchen or, worse, the house burns down. When we become disaffected and ignore the need to balance reflection *and* action, we have become Indifferent Thinkers. We are nowhere near Open Thinking. The cleanup is incredibly arduous. The result can be disastrous.

Throughout these pages I hope you have discovered that Open Thinking requires a continual flow of Creative, Critical, and Applied Thinking. Popcorn acts as my closing metaphor. Don't eat the kernels, don't burn it, and please try to prevent a fire. There ought to be a strong balance between reflection *and* action—thus between the three components of Open Thinking—if we are to provide a scrumptious, fluffy, and tasty result. Indeed, dream, decide, do, and repeat.

Hat Tip to the Millinery

As we close out *Open to Think*, let's pay one final visit to Karyn and the team at Lilliput Hats. When I ventured into the shop for the first time, it was without the intention to buy a hat. But the more I got to know Karyn, and the more I saw how this Open Thinking hive was operating, the more I wanted to experience the process for myself.

During a subsequent visit, I asked Karyn if she would make a hat for me—as a paying customer, of course. First, she reminded me that you can't cut corners when making a hat. There is always time for a good millinery pun.

Karyn started by asking about my intentions for the hat. "I'd like to occasionally wear it on stage, when delivering a keynote," I told her. "I might even wear it at formal, personal events," I added. From there we moved into shapes and sizes where Karyn explained the difference between a hat's brim, taper, bond, and crown. Finally, we discussed some of my personal inspirations, which led us to chat about colors, ribbons, feathers, and felts.

She showed me a video of her hats in action. One video contained a commercial that highlighted a bunch of her hats. She also flipped through a few photos of her hats worn by various people. A photo of Gord Downie, lead singer of The Tragically Hip, was shown. "That's pretty neat," I exclaimed in subdued awe. Karyn went to another area of the shop and pulled out the mold used for his hats. I was mightily impressed.

During this part of our conversation, Karyn was clearly in a Creative Thinking moment. She was dreaming about the art of the possible with me, and my hat aspirations. It may have only been 30 minutes or so, but it contained all the elements of Creative Thinking. From there, we moved on to some decisions and the Critical

Thinking phase. The color and brim size were decided. The act of creating the hat began next, a nod to Applied Thinking. Karyn began to
take several measurements of my head. She had me try on 10 different
hats and several molds. All the while, I could tell she had personally
gone back into Creative Thinking because she was asking additional
questions, and her note-taking took on a feverish pitch.

Meanwhile, the other milliners continued to steam, sew, stitch,
and sell hats in other parts of the store. Karyn then went to the very
back of the shop and emerged with another prototype. It was not the
color but the shape of the hat that struck me. Specifically, the crown
and taper in combination with the brim were exactly what I was hoping for. I tried it on, looked in one of several full-length mirrors, and
instantly smiled. So did Karyn.

Having decided on the type of hat and specific shape as well as the
color, it was on to the next stage. We were back in the Creative Thinking phase. Karyn said, "You mentioned you wanted to pay homage to
First Nations, right?" She began looking at a combination of feathers,
ribbons, and stone. "Leave it with me and the team. We'll have it ready
for you in a few days."

I arrived at the shop later that week to pick up my new hat. I was
excited. I had never been part of a custom-hat process before. Between
our conversation on the Monday and the Thursday when I came back
to try it on for the first time, Karyn and the Lilliput Hats team continued to go through Creative, Critical, and Applied Thinking categories.
They dreamed a little more, made a few more decisions, and crafted
what is now my favorite hat in a collection of over 30. Knowing the
high regard I had for Gord Downie, Karyn went the extra mile and
lined the inside of the hat with his writing:

> Done and done
> Night accomplished
> If I had a wish
> I'd wish for more of this

I was touched. The hat was a work of art. Indeed, it was "Music
at Work." Who knew I would learn so much about thinking from a

millinery? To Karyn and the team at Lilliput, keep doing what you're doing. The world could use a little more of your Open Thinking ways. If I had a wish, I'd wish for more of this.

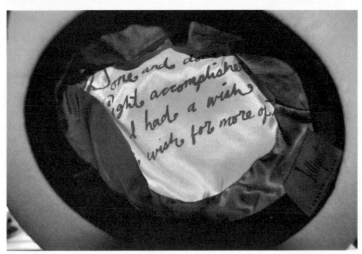

Afterword

You only have one short life. Don't waste a second
of it wishing you were someone else.

CLAIRE PONTEFRACT

W HEN OUR ELDEST daughter, Claire, was six years old, she begged us to let her learn the violin. As parents, we were delighted and promptly found her a violin teacher. Over the ensuing six years, her skills as a violinist grew proportionally to the teachers she had and the number of hours she practiced. The graceful sounds of Bach, Reger, and Tartini would float down the stairs from her bedroom. When friends or relatives gathered for a meal in our home, Claire emerged, eager to put on a performance. By her sixth year of playing violin, Claire had become the concert master in her school's orchestra. When she played in a public recital, judges were quick to praise her talent.

But as her grade six school year wound down in June, and Claire contemplated the summer ahead, she made a decision. "I've been thinking a lot lately, and I have decided to quit violin lessons. I love playing it, but I want to try something different. I hope you're not mad."

At the beginning of summer, Claire borrowed her younger brother's mini acoustic guitar, a Christmas gift that had gone untouched for months. She then started to teach herself how to play guitar, watching YouTube videos, experimenting, practicing.

While going through this autodidactic phase, Claire never performed in front of an audience. She just learned and practiced, alone and for hours at a time. Claire was being creative, choosing and learning chords and songs. She was being critical, analyzing what she was doing well, what needed more work. She was judging and critiquing her own skill development.

Later that year, we flew to Australia for a family holiday. On Christmas Eve, we found ourselves at a restaurant in Byron Bay, where they were hosting an "open mic" night. As we waited for our desserts to arrive, Claire surprised us all when she approached the stage, volunteering to perform.

"Umm, hi, I'm Claire," she said into the microphone. "My family and I are here from Canada on holiday. I thought it would be a good time to play a song. I've never done this before, I've never played guitar in front of a live audience, so here goes." She then launched into a version of "Grow Old With Me" by Tom Odell. Needless to say, we clapped like mad at the end of her performance. Later, I asked Claire a simple question. "What did it feel like when you went on stage in Byron Bay, playing guitar in front of people for the first time?"

Her answer was telling. "I was excited, a little scared, but I also felt a sense of accomplishment. I had been working on it for six months and I guess I felt confident enough to play in front of strangers. It was fun. You should have seen the look on your face. Oh, and I got an extra dessert."

Ever since that night in Byron Bay, Claire has continued to demonstrate the three stages of Open Thinking, the cyclical nature of thinking we have discovered throughout this book. These days she is thinking about new songs to play, learning new chords, deciphering whether or not her playing is up to snuff, and picking her spots to sing and strum the new songs in public settings. She now plays her guitar around family campfires, at parties with our friends, at school, in chapel, and she even plays to family members scattered across the world on Skype or FaceTime. In 2017 she played both at a funeral and a wedding. Recently she has added the ukulele to her repertoire.

Open to Think is about the never-ending and cyclical journey of dreaming, deciding, and doing. We are only as good as our ability to exhibit Creative, Critical, and Applied Thinking. We must balance reflection with action, always. Claire's story, while deeply personal to me, illustrates the beauty of the *Open to Think* journey.

Keep open. Keep thinking. Keep Open Thinking.

Quod erat demonstrandum.

TEN ESSENTIAL GUIDELINES FOR OPEN THINKING*

1. Time is a crucial component of thinking, for anything and everything can go wrong based on your inappropriate use of it.

2. Do not reflect to the point of impairment, for only the single-minded dreamer remains at the start line.

3. Take action only when deemed appropriate, for it is the foolish who rush blindly into completing an objective.

4. Be flexible with your verdicts, revisit decisions when necessary, for there is no chance for happiness when being dogmatic.

5. Do not hold thoughts solely in your head, for if you do they will undoubtedly be lost.

6. Be organized and prepared, for the scatterbrained can leave a trail of confusion.

7. Find your contentment in periodic breaks rather than with steadfast busyness, for, if you value progress as you should, the former unleashes better results than the latter.

8. Do not allow a dearth of information or facts to act as an excuse, for negligence to seek out the truth lies at the heart of your indifference.

9. Be deliberately focused on what matters most in the moment, for you squander the moment when you succumb to the allure of distractions.

10. Open Thinkers continuously dream, decide, and do, for it is those who close themselves off that suffer the ignominy of regret.

* An homage to Bertrand Russell

REFERENCES

INTRODUCTION

Einstein, Albert. 1946. "Atomic Education Urged by Einstein." *New York Times*, May 25, 1946.

Frost, R. 1906. "The Trial by Existence." *Independent*, 61, (January 1): 3019.

Frost, R., & Untermeyer, L. (commentary). 2008. *The Road Not Taken: A Selection of Robert Frost's Poems*. New York, NY: St. Martin's Griffin.

Lewandowsky, S., Ecker, U.K.H., Seifert, C.M., Schwarz, N., & Cook, J. 2012. "Misinformation and Its Correction." *Psychological Science in the Public Interest*, 13, 3, (September 17): 106–31.

Orr, D. 2016. *The Road Not Taken: Finding America in the Poem Everyone Loves and Almost Everyone Gets Wrong*. New York, NY: Penguin Group USA.

Puritt, Jeffrey. 2015. "Marinating in the moment" in conversation with the author.

The Road Less Traveled. Accessed on February 17, 2017, in Wikipedia.

CHAPTER 1: COGITO ERGO SUM

Ansoff, H. Igor. 1965. *Corporate Strategy: An Analytic Approach to Business Policy for Growth and Expansion*. New York, NY: McGraw-Hill.

Brown, B. 2012. *Daring Greatly: How the Courage to be Vulnerable Transforms the Way We Live, Love, Parent, and Lead*. New York, NY: Gotham Books.

Carnegie, D., & O'Reilly, T. 2017. *How to Win Friends and Influence People*. New York, NY: Collins.

DiSalvo, D., & Herbert, W. 2014. *What Makes Your Brain Happy and Why You Should Do the Opposite*. Amherst, NY: Prometheus Books.

D'Souza, S., & Renner, D. 2016. *Not Knowing: The Art of Turning Uncertainty into Opportunity*. Lid Editorial.

Duhigg, C. 2012. *The Power of Habit: Why We Do What We Do in Life and Business*. New York, NY: Random House.

Economic Policy Institute. 2016. "Top Charts of 2016 Show There's Still Work to Do to Boost the Incomes and Wages of Working People." Press release, December 22, 2016. http://www.epi.org/press/top-charts-of-2016/.

Greengard, Samuel. 2009. *Communications of the* ACM, 52, 7, (July): 18–19. 10.1145/1538788.1538796.

Helps, Lisa. 2017. In conversation with the author.

Kahneman, D. 2011. *Thinking, Fast and Slow*. New York, NY: Farrar, Straus and Giroux.

Kerber, Ross. 2016. "CEO-Worker Pay Gap Stays Wide Despite Wage Hikes: Unions." Reuters, May 17, 2016.

Kielburger, Marc. 2016. In conversation with the author.

Lazonick, W., & Hopkins, M. 2016. "Corporate Executives Are Making Way More Money Than Anybody Reports." *Atlantic*, September 15, 2016. http://www.theatlantic.com/business/archive/2016/09/executives-making-way-more-than-reported/499850/.

Leski, Kyna. 2016. In conversation with the author.

Moore, Greg. 2017. In conversation with the author.

Nastasi, Alison. 2016. "How Long Does It Really Take to Break a Habit?" September 21, 2016. http://www.hopesandfears.com/hopes/now/question/216479-how-long-does-it-really-take-to-break-a-habit.

Nichols, Tom. 2017. *The Death of Expertise: The Campaign Against Established Knowledge and Why It Matters*. New York: Oxford University Press.

Pontefract, D. 2013. *Flat Army: Creating a Connected and Engaged Organization*. John Wiley & Sons. Republished 2018 Figure 1 Publishing.

Pontefract, D. 2016. *The Purpose Effect: Building Meaning in Yourself, Your Role, and Your Organization*. Boise, ID: Elevate Publishing. Republished 2018 Figure 1 Publishing.

Port Arthur News. 1974. "Ali Wants Both Joe, Foreman at Same Time (UPI news service)." Quote Page 11, Column 3, (November 30). Port Arthur, Texas.

Sandberg, Sheryl. 2015. Facebook, June 3, 2015. https://www.facebook.com/sheryl/posts/10155617891025177:0.

Schwartz, B. 2016. *The Paradox of Choice: Why More Is Less: How the Culture of Abundance Robs Us of Satisfaction*. New York, NY: Ecco Press.

Shirky, C. 2010. *Cognitive Surplus: Creativity and Generosity in a Connected Age*. New York, NY: Penguin Press.

Society of Actuaries. 2016. "The Society of Actuaries Publishes Annual Update to Mortality Improvement Scale." October 20, 2016. https://www.soa.org/press-releases/2016/soa-publishes-mortality-improvement-scale-update/.

Toffler, A. 1981. *The Third Wave*. New York, NY: Bantam Books.

The website for The Tragically Hip can be found at http://www.thehip.com.

The WE website can be found at https://www.we.org/.

World Health Organization. 2012. "Depression: A Global Crisis." October 10, 2012. http://www.who.int/mental_health/management/depression/wfmh_paper_ depression_wmhd_2012.pdf.

CHAPTER 2: AT THE LONELY END OF THE THINK

Adobe. 2016. "Work in Progress." PowerPoint presentation, May 2016. http://www.adobe.com/content/dam/acom/en/aboutadobe/pdfs/Future-of-Work-2016.pdf.

Aon Hewitt. 2016. "Trends in Global Employee Engagement." http://www.aon. com/human-capital-consulting/thought-leadership/talent/2016-Trends-in-Global-Employee-Engagement.jsp.

Baer, D. 2017. "Kahneman: Your Cognitive Biases Act Like Optical Illusions." *New York Magazine*, January 13, 2017.

Baumeister, R.F., Bratslavsky, E., Finkenauer, C., & Vohs, K.D. 2001. "Bad is Stronger than Good." *Review of General Psychology*, 5, 323–70.

Brand, S. 2008. *Clock of the Long Now: Time and Responsibility.* New York, NY: Basic Books.

Campbell, J. 1949. *The Hero with a Thousand Faces.* Princeton, NJ: Princeton University Press.

Choi, J.N., Anderson, T.A., & Veillette, A. 2009. "Contextual Inhibitors of Employee Creativity in Organizations: The Insulating Role of Creative Ability." *Group & Organization Management*, 34 (3), 330–57.

Elangovan, Elango. 2015. In conversation with the author.

Elop, Stephen. 2011. "Full Text: Nokia CEO Stephen Elop's 'Burning Platform' Memo." *Wall Street Journal*, February 9, 2011. http://blogs.wsj.com/ tech-europe/2011/02/09/full-text-nokia-ceo-stephen-elops-burning-platform-memo/.

FAAS Foundation. 2017. "Mind the Workplace." Retrieved on November 12, 2017. https://www.mentalhealthamerica.net/sites/default/files/Mind%20the%20 workplace%20-%20MHA%20workplace%20Health%20survey%202017%20 FINAL.pdf.

Gallup poll. 1998. "History Shows Presidential Job Approval Ratings Can Plummet Rapidly." Gallup, February 11, 1998. http://www.gallup.com/ poll/4258/history-shows-presidential-job-approval-ratings-can-plummet-rapidly.aspx.

Gallup poll. 2016. "U.S. Employee Engagement Reaches New High in March." Gallup, April 13, 2016. http://www.gallup.com/poll/190622/employee-engagement-reaches-new-high-march.aspx.

IBM. 2016. "Redefining Competition: The CEO Point of View." http://www-935.ibm.com/services/c-suite/study/studies/ceo-study/.

ICIMS. 2016. "A Snapshot of Competition for Talent in the U.S." Retrieved on
    October 4, 2017. https://www.icims.com/sites/www.icims.com/files/public/
    A_Snapshot_Of_Competition_For_Talent%20Final_0.pdf.
Jordan, Eric. 2016. In conversation with the author.
Jung, C.G. 1969. *Phenomenology of the Spirit in Fairy Tales* (R.F.C. Hull, trans.). In
    H. Read et al. (series eds.), The Collected Works of C.G. Jung (Vol. 9 pt. 1,
    2nd. ed., 207–54). Princeton, NJ: Princeton University Press. (Original work
    published 1948).
Kahneman, D., & Tversky, A. 1979. "Prospect Theory: An Analysis of Decision
    under Risk." *Econometrica*, 47, 2, (March): 263–92.
Kahneman, D., & Tversky, A. 2003. *Choices, Values, and Frames.* Cambridge:
    Cambridge University Press, 372.
Lee, Y. 2016. "Samsung Says Galaxy Note 7 Recall to Cost at Least $5.3 Billion."
    Toronto Star, October 14, 2016. https://www.thestar.com/business/2016/10/14/
    samsung-says-galaxy-note-7-recall-to-cost-at-least-53-billion.html.
Levitin, Daniel. 2016. In conversation with the author.
The Long Now website can be found at http://longnow.org/about/.
Miettinen, A. 2013. "HS:n laaja Stephen Elop -artikkeli syyskuussa 2013: Mies,
    joka teki myyjän työn." September 29, 2013. http://www.hs.fi/sunnuntai/
    art-2000002677474.html?ref=hs-hitaat-e-1.
Nykänen, Pekka, & Salminen, Merina. 2014. "Operation Elop." Helsinki: Teos.
Oldham, G.R., & Cummings, A. 1996. "Employee Creativity: Personal and
    Contextual Factors at Work." *Academy of Management Journal*, 39(3), 607–34.
    doi:10.2307/256657.
Parrey, D. 2014. "Six Talent Practices that Boost Employee Engagement and
    Market Performance." i4cp, January 22, 2014. https://www.i4cp.com/
    trendwatchers/2014/01/22/six-talent-practices-that-boost-employee-
    engagement-and-market-performance.
Rossi, J. 2013. "Elop Was Second Choice as Nokia CEO." WSJ (blog),
    October 17, 2013. http://blogs.wsj.com/tech-europe/2013/10/17/
    elop-second-choice-as-nokia-ceo/?mod=rss_Europe_Technology.
Ruiz, Karyn. 2016. In conversation with the author.
Skypek, T. 2013. "In Defense of Net Assessment." *The National Interest*, November
    16, 2013. http://nationalinterest.org/commentary/defense-net-assessment-9411.
Smallwood, J., & Schooler, J. W. 2015. "The Science of Mind Wandering:
    Empirically Navigating the Stream of Consciousness." *Annual Review of
    Psychology*, 66, (January 1): 487–518.
Starkey, S., Hanks, T., Rapke, J. (producers), & Zemeckis, R. (director). 2002.
    Cast Away [Motion Picture]. United States of America: 20th Century Fox
    Home Entertainment.

Suoninen, S. 2014. "Elop's Nokia 'Golden Parachute' Swells to $33 Million."
    Reuters, April 30, 2014. http://www.reuters.com/article/
    us-nokia-ceo-payout-idUSBREA3T0KD20140430.
World Economic Forum. 2016. "The Future of Jobs." World Economic Forum,
    January 18, 2016. https://www.weforum.org/reports/the-future-of-jobs.

CHAPTER 3: COME TO THINK OF IT
Amabile, T.M. 1996. *Creativity in Context*. Boulder, CO: Westview Press.
Baror, S., & Bar, M. 2016. "Associative Activation and Its Relation to Exploration
    and Exploitation in the Brain." *Psychological Science*, 27, 6, (June 1): 776–89.
Biography: Joel Plaskett. 2016. Billboard. Retrieved on July 15, 2017.
    http://www.billboard.com/artist/304862/joel-plaskett/biography.
Catmull, E. 2008. "How Pixar Fosters Collective Creativity." *Harvard Business
    Review*, September 2008.
Collins, J., & Porras, J. 1994. "Built To Last: Successful Habits of Visionary
    Companies." *HarperBusiness*, 113.
Desjardins, Mike. 2016. In conversation with the author.
Downie, Gord. 2007. In conversation with the author.
Duncker, K. 1945. "On Problem Solving." *Psychological Monographs*, 58(270).
Durgahee, A. 2006. "Richard Branson Shares His Travel Tips." CNN, May 5, 2006.
    http://edition.cnn.com/2006/TRAVEL/04/25/branson.tips/.
Guth, R. 2005. "In Secret Hideaway, Bill Gates Ponders Microsoft's Future."
    Wall Street Journal, March 28, 2005. https://www.wsj.com/articles/
    SB111196625830690477.
Hagstrom, R.G. 2005. *The Warren Buffett Way*. Hoboken, NJ: John Wiley.
Holmes, R. 2016. "The One Skill Too Many CEOs Lack." *Fortune*, March 20, 2016.
IBM. 2016. "Redefining Competition: The CEO Point of View." Retrieved on
    January 14, 2017. http://www-935.ibm.com/services/c-suite/study/studies/
    ceo-study/.
Kielburger, Marc. 2016. In conversation with the author.
Levinthal, D.A., & March, J. G. 1993. "The Myopia of Learning." *Strategic
    Management Journal*, 1495–5112.
Lindgren, A., Glanzman, L.S., & Johnson, F.L. 1950. *Pippi Longstocking*. New York,
    NY: Viking Press.
Martin, R. L. 2007. *The Opposable Mind: How Successful Leaders Win Through Integrative
    Thinking*. Boston, MA: Harvard Business School Press.
McAfee, A. 2009. *Enterprise 2.0: New Collaborative Tools for Your Organization's Toughest
    Challenges*. Boston, MA: Harvard Business Press.
McDermott, B. 2011. "Great Leaders Teach and Don't Leave People Behind"
    [Video Interview]. Skillsoft Ireland Limited.

McLuhan, E., & Zingrone, F. 1997. *Essential McLuhan.* London: Taylor and Francis.

Mintzberg, H. 1987. "Crafting Strategy." *Harvard Business Review,* July–August, 1987.

Moore, Karl. 2017. In conversation with the author.

Mueller, J. 2017. *Creative Change: Why We Resist It … How We Can Embrace It.* New York, NY: Mariner Books.

Nin, A. 1983. *The Early Diary of Anaïs Nin: Volume three.* New York, NY: Mariner Books.

Patel, Sameer. 2017. In conversation with the author.

Plaskett, Joel. 2017. In conversation with the author.

Ruiz, Karyn. 2016. In conversation with the author.

Scudamore, Brian. 2017. In conversation with the author.

Senge, P.M. 1990. *The Fifth Discipline: The Art and Practice of the Learning Organization.* New York, NY: Doubleday/Currency.

Shen, L. 2017. "Warren Buffett's Net Worth Has Risen $6.4 Billion Since 'Trump Rally.'" *Fortune,* January 31, 2017. http://fortune.com/2017/01/31/warren-buffett-net-worth-trump-rally/.

Vernimmen, T. 2016. "Where Creativity Comes From." *Scientific American,* September 16, 2016. https://www.scientificamerican.com/article/where-creativity-comes-from/.

Wettläufer, Brianna. 2016. In conversation with the author.

Wharton School. 2014. "Can Creativity Be Taught?" *Knowledge@Wharton,* August 27, 2014. http://knowledge.wharton.upenn.edu/article/can-creativity-be-taught/.

CHAPTER 4: THINK HOLE

APA. 2017. "APA's Survey Finds Constantly Checking Electronic Devices Linked to Significant Stress for Most Americans." February 23, 2017. http://www.apa.org/news/press/releases/2017/02/checking-devices.aspx.

APA. 2017. "Stress in America." February 23, 2017. http://www.apa.org/news/press/releases/stress/2017/technology-social-media.PDF.

Argyris, C., & Schön, D.A. 1974. *Theory in Practice: Increasing Professional Effectiveness.* San Francisco, CA: Jossey-Bass.

Barr, N., Pennycook, G., Stolz, J., & Fugelsang, J. 2015. "The Brain in Your Pocket: Evidence that Smartphones are Used to Supplant Thinking." *Computers in Human Behavior,* 48, 473.

Carr, N.G. 2011. *The Shallows: What the Internet is Doing to Our Brains.* New York, NY: W.W. Norton.

Carreyrou, J. 2015. "Hot Startup Theranos Has Struggled with Its Blood-Test Technology." *Wall Street Journal,* October 16, 2015. https://www.wsj.com/articles/theranos-has-struggled-with-blood-tests-1444881901.

Carreyrou, J. 2016. "Theranos Whistleblower Shook the Company—And His Family." *Wall Street Journal*, November 17, 2016.

Centres for Medicare & Medicaid Services. 2016. "Important Notice." Department of Health and Human Services, San Francisco, January 25, 2016. https://cdn2.vox-cdn.com/uploads/chorus_asset/file/5969923/Theranos_Inc_Cover_Letter_01-25-2016.0.pdf.

Consumer Financial Protection Bureau. 2016. "Consumer Financial Protection Bureau Fines Wells Fargo $100 Million for Widespread Illegal Practice of Secretly Opening Unauthorized Accounts." Consumer Financial Protection Bureau Web page, September 8, 2016. https://www.consumerfinance.gov/about-us/newsroom/consumer-financial-protection-bureau-fines-wells-fargo-100-million-widespread-illegal-practice-secretly-opening-unauthorized-accounts/.

Duhaime-Ross, A. 2016. "U.S. Government Says Theranos Lab Poses 'Immediate Jeopardy to Patient Safety'." *The Verge*, January 27, 2016. http://www.theverge.com/2016/1/27/10853340/government-says-theranos-lab-poses-immediate-threat-to-public-safety.

Eliot, T.S. 2014. *Four Quartets*. New York, NY: Houghton Mifflin Harcourt.

Festinger, L. 1962. *A Theory of Cognitive Dissonance*. Palo Alto, CA: Stanford University Press.

Festinger, Leon, & Carlsmith, James M. 1959. "Cognitive Consequences of Forced Compliance." *Journal of Abnormal and Social Psychology*, 58, 203–10.

Glazer, E., & Rexrode, C. 2016. "Wells Fargo CEO Defends Bank Culture, Lays Blame With Bad Employees." *Wall Street Journal*, September 13, 2016. http://www.wsj.com/articles/wells-fargo-ceo-defends-bank-culture-lays-blame-with-bad-employees-1473784452.

Goleman, D. 2013. *Focus: The Hidden Driver of Excellence*. New York, NY: Bloomsbury.

Herper, M. 2016. "From $4.5 Billion to Nothing: Forbes Revises Estimated Net Worth of Theranos Founder Elizabeth Holmes." *Forbes*, June 1, 2016. https://www.forbes.com/sites/matthewherper/2016/06/01/from-4-5-billion-to-nothing-forbes-revises-estimated-net-worth-of-theranos-founder-elizabeth-holmes/.

Holmes, E. 2016. "An Open Letter From Elizabeth Holmes." Theranos website, October 5, 2016. https://news.theranos.com/2016/10/05/an-open-letter-elizabeth-holmes/.

Kushlev, K., & Dunn, E. W. 2015. "Checking Email Less Frequently Reduces Stress." *Computers in Human Behavior*, 43, 220–28.

The Lord Mayor's Show website can be found at https://lordmayorsshow.london/day/pageantmaster.

Martin, R.L. 2007. *The Opposable Mind: How Successful Leaders Win Through Integrative Thinking*. Boston, MA: Harvard Business School Press.

Maynard Keynes, J. 1963. *Essays in Persuasion*. New York, NY: W. W. Norton & Co., 358–73.

McCord, P. 2014. "How Netflix Reinvented HR." *Harvard Business Review*, January 1, 2014.

McElwee, J. 2016. "Francis Tells U.S. Catholics to Vote Their Conscience in November Election." NCR Online, October 2, 2016. https://www.ncronline. org/news/vatican/francis-tells-us-catholics-vote-their-conscience-november-election.

McSpadden, K. 2015. "You Now Have a Shorter Attention Span Than a Goldfish." *Time*, May 13, 2015. http://time.com/3858309/attention-spans-goldfish/.

Microsoft. https://advertising.microsoft.com/en/wwdocs/user/display/cl/ researchreport/31966/en/microsoft-attention-spans-research-report.pdf.

The Netflix website can be found at https://jobs.netflix.com/life-at-netflix.

Newport, C. 2016. *Deep Work: Rules for Focused Success in a Distracted World*. New York, NY: Grand Central Publishing.

Plaskett, Joel. 2016. In conversation with the author.

Plato, & Scully, S. 2003. *Plato's Phaedrus*. Newburyport, MA: Focus Pub./ R. Pullins Co.

Reid, Dominic. 2017. In conversation with the author.

Ring, T., Salkin, R., & Boda, S. 1996. *International Dictionary of Historic Places: Southern Europe*. Routledge, 66.

Ruiz, Karyn. 2016. In conversation with the author.

Stross, R. 2016. "Don't Blame Silicon Valley for Theranos." *New York Times*, April 27, 2016.

The Examiner. 1710. Number 15, (Article by Jonathan Swift). November 2 to November 9, 1710. Quote Page 2, Column 1, Printed for John Morphew, near Stationers-Hall, London.

Waterloo News. 2015. "Reliance on Smartphones Linked to Lazy Thinking." March 5, 2015. Retrieved from https://uwaterloo.ca/news/news/ reliance-smartphones-linked-lazy-thinking.

Weaver, C. 2017. "Second Theranos Lab Failed U.S. Inspection." *Wall Street Journal*, January 17, 2017.

The Wells Fargo websites can be found at https://www.wellsfargo.com/about/ corporate/vision-and-values/our-values/; https://www.wellsfargo.com/about/ corporate/vision-and-values/our-culture; https://www08.wellsfargomedia. com/assets/pdf/about/press/2017/january-customer-activity.pdf.

WTOE 5 News. 2016. "Pope Francis Shocks World, Endorses Donald Trump for President, Releases Statement." Way Back Machine, July 10, 2016. https://web.archive.org/web/20161115024211/http://wtoe5news.com/us-election/pope-francis-shocks-world-endorses-donald-trump-for-president-releases-statement/.

CHAPTER 5: GREAT MINDS DON'T THINK ALIKE

Abraham Lincoln's first inaugural address (March 4, 1861) can be accessed at http://avalon.law.yale.edu/19th_century/lincoln1.asp.

The APA Delphi Report. 1990. "Critical Thinking: A Statement of Expert Consensus for Purposes of Educational Assessment and Instruction." ERIC Doc. NO.: ED 315 423.

Atlassian. https://www.atlassian.com/time-wasting-at-work-infographic.

Bain & Company. 2014. *Managing Your Scarcest Resource: Time Management Study and Impact on Organizations.*

Berkshire Hathaway letter. http://www.berkshirehathaway.com/letters/1996.html.

Bevelin, P. 2013. *Seeking Wisdom: From Darwin to Munger.* Malmö, Sweden: PCA Publications.

Birkinshaw, J., & Cohen, J. 2013. "Make Time for the Work That Matters (Digest Summary)." *Harvard Business Review,* 91, 1, (September): 2–5.

Bungay, S. 2012. *The Art of Action: How Leaders Close the Gaps Between Plans, Actions and Results.* London, UK: Nicholas Brealey.

Condell, B., & Zabecki, D. T. 2009. *On the German Art of War: Truppenführung.* Mechanicsburg, PA: Stackpole Books.

De Smet, A., Lackey, G., & Weiss, L. 2017. "Untangling Your Organization's Decision Making." June 2017. http://www.mckinsey.com/business-functions/organization/our-insights/untangling-your-organizations-decision-making.

Devine, Allen. 2016. In conversation with the author.

Drucker, P.F. 2004. "What Makes an Effective Executive." *Harvard Business Review,* 82, 6, (January 1): 58–63.

Facione, Peter A. 1990. *Critical Thinking: A Statement of Expert Consensus for Purposes of Educational Assessment and Instruction.* Newark, Del: APA.

Galloway, Alison. 2017. In conversation with the author.

Glaser, Edward M. 1941. *An Experiment in the Development of Critical Thinking.* Teacher's College, Columbia University.

Gokhale, A.A. 1995. "Collaborative Learning Enhances Critical Thinking." *Journal of Technology Education,* 7, 1, (January 1): 22–30.

Google Books. https://books.google.com/intl/en/googlebooks/about/index.html.

Google Search Help. https://support.google.com/websearch/answer/2466433?hl=eN&visit_id=1-636259749362819857-941055816&rd=1.

Gore, A. 2007. "Al Gore: The Nobel Peace Prize 2007: Nobel Lecture." December 10, 2007. Oslo: Nobel Foundation.

Hinchcliffe, Dion. 2017. In conversation with the author.

Learning Forward. https://learningforward.org/who-we-are.

Levitin, Daniel. 2016. In conversation with the author.

Makerspace Playbook. 2013. San Francisco, CA: Maker Media.

Mark, G., Gudith, D., & Klocke, U. 2008. "The Cost of Interrupted Work: More Speed and Stress." *Chi Conference*, 1, (January 1): 107–10.

NMC. 2015. "NMC Horizon Report: 2015 K-12 Edition." http://cdn.nmc.org/media/2015-nmc-horizon-report-k12-EN.pdf.

Perry, James. 2016. In conversation with the author.

The Promoting and Assessing Critical Thinking website can be found at https://uwaterloo.ca/centre-for-teaching-excellence/teaching-resources/teaching-tips/developing-assignments/cross-discipline-skills/promoting-assessing-critical-thinking.

The Radicati Group. 2017. "Email Statistics Report, 2017–2021 – Executive Summary." March 2017. https://www.radicati.com/wp/wp-content/uploads/2017/01/Email-Statistics-Report-2017-2021-Executive-Summary.pdf.

Reid, Dominic. 2017. In conversation with the author.

Ruiz, Karyn. 2016. In conversation with the author.

Stangel, Luke. 2016. "John Donahoe: Dump the Myth of the High Achiever." November 3, 2016. https://www.gsb.stanford.edu/insights/john-donahoe-dump-myth-high-achiever.

Stewart, James. 2017. In conversation with the author.

Vatican News. http://www.vaticannews.va/en/pope/news/2018-01/pope-world-communications-day-message-2018-truth-journalism-fake.html.

Way Back Machine. https://archive.org/web/.

WorldCat. http://www.worldcat.org/whatis/default.jsp.

CHAPTER 6: SOONER THAN YOU THINK

Bar-Eli, M., Azar, O. H., Ritov, I., Keidar-Levin, Y., & Schein, G. 2007. "Action Bias Among Elite Soccer Goalkeepers: The Case of Penalty Kicks." *Journal of Economic Psychology*, 28, 5, (January 1): 606.

Bergin, C. 2007. "Remembering the Mistakes of Challenger." January 28, 2007. https://www.nasaspaceflight.com/2007/01/remembering-the-mistakes-of-challenger/.

Bloomgarden, K. 2016. "How Saying 'No' Can Actually Motivate Your Team." *Fortune*, June 2, 2016. http://fortune.com/2016/06/02/leadership-teams-how-to-say-no/.

Bruch, H., & Ghoshal, S. 2002. "Beware the Busy Manager." *Harvard Business Review*, 80, 2, (January 1): 62–9.

Chaplin, C. (producer and director). 1936. *Modern Times* [Motion Picture]. United States of America: United Artists.

Clark, E. 2011. "The Shift in Leadership." February 17, 2011. https://www.td.com/about-tdbfg/corporate-information/thought-leadership/speech.jsp?id=50.

De Bono, Edward. 1981. *Edward de Bono's Atlas of Management Thinking*. London, UK: Temple Smith.

Duarte, N., & Sanchez, P. 2016. *Illuminate: Ignite Change Through Speeches, Stories, Ceremonies, and Symbols.* New York, NY: Portfolio/Penguin.

Entwistle, D. 2010. TELUS Leadership Philosophy.

Funahashi, S. 2001. "Neuronal Mechanisms of Executive Control by the Prefrontal Cortex." *Neuroscience Research,* 39, 2, (January 1): 147–65.

Hockey, Tim. 2016. In conversation with the author.

Hougaard, R., Carter, J., & Coutts, G. 2016. *One Second Ahead: Enhance Your Performance at Work with Mindfulness.* Basingstoke, UK: Palgrave Macmillan.

Kirby, J. 2014. "Why Businesspeople Won't Stop Using that Gretzky Quote." Accessed September 24, 2014. http://www.macleans.ca/economy/business/why-business-people-wont-stop-using-that-gretzky-quote/.

Lamarche, Denise. 2016. In conversation with the author.

Lezak, M.D. 1982. "The Problem of Assessing Executive Functions." *International Journal of Psychology,* 17, (January 1): 281–97.

Macdonnell, D. 1798. *Monthly Review,* 467.

McKeown, G. 2014. *Essentialism: The Disciplined Pursuit of Less.* New York, NY: Crown Business.

McRaney, D. 2014. *You Are Now Less Dumb: How to Conquer Mob Mentality, How to Buy Happiness, and All the Other Ways to Outsmart Yourself.* New York, NY: Gotham Books.

Medina, J. 2008. *Brain Rules: 12 Principles for Surviving and Thriving at Work, Home, and School.* Seattle, WA: Pear Press.

Nyhan, B., & Reifler, J. 2010. "When Corrections Fail: The Persistence of Political Misperceptions." *Political Behavior.* Springer. 32, 2, (June): 303–30.

Pascal, B. 2016. *Pascal's Pensees.* Lanham: Dancing Unicorn Books.

Patel, Sameer. 2017. In conversation with the author.

Report of the Presidential Commission on the Space Shuttle Challenger Accident can be found at https://history.nasa.gov/rogersrep/v1p252.htm.

Ruiz, Karyn. 2016. In conversation with the author.

Seneca, L.A., Lipsius, J., Lodge, T., Stansby, W., Hole, W., Ellesmere, T.E., Prince, C.L., et al. English Printing Collection (Library of Congress). 1614. *The workes of Lucius Annaeus Seneca, both morrall and naturall.* London: Printed by William Stansby.

Sull, D., Homkes, R., & Sull, C. 2015. "Why Strategy Execution Unravels— and What to Do About It." *Harvard Business Review,* (January 1): 1–10.

TELUS annual results can be found at http://about.telus.com/investors/annualreport2016/?lang=en.

Wansink, B., Painter, J.E., & North, J. 2005. "Bottomless Bowls: Why Visual Cues of Portion Size May Influence Intake." *Obesity Research,* 13, 1, (January 31): 93–100.

Zelazo, P. 2010. "Executive Function Part One: What is Executive Function?" May 28, 2010. http://www.aboutkidshealth.ca/En/News/Series/ExecutiveFunction/Pages/Executive-Function-Part-One-What-is-executive-function.aspx.

CHAPTER 7: YOU HAVE ANOTHER THINK COMING

Becher, Jonathan. 2017. In conversation with the author.

Boyatzis, R. 2012. "Neuroscience and the Link Between Inspirational Leadership and Resonant Relationships." *Ivey Business Journal*, (January/February). http://iveybusinessjournal.com/publication/neuroscience-and-the-link-between-inspirational-leadership-and-resonant-relationships-2/.

Boyatzis, R.E., Passarelli, A.M., Koenig, K., Lowe, M., Mathew, B., Stoller, J.K., & Phillips, M. 2012. "Examination of the Neural Substrates Activated in Memories of Experiences with Resonant and Dissonant Leaders." *Leadership Quarterly*, 23, 2, (January 1): 259–72.

Brockman, A. 2017. "Argentine Climber Survived 4 days on Mount Logan with Thoughts of Love and Family." May 6, 2017. http://www.cbc.ca/news/canada/north/natalia-martinez-survival-mountain-1.4103171.

Dalla Costa, John. 2017. In conversation with the author.

The DDI website can be found at http://www.ddiworld.com/hirezleadership.

Della Cava, M. 2017. "Microsoft's Satya Nadella is Counting on Culture Shock to Drive Growth." *USA Today*, February 20, 2017. https://www.usatoday.com/story/tech/news/2017/02/20/microsofts-satya-nadella-counting-culture-shock-drive-growth/98011388/.

Diamond, A. 2014. "Executive Functions: Insights into Ways to Help More Children Thrive." *Zero to Three*, 35, 2, (November): 9–17.

Dishman, L. 2016. "Here's the Email Kind Snacks CEO sent to Staff About Trump's Win." *Fast Company*, November 10, 2016. https://news.fastcompany.com/heres-the-email-kind-snacks-ceo-sent-to-staff-about-trumps-win-4024619.

Drucker, P. 1967. *The Effective Executive*. Oxford, UK: Butterworth-Heinemann.

Duckworth, A. 2016. *Grit: Why Passion and Resilience are the Secrets to Success*. New York, NY: Simon & Schuster.

Dutton, J.E., Workman, K.M., & Hardin, A.E. 2014. "Compassion at Work." *Annual Review of Organizational Psychology and Organizational Behavior*, 1, 1, (March 21): 277–304.

Gentry, W.A., Weber, T.J., and Sadri, G. 2007. "Empathy in the Workplace." Center for Creative Leadership, (April).

Goldsmith, Oliver. "1762, The Citizen of the World: or, Letters from a Chinese Philosopher, Residing in London, to His Friends in the East by Lien Chi Altangi (Oliver Goldsmith), Letter VII and Letter XXII." Printed for George and Alex. Ewing, Dublin, Ireland.

Harford, T. 2012. *Adapt: Why Success Always Starts with Failure*. London, UK: Abacus.

Kandel, E.R. 2006. *In Search of Memory: The Emergence of a New Science of Mind*. New York, NY: W.W. Norton.

Konrath, S.H., O'Brien, E.H., & Hsing, C. 2011. "Changes in Dispositional Empathy in American College Students Over Time: A Meta-Analysis." *Personality and Social Psychology Review*, 15, 2, (May 1): 180–98.

Leroy, S. 2009. "Why Is It So Hard to Do My Work? The Challenge of Attention Residue When Switching Between Work Tasks." *Organizational Behavior and Human Decision Processes*, 109, 2, (January 1): 168–81.

Li, Charlene. 2016. In conversation with the author.

Light, Rohan. 2017. In conversation with the author.

Mattson, Mark. 2016. In conversation with the author.

Miller, Tania. 2016. In conversation with the author.

Myers, C. 2017. "How to Become a More Decisive Leader." *Forbes*, April 28, 2017. https://www.forbes.com/sites/chrismyers/2017/04/28/how-to-become-a-more-decisive-leader/#430972274336.

Orin, A. 2017. "I'm Brad Smith, CEO of Intuit, and This Is How I Work." *Lifehacker*, April 12, 2017. http://lifehacker.com/im-brad-smith-ceo-of-intuit-and-this-is-how-i-work-1794268430.

Pagonis, W. 2001. "Leadership in a Combat Zone." *Harvard Business Review*, 79, 11, (January 1): 107–16.

Patel, Sameer. 2016. In conversation with the author.

Pontefract, D. 2013. *Flat Army: Creating a Connected and Engaged Organization*. John Wiley & Sons. Republished 2018 Figure 1 Publishing.

Reid, Dominic. 2017. In conversation with the author.

Rosen, L., & Samuel, A. 2015. "Conquering Digital Distraction." *Harvard Business Review* [serial online], 93, 6 (June): 110–13. Business Source Corporate Plus, Ipswich, MA.

Ruiz, Karyn. 2016. In conversation with the author.

Scudamore, Brian. 2016. In conversation with the author.

Sostrin, J. 2017. "How to Act Quickly Without Sacrificing Critical Thinking." *Harvard Business Review*, April 27, 2017.

Winfrey, O. 2009. "Why Right-Brainers Will Rule This Century." CNN, May 7, 2009. http://www.cnn.com/2009/LIVING/worklife/05/07/o.Oprah.Interviews.Daniel.Pink/.

Zaki, J., & Ochsner, K. N. 2012. "The Neuroscience of Empathy: Progress, Pitfalls and Promise." *Nature Neuroscience*, 15, 5, (January 1): 675–80.

CHAPTER 8: THINK AGAIN

Antinori, A., Carter, O.L., & Smillie, L.D. 2017. "Seeing It Both Ways: Openness to Experience and Binocular Rivalry Suppression." *Journal of Research in Personality*, 68, (June 1): 15–22.

Becher, Jonathan. 2017. In conversation with author.

The Businessolver website can be found at https://www.businessolver.com/2017-empathy-monitor-executive-summary?hsCtaTracking=9e006e63-8034-41e9-ac00-19227993b694%7Cd49f67a6-5d50-4439-9241-5ec2bb24321f.

Calder, Kathryn. 2017. In conversation with the author.

Carnegie, D. 1938. *How to Win Friends and Influence People*. New York, NY: Simon and Schuster.

Clayton, Eva. 2017. In conversation with the author.

Couros, G. 2015. *The Innovator's Mindset: Empower Learning, Unleash Talent, and Lead a Culture of Creativity*. Dave Burgess Consulting, Inc.

Dalla Costa, John. 2017. In conversation with the author.

D'Souza, Steven, & Renner, Diana. 2014. *Not Knowing: The Art of Turning Uncertainty into Opportunity*. LID Editorial.

Gilmore, Peter. 2017. In conversation with the author.

Gray, D. 2016. *Liminal Thinking: Create the Change You Want by Changing the Way You Think*. Brooklyn, NY: Two Waves Books.

Gray, Dave. 2017. In conversation with the author.

Hinchcliffe, Dion. 2017. In conversation with author.

Kielburger, Marc. 2016. In conversation with the author.

Lathrop, G.P. 1890. "Talks with Edison." *Harper's Magazine*, 80, (February): 425.

Levitin, Daniel. 2016. In conversation with the author.

Li, Charlene. 2016. In conversation with the author.

Mattson, Mark. 2016. In conversation with the author.

Miller, Tania. 2016. In conversation with the author.

Perry, James. 2016. In conversation with the author.

Popova, M. 2012. "John Cleese on the Five Factors to Make Your Life More Creative." *Brainpickings*, April 12, 2012. https://www.brainpickings.org/2012/04/12/john-cleese-on-creativity-1991/.

Rilke, R.M. 1995. *Ahead of All Parting: The Selected Poetry and Prose of Rainer Maria Rilke*. New York, NY: The Modern Library.

Ruiz, Karyn. 2016. In conversation with the author.

Schein, E.H. 2004. *Organizational Culture and Leadership*. Hoboken, NJ: John Wiley & Sons.

Scudamore, Brian. 2016. In conversation with the author.

World Economic Forum. 2016. "The Future of Jobs." http://reports.weforum.org/future-of-jobs-2016/.

Zhao, Yong. 2017. In conversation with the author.

INDEX

ABOUT THE AUTHOR

DAN PONTEFRACT IS Chief Envisioner at TELUS, a Canadian telecommunications company, where he heads the Transformation Office, a future-of-work consulting group that helps organizations enhance their corporate cultures and collaboration practices. Previously as Chief Learning Officer at TELUS, Dan introduced a new leadership framework—called the TELUS Leadership Philosophy—that dramatically helped to increase the company's employee engagement to record levels of nearly 90 percent. He has also held senior leadership roles at SAP, Business Objects, and BCIT.

Dan is an adjunct professor at the University of Victoria Gustavson School of Business, and is the author of *The Purpose Effect: Building Meaning in Yourself, Your Role, and Your Organization* as well as *Flat Army: Creating a Connected and Engaged Organization*. A renowned keynote speaker, Dan has presented at multiple TED events and also writes for *Forbes*, *Harvard Business Review*, and *The Huffington Post*. Dan and his wife, Denise, have three young children (aka goats) and live in Victoria, Canada. He is hard at work researching his next book, *Six Degrees of Leadership*, publishing January 26, 2021.

You can reach Dan at his website (www.danpontefract.com), on Twitter (@dpontefract), Instagram (@dan.pontefract), Facebook (@danpontefractauthor), or via email (dp@danpontefract.com).

Dan's declaration of purpose is as follows: "We're not here to see through each other; we're here to see each other through." What are you doing to help see others through their day, their life? It's the ultimate question.

ALSO BY **DAN PONTEFRACT**